Medieval
BATH
Uncovered

To my parents, who never made me get a proper job, and my wife, who shares my enthusiasm for this strange profession

Medieval BATH *Uncovered*

PETER DAVENPORT

TEMPUS

First published 2002

PUBLISHED IN THE UNITED KINGDOM BY:
Tempus Publishing Ltd
The Mill, Brimscombe Port
Stroud, Gloucestershire GL5 2QG

PUBLISHED IN THE UNITED STATES OF AMERICA BY:
Tempus Publishing Inc.
2 Cumberland Street
Charleston, SC 29401

British Library Cataloguing in Publication Data.
A catalogue record for this book is available from the British Library.

ISBN 0 7524 1965 X

Typesetting and origination by Tempus Publishing.
Printed in Great Britain by Midway Colour Print, Wiltshire

Contents

List of illustrations   6

Acknowledgements   8

Introduction   9

1   The end of the beginning   11

2   From convent to most celebrated monastery   31

3   After Offa: Alfred and the town reborn   39

4   Vikings, kings and abbots   57

5   Cathedral city   71

6   City and Guilds   97

7   Topography and townscape: the shape of the later medieval city   123

8   The later Middle Ages in Bath   151

Epilogue   169

Appendices   I   Mayors of Bath in the Middle Ages   172
           II   Abbots, Bishops and Priors of Bath   174
          III   Pounds, shillings and pence   183

Bibliography   184

Index   186

List of illustrations

1   Fallen Roman buildings in the temple precinct
2   A page of The Ruin, the Saxon poem describing the Roman remains
3   Fifth-century paving in the temple precinct
4   Heavy wear in the fifth century paving in the doorway to the Sacred Spring
5   Plan of Bath c.400
6   Plan of the sub-Roman west
7   Wear patterns in the late Roman paving by the Great Bath
8   Plan of Bath c.550
9   The Wansdyke: excavations in the 1990s
10   Plan of Bath c.700
11   The *burhs* of Wessex
12   Reconstruction of the Alfredian defences
13   Saxon Bilbury Lane
14   Alfred's *burh* and the units of survey
15   Coins from the Bath mint and a continental sceat
16   Saxon burials at the abbey
17   Tenth-century memorials: a grave slab and the Eadgyvu plaque
18   The late Saxon bank blocking the Alfredian street
19   Finds from the Saxon cloth industry
20   The tenth-century seal of the abbey
21   A late Saxon stone-sculpted angel from St Lawrence's Church, Bradford-on-Avon
22   The sword from Upper Borough Walls
23   Late Saxon carved cross heads from Bath
24   The dedication page of Aelfric's gospel of St Matthew
25   The way to the Cross Bath, late Saxon(?) cobbling
26   The city of Bath after c.1100
27   The Norman masonry in the east end of the present church after Bligh Bond's drawing of 1918
28   Excavations at Orange Grove: the north eastern apse of John of Tours' Cathedral
29   The twelfth-century cloister wall during excavations in 1993
30   Excavations on the site of the Bishop's Palace
31   The 1725 map of the Duke of Kingston's estates in Bath
32   Plan of the bishop's palace as excavated
33   Reconstruction drawing of the earliest Bishop's Palace, c. 1100
34   Reconstruction of John of Tours' Cathedral: a view from the south east

35   Reconstruction of John of Tours' Cathedral: the nave arcades
36   Plan of John of Tours' Cathedral
37   The steps up to the north transept from the nave aisle, as recorded by Irvine
38   Architectural fragments from John of Tours' Cathedral
39   The King's Bath and the building to its north as it might have appeared *c.*1150
40   Plan of the King's Bath *c.*1150
41   The charter of 1189
42   The city hundred boundaries
43   The forinsecum or foreign hundred
44   An impression of the medieval guildhall
45   The early fourteenth-century seal of the Guild Merchant of Bath
46   The lands of St Mary Magdalen and stone quarries
47   Twelfth-century saw pits at Saw Close
48   St Mary Magdalen Chapel
49   Philips' Almshouses, the Black Alms: a view of 1825
50   Speed's map of Bath, published 1610
51   Savile's map of Bath, after *c.*1603
52   Gilmore's map of Bath of 1694
53   Johnson's view of the King's Bath, 1672
54   The city wall during excavations in the 1950s
55   Upper Borough Walls: the city walls today from the small eighteenth-century graveyard
56   Rev. Lockey's 1840s photograph of the city wall by the east gate
57   The east gate and city wall in a watercolour of *c.*1850
58   The medieval bridge as engraved in 1718
59   Plan of St James' Church as excavated in 1959
60   The city and its suburbs
61   The High Street today
62   Union Passage today
63   The archaeological drawing of the timbers at 21 High Street
64   Reconstruction of 21, High Street as originally built
65   A contemporary drawing of the houses along Stall Street in 1806
66   Priory Seal showing the cathedral with a spire, dating from about 1300
67   The tile floor in the crossing of the Norman cathedral
68   The Prior's Lodging as seen in Gilmore's map of 1694
69   Oliver King's rebus on the west front of his new cathedral
70   The crossing and east end of King's church showing the fan vaulting
71   West front as drawn in 1798 for the Society of Antiquaries
72   The heraldic bosses of Prior Bird and Cardinal Bishop Adriano in the choir aisle vaults
73   Oliver King's statement, the present 'Abbey'
74   The Norman arch in the present south choir aisle, the entry into the transept in the old church
75   Prior Bird's chantry of *c.*1520

Acknowledgements

Professor Barry Cunliffe first brought me to the city to run excavation projects for the Bath Archaeological Trust. It was then I first encountered medieval Bath. My work for the Trust has involved excavating, writing up or editing several medieval sites and I am grateful to colleagues for their co-operation, especially Robert Bell for allowing me to refer to the work on the Abbey in 1992-3.

The Survey of Bath and District, essentially Elizabeth Holland and Mike Chapman, have been exceedingly generous in assisting with the medieval documentary sources, especially as they relate to the topography of the town, and for providing helpful discussion of chapters 6 and 7. I must also thank freelance historian Jean Manco, for discussions over the years and her interest in the medieval town. Mike Heaton of ASI Heritage gave me free access to his records of 21 High Street. Of course, all errors are my responsibility. I should also like to thank Colin Johnston, the Bath and North East Somerset Council Archivist, for helping me with sources and for allowing me to reproduce **41** without charge. The master and Fellows of Corpus Christi College, Cambridge were likewise generous with **24**, as was Avon Archaeological Unit who supplied figure 9. Linda Smith of the Abbey Heritage Vaults very kindly allowed me and my camera the run of her museum. All other pictures without acknowledgements are a small thing but mine own.

Finally, I would like to thank my wife, Lisa Brown, who encouraged me to keep going, tolerated my effective absence from family duties and house maintenance for nearly a year, and put up with all the extra work this entailed.

Introduction

Almost the first job I did when I came to Bath in 1980 was to record the Roman and medieval walls of the King's Bath, exposed during works for the new displays in the Roman Baths Museum. The plan was to relay a floor which had been built in the 1880s, and to create modern records of whatever was revealed. Rather good accounts of the Roman structures had been made the first time around, so I had a fair idea of what to expect; but I was puzzled by what I saw when the old floor was taken up. The Roman walls were certainly there, but were obscured by all sorts of other structures – in particular, by a massive wall with semicircular niches in one face. I soon realised that this was the northern wall of the medieval King's Bath, built over the Roman wall: but why did it not appear on the old drawings? It was big enough and clear to see. The notes of the archaeologists at the time make it clear that they realised what was there; but in a sense, they simply did not see it. The Roman remains were what they sought: medieval Bath was invisible.

To the visitor today, medieval Bath is similarly invisible. The signs, the guide books, the tours and the publicity all talk about *Bath, the Roman City* and *Bath, the Georgian City*: it is as if there were nothing in between. Indeed, one could say that for the modern visitor this is true: Bath has no timber-framed houses overhanging narrow streets, no ancient parish churches, no castle – and the only publicised 'medieval building', Sally Lunn's House, was in fact built in 1622. Yet, overshadowed by the Roman/Georgian double act, even the one great, unmissable, top quality, show-stopping bit of medieval Bath that the visitor *can* see is strangely dimmed. Perhaps it is too much to say that the Abbey is invisible. Yet somehow it is not noticed, or rather, it is re-categorised into something *sui generis*: not Georgian, but not really anything else either. Visitors go as much in search of famous Georgian epitaphs as to see the church itself, or regard it as part of the generalised city-wide ambience of golden Bath stone, despite the fact that in terms of style, position and status the Abbey is surely the most striking building in Bath. After all, it is the last medieval cathedral built in England, planned by a bishop in royal service and designed by the king's own masons, the best architects in England. Cleaned and given its own museum in honour of its quincentenary, the Abbey is at last coming into its own. But, stripped of all vestiges of its contemporary surroundings, it still seems like a beached hulk abandoned after the medieval tides have receded, left without the wreckage of its past around it, and even devoid of its original identity.

My main motive in writing this book was simply to fill this huge gap in our perception of the City of Bath, these centuries of historical amnesia. The Romans came, the Romans left. It was 1300 years before the Georgian spa town began its century of heady growth, before medieval Bath, already undergoing many changes in the seventeenth century, was transformed by the vision of Nash, Allen and Wood. The chapters that follow attempt to show that the history and archaeology of these centuries are not only interesting and important in their own right, deserving to be known by a wider audience, but have left an indelible, if subtle, imprint on the city today. My book begins with the Abbey and ends with it. I shall be pleased if I have given it a deeper context, and if I have helped anyone to see the invisible: to discover medieval Bath.

1 The end of the beginning

In the early eighth century, we may imagine a member of the recently-founded Saxon monastic community at Bath walking a short distance from the dormitory and clambering over mounds of bricks and Bathstone blocks to stand and wonder at the massive, ruinous buildings that dominated the religious precinct (**1**).

> Wondrous is this masonry, shattered by the fates . . . the buildings raised by giants are crumbling . . . the owners and builders are perished and gone . . . and so these courts lie desolate, and the framework of the dome with its red arches sheds it tiles . . . the wall enfolded within its bright bosom the whole place which contained the hot flood of the Baths.

Expressing the awesome impression the ruins made, these words come from a poem, large fragments of which luckily survive, known to us by its modern title 'The Ruin'. It is the oldest description of the site of Bath, and astonishingly detailed; and modern

1 '. . . *shattered by the fates . . . the buildings raised by giants are crumbling.*' *The collapsed masonry from the Roman monuments around the Temple Precinct, burying the courtyard of the Temple of Sulis Minerva.* Bath Archaeological Trust/Institute of Archaeology, Oxford

2 *The first page of the manuscript of* The Ruin. *This tenth-century copy from the Exeter Book is the earliest in existence, but the poem is thought to be of eighth- or even seventh-century date.* Reproduced by permission of the Dean and Chapter of Exeter Cathedral

excavation shows it to be remarkably accurate. It is also a marvellous and lucky survival of a fragment of great poetry from the earliest period of English writing (**2**). Much has been written about this poem since its recognition by scholars in the eighteenth century. It survives in a collection of verse left to the cathedral at Exeter in 1072; the manuscript itself is later tenth century, but the poem is generally thought to date from the late seventh or eighth century. Given the distribution of literacy in this period, it is generally assumed the author was a religious, probably a member of the religious house at Bath, which is first mentioned in a document of 675 (albeit one of slightly uncertain authenticity). There it is described as a *convent of holy virgins*. No one seems to have considered up to now the possibility that the author was, in that case, a woman.

Yet although this poem has been dug into almost as much as the ground itself to provide evidence for the buildings of the Baths and Temple of the Roman city, it also speaks to us directly on the state of Bath in the middle Saxon period. The 24-acre central area, encircled by the Romans with a great stone wall, was clearly still occupied by massive and impressive buildings, albeit gaunt and ruinous; by pools of hot water, carpets of moss-covered rubble – and, presumably, the community in which our author lived. What kind of a place was this eighth-century Bath, and how had it got this way?

By the early third century, Roman Bath, *Aquae Sulis* (the waters of the goddess Sulis), had reached its zenith. The baths and temple were set among several other grand public buildings, along with smaller-scale structures with mosaic floors and underfloor heating, possibly houses for the officials of the complex. This set of central buildings, enclosed by a ditch and earthen bank, formed a religious and perhaps administrative centre, with little or no evidence of craft, commerce or industry, or even much indication of the homes of the population who serviced the facilities and made a living from the tourist trade. Excavation has now been extensive enough to show that in this part of the town, the normal spread of domestic finds common in Roman urban centres is also missing. Such evidence does occur in excavations of the town at modern day Walcot, which had developed in the mid-first century around the road junction and river crossing nearly a kilometre to the north, on the way to London and Cirencester, and had spread down the road to merge with the ceremonial centre by the early second century at the latest. This part of town contained shops, workshops and studios, and housing for all social levels. As well as the civic centre and the town, there were also a number of villas in the countryside nearby, so close that we might consider them to be suburban villas rather than country houses.

By the mid-fourth century things were changing. At least one spacious and well-appointed house along Walcot Street had fallen into ruin and been converted to a tile factory; one of the suburban villas a few hundred yards west of town at Lower Common had its bath suite converted to a workshop for recycling coloured glass. In the centre, a blacksmith had set up shop, in quite a big way, in a converted house just south of the baths, and a pewter vessel workshop had been erected just east of the baths, its walls incorporating a recycled column-base from a grander building. To the west of the outer courtyard of the Temple of Sulis Minerva,

3 *The probably fifth-century paving in the Temple precinct, in use after the religious monuments had been destroyed. The large blocks at the rear are from a dismantled Roman building, and form the pavement that the 'step' in* **4** *belongs to.* Bath Archaeological Trust/Institute of Archaeology, Oxford

another iron-working workshop was set up. In contrast, but almost more shocking a change, the outer courtyard itself was built over with expensive houses with underfloor heating and mosaics, and the inner courtyard was no longer being carefully maintained. The earthen bank had been replaced by a defensive stone wall 3m thick and 5-6m high.

These changes are shown in detail in the inner precinct of the Temple, excavated in the early 1980s. From 350 to perhaps 450 or even later, the inner precinct went through a series of remarkable transformations. For the first time, mud and rubbish were allowed to accumulate: a cobble floor and then a mortar floor were laid over this layer (**3**). While more mud and debris was being allowed to build up, the central outdoor altar, the focus of religious ceremony at the site for over 300 years, was thrown down; this occurred *c.*380 or 390, and must represent the end of overt pagan worship at the site. Cobble floors continued to be laid, alternating with layers of mud and domestic refuse, and the cobbling now starts to include recognisable fragments of temple stonework and other known monuments from around the courtyard. By some time in the first half of the fifth century, both religious sculpture taken from the temple pediment and the Façade of the Four Seasons (a richly-carved monument well known from these fragments), was thrown face down to provide the paving – continuing on from the desecration of the altar, pagan references are being consciously destroyed or hidden. By the mid-fifth century, the centre of town might have already started to look familiar to our Saxon poet.

It seems obvious that these physical changes should imply economic, social and religious transformation. What is fascinating, and can only be superficially followed in this book, is that this change both began before and continued after the formal 'end of Roman Britain' in 410. The religious and architectural set piece of earlier years, reflecting and symbolising the classical grandeur of Roman civilization, was already being refashioned into a new, harsher, more practical form during the fourth century. The new city walls epitomised this change, insensitively recycling sculptured and inscribed stone blocks from demolished monuments including tombstones (a process also seen in the fourth-century riverside wall at *Londinium*).

What was this transformation for? It was of a piece with the transformation of the empire itself. The third century had been a period of crisis. The reforms of the emperors Diocletian (284-305) and Constantine I (306-37) saved the empire but, it might be said, at the cost of destroying it. Historians date the beginning of Late Antiquity from these reigns, a period that can almost be considered a transition into the Middle Ages. While it is true that viewed from some perspectives, Roman Britain enjoyed a cultural golden age in the fourth century, it is also true that it was a period of high taxes, oppressive administration and a growing obsession with military matters and the need to finance them. In general, the empire was increasingly insecure, and increasingly under attack from without. Towns and their administrations played a central rôle in collecting taxes, yet most large towns in Britain were showing the strain of this rôle – in few cases can large public buildings, such as baths, basilicas, or temples, be shown to survive far into the fourth century. Public squalor is reflected by private affluence: some large houses survive, but most are abandoned. They are usually surrounded by small houses, workshops, or cultivated ground, sometimes even by rubbish dumps.

Cutting across these economic and political currents was, of course, the impact of Christianity. Christians were in Britannia from at least the second century, and are attested in Bath in the third. After 312 they were not only tolerated, but encouraged and privileged, and there are clear indications that a proper system of bishoprics was established. It is uncertain how far the various measures against pagan cults from Constantine onwards were applied in Britain, though it is tempting to correlate the declining standards in the temple precinct to Constantine's appropriation of temple funds to the imperial treasury towards the end of his reign. The throwing down of altars and the defacing of pagan sculpture at Bath are not far removed in time from the edicts of Theodosius of 391 and 392 which forbade pagan worship. Many other pagan temples in the West Country continued to flourish in this period, and it has been suggested that the Theodosian laws were not enacted in Britain; but it seems almost certain that the temples of *Aquae Sulis* were closed at this period. If they had not already been closed, the Baths, at least in their full extent, could not have lasted much longer without the visitors.

Bath was a small town in the province, but its status was greatly enhanced by its tourist and pilgrim trade. Losing those aspects made it much more of a typical, late Roman 'small town'. Many 'small towns' in Britannia, often little more than villages to our way of thinking, received defensive circuits of walls in this period. Faulkner has suggested that they may have been part of a new imperial strategy: a network of strong-holds and central stores, each used for the collection, administration and safe storage of imperial taxes. If paid in gold coin, security was needed; if in kind, bulk storage. They often, in addition, contain workshops producing goods for the army, and administra-tion and accommodation for the administrators. We are reminded of the housing in the temple precinct, and the metalworking within the walls. These walled strongholds could also provide places of refuge for goods and people in the increasingly common periods of unrest in the later fourth and early fifth century. It seems that central Bath changed from cult centre and architecturally grandiose visitor attraction, a backdrop for the theatre of Roman urban life, to this much more mundane rôle. We have seen how the Temple and Baths of *Sulis Minerva* probably went out of use, or drastically declined. The hot springs themselves could not be stopped and we may imagine *ad hoc* bathing and clandestine religious observances continuing. The absence of baths and temple and the changed circumstances of the later empire would have reduced visitor numbers drastically. This modified the economic basis for the settlement outside the walls, which lost its better quality houses, but struggled on into the fifth century, again with produc-tive 'industry' in the ruins. The medieval village of Walcot may have been the remnants of this part of the town, never quite disappearing.

While in some respects this looks like decline, it was, perhaps, only transforma-tion. A new function produced a new form. Wear on the cobble floors in the temple precinct showed that the hot spring was still being frequently visited well into the fifth century (**4**), and a curious arrangement of whole pottery vessels along the side of one of the porticoes in the precinct suggests some kind of informal religious rites still being carried out after the demolition of the altar. The grand religious complex and plush visitor attractions and facilities were closed. Many were being quarried for building materials; yet some authority, driven by different priorities, was still making a practical, no-nonsense investment in the town.

Thus, by 400 the industrial town inside and outside the walls was already hugely different from the earlier resort (**5**). A new kind of town was evident. The huge buildings still stood, the springs continued to flow, but provincial officials, craftsmen, military officials perhaps, staffed a secure storage depot and production centre, perhaps also a local market, rather than a tourist resort. It may have also acquired some administrative rôle for the local region: the large bronze buckle found at Bath Street, might be part of a late Roman official's belt of office. Inside and out, the shells of the older buildings were demolished or converted into workshops, store houses, and official residences.

Yet these changes themselves were ephemeral: political changes altered the economic basis of the town once again. Repeated barbarian incursion, military rebellion and imperial reconquest in the last 30 years of the century left the province economically, militarily and politically exhausted. In 407, Britain had lost yet another home-grown usurping emperor, Constantine III, to war in Gaul and Italy (he was killed in 411). In 410 Honorius, the official emperor, effectively if not deliberately, abandoned the province. History enters the Dark Ages and the course of events is very poorly under-stood. This is both because written sources are extremely scant and difficult to interpret,

4 *This deeply-worn block in the door to the Sacred Spring is not a door step but the last remnant in this area of the pavement seen in* **3**. *The rest of the pavement here was removed in 1879, but there was some evidence in the excavations of 1983 that there was a wide cone of wear of this depth leading to the doorway into the Sacred Spring. This suggests intensive or long-lived use of the Roman spring and courtyard into the late fifth or even sixth centuries.* Bath Archaeological Trust/Institute of Archaeology, Oxford

and because archaeological evidence changes its nature so much at this point that it is missed, dismissed or misunderstood. Like most discussions of this period, what follows is therefore a personal choice of interpretation based on very little and very difficult evidence. For example, at some point in the fifth century the Roman pottery industries ceased production, probably by 420. Apart from the rather surprising appearance of imported Mediterranean wine amphorae and some very rare, crude organic tempered examples, no pottery is found in western Britain (apart from Cornwall) until the late ninth century. Since coins ceased being imported to Britain in about 402, two of the major dating methods and indicators of settlement are therefore missing from this period. In Bath itself, the extensive redevelopment of the eighteenth century has removed most of the layers from this period, while deeper, Roman levels survive.

Some traces of this period have been found in Bath, but in common with most of the rest of Britain, they are slight and difficult to interpret. By the early fifth century the monumental gateway into the temple precinct had been demolished and

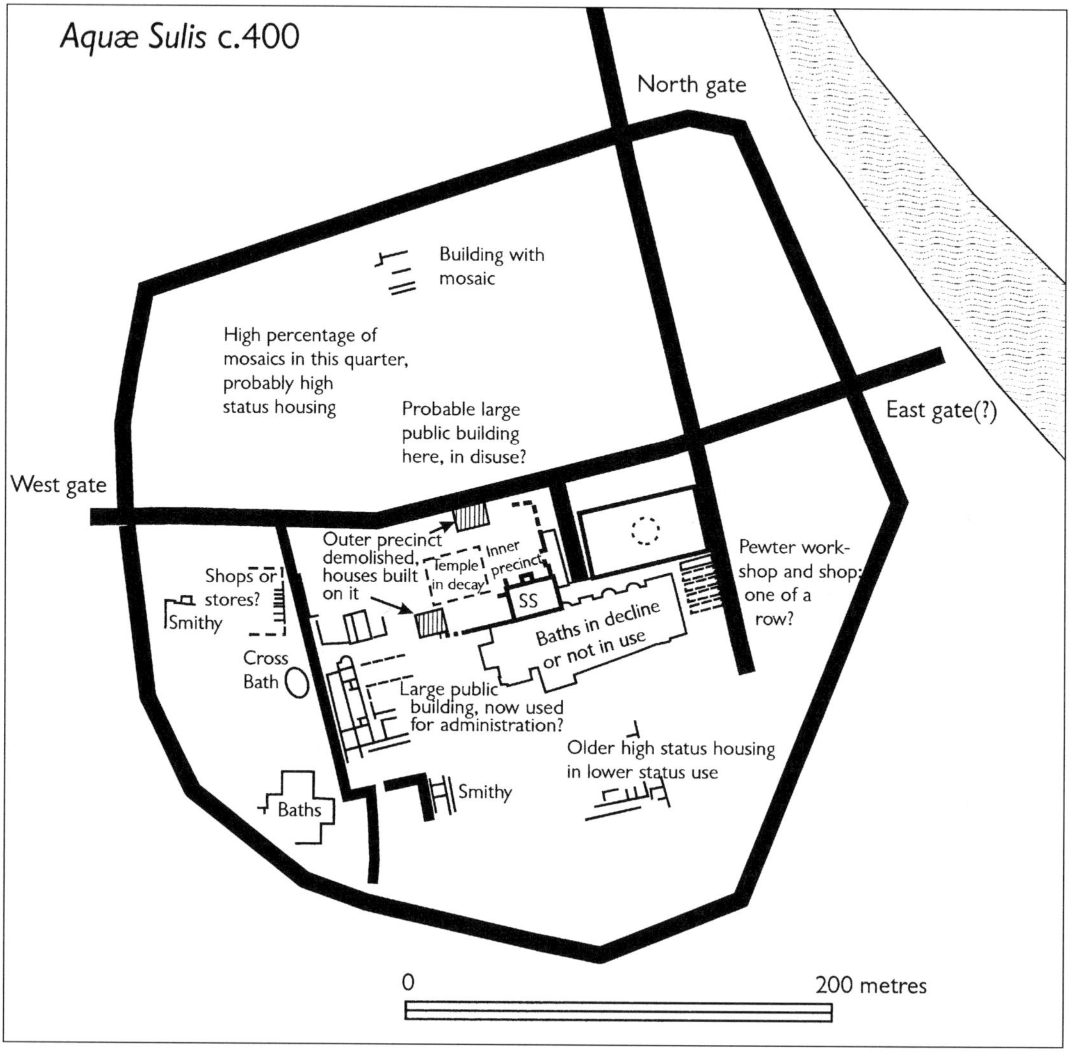

Aquæ Sulis c.400
North gate
Building with mosaic
High percentage of mosaics in this quarter, probably high status housing
Probable large public building here, in disuse?
East gate(?)
West gate
Outer precinct demolished, houses built on it
Temple in decay
Inner precinct
SS
Shops or stores?
Smithy
Pewter work-shop and shop: one of a row?
Baths in decline or not in use
Cross Bath
Large public building, now used for administration?
Older high status housing in lower status use
Baths
Smithy
0
200 metres

5 *Plan of late Roman Bath around AD 400. The blank areas are simply where we have no evidence. The street pattern is the maximum that can be inferred, but there would have been more streets. The Baths in the south-west corner might well have also been out of use*

some time later, possibly well into the century, a cobbled floor was laid over it. Only a tiny fragment of this floor survived later disturbances, but set in it was the slot for a large timber ground beam. This is interpreted as the fragmentary remains of a substantial timber building, built in the very shadows of the Roman monuments. Contemporary with this was a massive paving outside the door which led from the precinct to the hot spring itself. This consisted mainly of reused Roman architectural blocks, and was worn by the continual passage of feet into a fan-shaped hollow up to six inches (15cm) deep. Possibly at this time, another large timber building was erected on stone footing pads over the demolished hypocaust of a public building recently excavated between Bath Street and Beau Street. This suggests use of the area well into the mid-fifth century if not later, a use involving a considerable investment of time and resources. Conventionally, *Aquae Sulis* disappears from archaeological sight by shortly after 400, but it has been apparent for some time that this is not the case. We are usually presented with a picture of an *Aquae Sulis* that within a few short years had become an empty wreck of a town: ruins and wasteland half-hidden behind a massive defensive wall. We will investigate the evidence against this view a little later, but before investigating the state of Bath in the fifth and sixth centuries we need to describe, as far as we can, the events of the period that provide the larger framework. What was going on around Bath in the fifth and sixth centuries and what might we therefore expect to find at Bath itself?

The regional governments of Britannia (*civitates*) were effectively abandoned by Rome when the Emperor Honorius wrote to them in 410 advising and authorising them to look to their own defence. This may have been in response to one of the occasions when, as we are told by Gildas, the Britons asked for military assistance from Rome. The rebellion of Constantine III had drawn the last troops from the province in 407. The *civitates* were the only governmental organisations left, and it seems that the Roman regional administrative structure did form the basis of the post-Roman government. Curiously, there is some evidence that the very upper echelons of late Roman society were actually excluded from this government, by a sort of middle and lower class revolt. In any case, the levers of power which had long been manipulated by the rich and powerful of the province were used to quickly create a political and military structure, one that moreover seems to have been intended to provide a unified political entity.

This we can infer from the fragments of historical information that we have to work with. Gildas, a monk writing in southern Britain in the mid-sixth century, tells us that the Britons, faced with invasion by barbarians (broadly, the Anglo-Saxons, Scots and Picts) successfully organised themselves, and won a great victory. This seems to have held the line for a generation. During this time there emerged a 'great tyrant', unnamed by Gildas, but known to us as Vortigern. Vortigern seems to have controlled the whole of southern Britain, including (following the dates in Bede and the *Anglo-Saxon Chronicle*) Kent in the 450s; for by then, following good Roman precedent, he had settled Saxon mercenaries there in return for military service.

The famous rebellion against Vortigern by the mercenaries in the 450s (although Gildas puts it some time later), traditionally led to the massive influx of settlers from across the North Sea, and the loss of the eastern provinces to the invaders. However, another British leader arose, Ambrosius Aurelianus, 'the last of the Romans', who stopped the collapse; and while his was an age of continuing and indecisive warfare, it culminated in the unlocated siege of Mons Badonicus in *c*.490 AD. This was the defining victory which stopped the Saxon advance and gave peace and stability to the western, British half of the island until Gildas' own days, 50 or 60 years later. This much is broadly agreed, but almost every other detail is argued over by historians. Yet there are intriguing details that support much of what the sources say. On linguistic grounds there has long been recognised a major migration of Britons from south central England to Armorica in the mid-fifth century, causing the transformation of Latin-speaking Armorica into British-speaking Brittany. Gildas refers to this, placing the flight between the Saxon rebellion and the recovery of Ambrosius Aurelianus – say by 500. There is also evidence that some Saxons returned to the continent at this time. The detailed relationship of these political events to real settlement of Saxons is not straightforward, but it is true that place name and archaeological evidence strongly suggests that the Britons successfully created a stop line in *c*.490 which ran (very roughly) through the Hampshire-Wiltshire border and the western side of Oxfordshire, and northwards in a hazy line towards the southern tip of the Pennines. Behind this line the Britons maintained political control (**6**).

We have only the haziest idea of how that political control was exercised. Gildas makes it clear that in his day, in the mid-sixth century, there were kings in Britain, each ruling a relatively small area, such as north Wales, Cornwall, the Welsh marches and so on; but he also mentions *rectores* or governors, implying some kind of non-monarchical government in some places. It is likely that this pattern arose early, and may have been based on the Roman *civitates* (ruled by *rectores*?) and, in the less Romanised areas such as Wales and Cornwall, on tribal areas (which, of course, the *civitates* were originally), ruled by kings. Indeed, the unity of control suggested by the story of Vortigern is almost certainly that of a federation of smaller 'polities' under an overall leader at a time of crisis. Vortigern's unconstitutional rôle (the real meaning of *tyrant*) may have been as military overlord of these smaller rulers. Ambrosius Aurelianus also seems to be more of a war leader than a king. Bath may have had a place in the power politics of the region, remote as it was from the possible political centres of Gloucester and Cirencester, and cut off by the stop line from its Roman administrative centre, Winchester. It might have become a centre for local or regional politics, a defensive stronghold for local leaders who emerged to fill the power vacuum of this uncertain period. Its defensive walls and ditch, and relatively small size, would make it an ideal stronghold. This idea is persuasive when we realise that Bath is specifically mentioned as one of the cities captured by the Saxons in 577 after the battle of Deorham (modern Dyrham, a few miles north of Bath), at which one of the British leaders captured may have been the 'king' or governor of Bath. Perhaps our poet, writing of ' . . . many a warrior . . . splendid in harness of battle' was not so mistaken after all. Can we find traces of this in the archaeology of the city?

We saw earlier how the archaeology of central *Aquae Sulis* could be followed well into the fifth century, when substantial timber buildings and stone floors were being

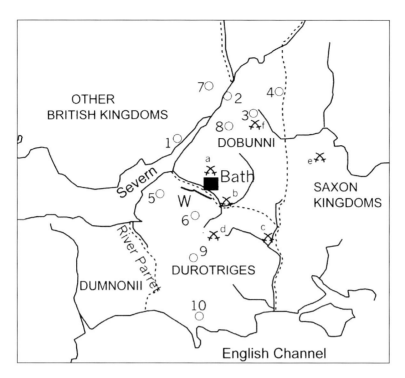

6 *Map of the sub-Roman west, c.550-650. The probable boundaries of the sub-Roman states are indicated with dashed lines. The circles are the candidates for regional centres, for trade and or administration, plus Bath. 1. Caerleon, 2. Gloucester, 3. Cirencester, 4. Bourton on the Water, 5. Congresbury, 6. Camerton, 7. Ariconium, 8. Kingscote. 9. South Cadbury, 10. Dorchester. Battles in the Anglo-Saxon Chronicle are marked: a. Dyrham (577), b. Bradford-on-Avon (652), c. Salisbury (Old Sarum, 552), d. Penselwood (658), e. Barbury (556), f. Cirencester (628). The Wansdyke is marked 'W'*

built in the vicinity of the springs. In addition, excavations at Abbeygate Street, south of the Baths, showed a long sequence of structural alterations and occupation running for an uncertain period after the late fourth century, and Cunliffe long ago suggested that it perhaps lasted until after 500 (though the famous 'skull in the oven', thought to symbolise a lapse in civilised standards, is probably a disturbed medieval burial). In the western part of the town, at Citizen House, timber buildings on stone foundations were built after 395, and were succeeded by first more timber structures, and then a timber building on dry stone foundations which was provided with a thick yard surface of dumped clay. This last building can be no earlier than the mid to late fifth century, and since it follows the earlier layout, there seems no doubt that it represents continuity of occupation. The lack of precision in dating is due as always to the absence of pottery and of coins referred to above. For the rest, this period was represented by layers of 'dark earth'.

Now this dark earth is a puzzle to archaeologists, though progress is being made in understanding it. Many Roman towns seem to have thick layers of this material blanketing the latest recognisable Roman buildings and deposits. Archaeologists have conventionally seen it as an abandonment layer, but are now realising that, in fact, it must represent *activity*. Contrary to the layman's view, thick soil layers do not magically appear on abandoned sites at a regular rate. It has to be put there by some agency. The big question is, what kind of agency? It has been investigated in three places in Bath: south of the baths at Swallow Street, and west, at Bath Street and Citizen House. At the former, next to the Abbeygate Street excavations and over the same Roman building, the dark gritty soil, darkened with many flecks of charcoal, contained streaks of mortar, and inside the buildings had been dumped or accumulated in discrete episodes. It contained animal bone food refuse, but only one sherd of the rare organically tempered pottery, of a type datable with no better precision than to 450-950, but found on early post-Roman sites in the *civitatis dobunnorum*, the Roman administrative area north of the city. Outside the Roman buildings the dark earth was a fine silt that had accumulated slowly and evenly, and was possibly cultivated. This implies different activities on the site of the old buildings, and outside them; and such a structure implies occupation. At Bath Street an extensive dark earth layer was seen, but not properly investigated, due to pressures of redevelopment. It, too, overlay more normal Roman deposits and was more like the external silt at Swallow Street. The food debris certainly suggests human activity. The material continued to accrete through the Saxon period, during which it was clearly interspersed with occupation levels and activity, and produced a fragment of a kind of brooch used in the late fifth to seventh centuries. An iron knife of this period was also found, albeit in later layers. At Citizen House in the west of the city, where buildings were certainly being erected and maintained in the fifth century, thick layers of 'soil' blanketed third-century workshops before more buildings were erected in the later fourth century, and continued accumulating after them. It is not at all obvious that this should be interpreted as abandonment, even if it is somewhat puzzling. On early medieval sites in northern Europe such dark earths have been interpreted as settlement debris, decomposed organic remains of everyday materials and rubbish, and even of timber and turf buildings: in fact, as indicating intensive activity. A hint that this may well be true for Bath comes when we recall that between the successive floors in the temple precinct are similar layers of dark earth with much animal bone. This material had built up slowly but surely *while* the floors were in use, and the bone evidence made it clear that the area was heavily utilised by people requiring a lot of meat joints. Not only that, but the age and animal-part profile was a typically urban one, with cows and sheep raised away from the site and pigs nearby (in backyard pigpens?). If the cobbling had not been laid, this material would have been a typical, mysterious, dark earth. Again, similar soils continued to build up in the early medieval period.

The generally poor survival of post-Roman archaeological deposits in Bath, and the difficulty in interpreting them, make the loss of what seem to have been wonderfully high quality examples, discovered when the baths were cleared in the 1880s and 90s, all the more tragic. If we were to wonder whether the Saxon poet's view of the baths as 'mead halls' and 'martial halls' 'where a host of heroes . . . shone in their armour' were true; if we were to ask whether the post-Roman rulers of the city and region lived here within the major public buildings,

7 *The wear on the broken-up surviving fragment of late Roman paving on the north side of the Great Bath can be seen lining up with that on the earlier large paving slabs. Note how unworn the slabs to the left are (which were also repaved, now missing), suggesting that the wear took place* through *the later paving in post-Roman times*

converting baths to barracks, precinct to palace, we should not be able to test that hypothesis easily by the use of archaeology. The evidence is gone, but there are hints. We have seen the evidence for late use of the temple precinct, and it is possible to look at the Baths and see signs of use in late-Roman, and perhaps early post-Roman, periods.

It has long been known that the massive Bath stone slabs which form the paving around the Great Bath show heavy wear. This is usually given as the reason for the re-paving of the area with pennant sandstone, fragments of which can still be seen today. However, it is possible to argue that the wear on the original slabs *post*-dates the pennant paving, which now mostly survives over flat and unworn older paving; and areas where it has been removed are also often unworn. The worn areas of original paving are usually bordered rather than covered by later paving. Some reason other than wear must have been the occasion for re-paving, perhaps in the early fourth century (as in the precinct). The visible wear in the paving seems, in fact, to cut *through* the later flooring, down and into the original slabs. In fact, wear polishing on surviving portions of later paving can be seen to continue the lines of the wear on the earlier slabs (**7**). The wear is strictly undated, but it must be late or post Roman. Its narrow, linear nature, east-west along the centre of the walkways north and south of the great swimming bath itself, seems to ignore the bath and be the result of quite determined foot traffic between the east and west bath suites, with the perpetrators perhaps picking their way between piles of rubble and rubbish, and occasionally rising over them. Could these suites have been converted into accommodation in the fifth and sixth centuries, or even (as suggested below) still be partly in use as very reduced baths, and the wear be the consequence of communication between them? The drains and conduits from the hot spring would certainly need some sort of continued maintenance, but this need not have been onerous at the beginning, when the Roman arrangements would continue to function – as in part they do now.

The evidence now makes it clear that, whatever the difficulties of dating and interpretation, *Aquae Sulis* was not deserted soon after 410, and neither was it simply a shell occupied by ragged survivors of the devastation of Roman rule. Wreck compared to its grand days it may have been, but everywhere that the evidence survives there are hints, and sometimes much more, of stone buildings, of the more common timber structures (of a scale and character that are clearly more than mere huts and *need* be no less than that of late medieval timber frame houses), of re-floorings and continued activity in the area around the spring and in the baths. We might compare the much more complete and extensive evidence of occupation of the largely demolished public buildings at the Roman town of Wroxeter in the fifth and sixth centuries, which may have been the base of Vortigern and his successors. This evidence is very ephemeral, and would have barely survived had the town continued to be occupied into modern times; yet it represents a continuing urban activity with high-status buildings and owners.

This impression of fifth and sixth century Bath corresponds with that known to be the case in Gaul and other parts of the continent, where towns are seen to lose both a large part of their population, and sometimes market functions, but retain political/administrative and perhaps religious significance as the centre of the region. This pattern pertains mostly to large cities, and may not be exactly applicable to Bath, but in its recognition of a model of transformation that still allows a town to exist even after major change, it is illuminating.

The late activity in post-Roman Bath also provides the context for a curious reference to Bath in the later Saxon period as *Acemannesceastre*, or *Achamanni* and *Aquamania*. The English generally called the town *Baðon* or *Baðan*, but in documents around the time of the coronation of King Edgar in 973 the town is referred to by these peculiar names. It has been suggested that this was a scholarly revival of a post-Roman name for Bath, replacing the pagan *Waters of Sulis* with a neutral or Christian-friendly *Place of Water* – *Aquæmann* (from the British *mann*: place). The name is only known to us from these sources, but it must have been in use long enough to give the Saxon name to the stretch of Roman road running to Bath from St Alban's – Akeman Street.

Outside Bath similar hints of continuity can be found. While the outward signs of Roman culture disappeared, farms and farming settlements carried on; and most of the medieval villages around Bath have Roman antecedents. Hartley Farm on Charmy Down, four or five miles northeast of Bath, is documented on the same site from the tenth century, and is set in a landscape of Roman and pre-Roman fields.

Excavations at Bathampton (which has a Roman villa at its centre) have showed continuous occupation within a few hundred yards of the present village core from the third century BC until the fifth century AD, with sporadic evidence from the seventh, early eighth and tenth centuries. The earliest documentary reference occurs in 940. Should we imagine the villagers all moved to some mysterious nowhere place and only returned to the villages and farms when historical documents once again start to record their existence in the ninth and tenth centuries? Despite the difficulties in recognising 'sub-Roman' archaeology, it is obvious that the Bath area as well as the town itself remained settled through the post-Roman centuries. Although conditions were quite different from the Roman period, where there were people, there must have been organisation – social, religious and political.

This organisation is also reflected in sites further afield that belong to the period of British resistance to the Saxon advance. One site that is surrounded by dubious claims to antiquity, but nonetheless has produced good evidence of British post-Roman Christianity, is Glastonbury. On the Tor, a monastery seems to have flourished in the fifth and sixth centuries, which maintained some sort of trading contacts with the Mediterranean (as did several British sites of this type and period). An organised church in the British zone is confirmed by the story of Patrick, and the West Country and Welsh origins of many of the saints who preached in Brittany at this time. A church of this period seems to have been established on the site of a pagan Roman temple at Uley, Gloucestershire. Secular sites, major enough to imply that they were the strongholds of a ruling elite, have been excavated at Cadbury Castle, near Ilchester (where the site may succeed the Roman town of *Lindinis*), and at Cadbury Hill at Congresbury, near Weston-super-Mare. Both these sites also show evidence of contact with the Mediterranean, and the probable import of wine.

A reading of Gildas suggests that Roman-style villa buildings had disappeared completely by his day. However, as he informs us that towns were 'not as populated as formerly they once were', and as land ownership was the basis of wealth in all such societies, not only must the population have been overwhelmingly rural (as indeed it had been in Roman times), but there must have been large country estates. These would have been owned by the leaders of society, and might well have been the very estates that were formerly run from the villas. The existence of such holdings, hardly surprising in itself, is proved by the granting of land to Glastonbury Abbey in 601 by the king of *Dumnonia* (which at this date comprised Cornwall, Devon and much of Somerset).

These estates are probably broadly those of Roman times, but controlled from bases that we simply cannot recognise. Excavations at Frocester Court and Barnsley Park (both Gloucestershire), show how the grand house is only one, often transient, element in the history of country estates. A huge cemetery at Cannington, near Bridgewater, Somerset, is one of a very small number excavated which shows apparent continuity of a rural population from Roman times into the seventh or eighth centuries. Henley Wood temple, which may have been the cemetery for Cadbury-Congresbury, is another example, and similar remains have been excavated at Shepton Mallet. Many more of these must await discovery, representing the normal continuity of life and community in this period.

Mick Aston has put forward the idea of a large estate centred on Bath, which may well have its origins in this or an earlier period. He has laid out evidence that the medieval Foreign Hundred of Bath was in origin a large sub-Roman estate, identifiable as the later parishes of the Hundred and almost certainly predating the formation of the Somerset boundary with Gloucestershire and Wiltshire (**43**). This area, in modern terms stretching from Kelston in the west to Warleigh in the east and from St Catherine's in the north to South Stoke, seems to have been the estate which was part of King Osric's gift in 675 (see below). He held it as Royal land, presumably inheriting it whole from ancestors who had taken it from the British. The head or *caput* of the estate may well have been in Bath or just outside in the Barton, an estate in Royal hands until the later Middle Ages. There may be an element of circularity in the argument for continuity, but it is also true that the great majority of farms and villages in the estate are those that have Roman antecedents.

The process of conquest of the British zone, as outlined in the Anglo-Saxon Chronicle, gives us a glimpse of how the little 'kingdoms' might have been organised geographically. It should perhaps be added here that there is much doubt in some quarters about the historicity of the Chronicle for the early years, and detailed analysis is unwise. Nonetheless, its account of the basic narrative trend from the mid-sixth century seems to me to be simple, consistent, and to fit well with what we know from the succeeding years, and is therefore followed here with little more comment.

The British 'stop line' started to be broken everywhere from about 550. The Britons were defeated at Old Sarum near Salisbury in 552, by the energetic West Saxon leader, Ceawlin, who four years later also fought the Britons at Barbury near Swindon, but is not recorded as having won. In 577, he defeated the Britons at *Deorham* (Dyrham, about 8 miles north of Bath) and took the cities of Gloucester, Cirencester and Bath. He also killed three 'cyningas' or kings. Their actual status is unclear, but they could be the rulers of the three cities, or simply generals. This is usually seen as the campaign that broke through to the Severn and separated the Britons in Wales from those in *Dumnonia*, the south west. This much is probably true and marks the passing of the political control of Bath to the Saxons. However, the story is certainly more complex (for example Ceawlin is still fighting the Britons in 584, and despite localised success seems to have withdrawn to his base). The capture of Gloucester, Cirencester and Bath in one battle implies the collapse of a political unit, and the three towns seem to have had some significance within it – they are hardly likely to have been mentioned if they were deserted ruins. This political unit is probably a British territory that grew out of the Roman *civitas Dobunnorum,* originally based on Cirencester. This view is reinforced by the discovery of an inscribed stone from Devon referring to a 'citizen of the Dobunni' in the late fifth or sixth century. The three cities were probably the local centres of government of the British polity, and the three 'kings' the regional leaders, or their military arm, based in or near them, together representing its government. Perhaps now after the years of peace, 'slaughter was widespread, pestilence was rife, and death took all those valiant men away. The martial halls became deserted places, the city crumbled, its repairers fell, its armies to the earth . . . '. There does indeed seem to have been an outbreak

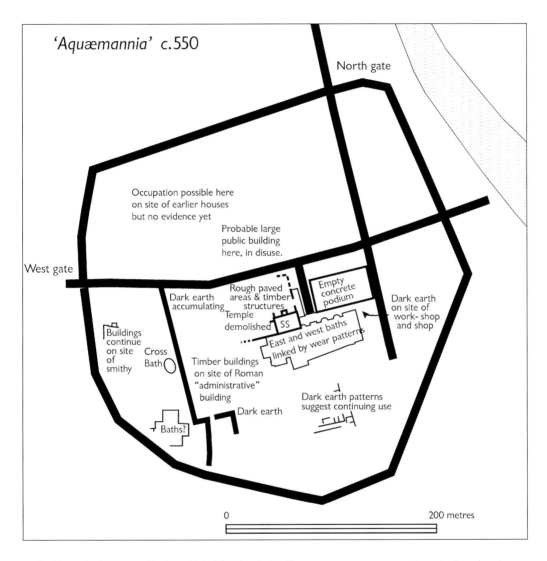

'Aquæmannia' c.550

North gate

Occupation possible here
on site of earlier houses
but no evidence yet

Probable large
public building
here, in disuse.

West gate

Rough paved
areas & timber
structures

Empty
concrete
podium

Dark earth
accumulating

Temple
demolished

SS

Dark earth
on site of
work-shop
and shop

Buildings
continue
on site
of
smithy

Cross
Bath

Timber buildings
on site of Roman
"administrative"
building

East and west baths
linked by wear patterns

Dark earth

Dark earth patterns
suggest continuing use

Baths?

0   200 metres

8 *Plan of sub-Roman Bath, c.550. This is admittedly an attempt to sum up a hypothesis rather than presenting knowledge, but may be nearer the truth than the traditional view. The dark earths in particular suggest areas of use or occupation, but are poorly dated*

of plague, the 'great mortality' of the chronicles, in the 540s and 50s. Was our poet simply telling the plain truth about its impact on the city?

Curiously, the only two archaeological finds from Bath that may relate to this period, an iron knife and a fragment of a bronze brooch, both have West Saxon affinities – yet the conquered province did not become part of the West Saxon Kingdom, or at least not for long. We know that by 626 it formed the bulk of the minor kingdom of the Hwicce. In 628 the West Saxon king, Cynegils, was defeated by Penda, the powerful Mercian king of central England and overlord of the Hwicce, at Cirencester, again suggesting some sort of political significance for the town. From that time the sub-kingdom was firmly in the orbit of Mercia, and by the end of the century it was absorbed into it.

The *Hwicce* are a fascinating people. It is interesting that Bede gives no conversion narrative for them and their first mention is when a Hwiccian princess, Eabae (Eafe), is described as coming from an already Christian people who, from the context, must have been so by the 650s at the latest. This suggests that the Hwicce may have been converted by some other means than an Augustinian mission. One theory is that the Dobunni might have converted the incomers, as the settlement was small-scale and peaceful, and the two groups formed a combined state, the Hwicce. The fighting with Wessex is then seen as political, not related to large-scale immigration at all. The archaeological evidence indicates that the English settlement of the Severn valley and the west midlands was a slow process, coming in the main from the north and east, and that pagan cemeteries are rare, indicating early conversion. As a general rule the British refused to preach to the heathen, and it happening here suggests a much more friendly relationship. It has been shown that a church at Worcester, a northern stronghold of the Hwicce and a late Roman small town, was probably founded in pre-Saxon times and retained its major ecclesiastical status well into the Saxon period, suggesting continuity of church administration from British to Saxon times. We might view the attachment of the Hwicce to Mercia rather than Wessex as the result of a sort of ethnic loyalty to the east, yet one leavened by intermingling with the locals. Ethnic reasons might also ensure good relations with the free British across the Severn. Within six years of the defeat of Cynegils, the latter were allied with the Mercians against the Northumbrian Angles. Was the sub-Roman kingdom defeated by Ceawlin in 577 already a British/English hybrid?

This idea is also supported by the boundaries of the Hwiccian kingdom, which can be deduced from those of the medieval diocese of Worcester. King Osric persuaded Archbishop Theodore to set up this bishopric in 679 or 680 and, as the diocese was meant to serve his kingdom, it seems likely that it reflected its boundaries. These are almost identical to our understanding of those of the Roman *civitas Dobunnorum* as it probably was in late Roman times. By whatever means its control by the Hwicce came about, this again suggests a continuity as a political unit.

In one way or another, Bath passed into the control of the English, and perhaps the last remnants of its civic functions sloughed away with the red roof tiles of the giants' work. The Britons seem to have held out in Somerset for another two or three generations. The Avon valley probably formed the boundary between them

9 *The Wansdyke, a sixth-century British defence against the north? This shows excavations into the two-phase bank in the 1990s. The size of the rampart, even in its denuded state, is obvious and impressive.* Avon Archaeological Unit

and the English to the north, with the modern boundary between Somerset and Wiltshire to the east. Bath would continue to be a frontier town on an important route junction, as the Roman roads and river crossings would remain in use. It would be likely to have been kept in some sort of order as a strongpoint, whether or not there was still an urban population. We know that it was in royal hands, and the estate based upon it continued to be administered.

The west was probably protected from the further advance of the English by the weakness of Wessex in the seventh century and the concentration of Penda's attacks on his enemies to north and east. That a well-organised polity survived in Somerset is shown by the creation of a frontier work, the west Wansdyke. This was a Roman-style ditch and bank with a timber revetment and palisade, which has stubbornly rebuffed archaeological attempts to date it securely but which fits most probably into this period (**9**). It ran along the high ground just south of the edge of the Avon valley, from Bath to Dundry Hill. As the course of this frontier work contains several pre-Roman hill forts in its line (which may have been re-occupied at this time as well), the boundary it defended may well have included Cadbury-Congresbury, and been defined as much by these forts as the Wansdyke itself. As we have seen, 'Cad-Cong' was a British stronghold, and is on high ground overlooking the low-lying Avon levels south of the Avon estuary. The grant of land by Geraint, the British king of Dumnonia, to Glastonbury in 601 suggests control of this area by the British after

Dyrham. Nonetheless, the Britons must have continued to feel under pressure. This is a period of renewed emigration to Brittany.

A lightning raid across this kingdom took place in 614 when the English defeated the British at Bindon in east Devon, but conquest seems to have been delayed until the 650s. In 652 Cenwalh of Wessex lost a battle – it is not clear against whom – at Bradford-on-Avon (which was likely to have been on the border), but in 658 he crossed into Somerset, defeated the British at Penselwood (about 21 miles south of Bath) and drove them to the River Parret, most of the way across the county. Both Cadbury and Glastonbury were now under English control. The British resistance in England outside Devon and Cornwall was over. Bath now had no choice but to find an English future.

Further reading

The best introduction to Roman Bath is Cunliffe 2000, where there is some discussion of the latest periods. My own article Davenport 2000 gives a less detailed account concentrating on the origins, character and development of the town. Archaeological detail is found in Cunliffe 1979, Cunliffe and Davenport 1985, Davenport 1991 and 1999. There is little written on the sub-Roman period, but a very clear if simplified treatment is available in Manco 1998, who also explains the case for 'Aquamann'. For The Ruin, Cunliffe 1983 is a good introduction to the work from an archaeological angle and gives good references. For a background to the period, four books stand out: Cleary 1989, Faulkner 2000 for an idiosyncratic but thought-provoking discussion and Dark 1994b and 2000, who is the most extreme in his belief that Roman society lasted for centuries after 410. The extent of disagreement among archaeologists will be evident from these three. Steven Basset has edited an interesting set of papers on the origins of Anglo-Saxon kingdoms (Bassett 1989b), and also Bassett 1992. Publications on Glastonbury and the Cadburys are Rahtz *et al.* 1992 and Rahtz 1993. The post-Roman cemeteries at Henley Wood and Cannington are in Rahtz *et al* 2000 and Watts and Leach 1996. For the Uley shrines see Woodward and Leach 1993. For the multiple estate around Bath see Aston 1986. These books and articles all give references to more detailed and specific work for those who wish to delve into site detail or academic argument.

2 From convent to most celebrated monastery

We have seen in the last chapter how, although hard information is scarce, there is enough circumstantial evidence to suggest that Bath must have retained some functions as a central place within a sub-Roman political structure. This is not to say that it remained as a bastion of *romanitas* through the years after the collapse of imperial authority, with its buildings and streets maintained in Roman manner. The evidence suggests that the town changed enormously between 410 and 600 (although the details of this transformation are perhaps irrecoverable). Yet the town functioned as the head of a major estate and perhaps a larger political unit, almost certainly forming a part of the sub-Roman polity of the Dobunni. Having accommodated the English infiltration already, it may have continued in much the same way under the Hwiccian kings.

The second date in Bath's history is 675, but this only appears in a twelfth-century copy of a charter held by the monks at Bath until the Dissolution of their abbey in 1539. It was held as evidence of the antiquity of the abbey and its royal founding. On 6 November 675, King Osric of the Hwicce gave land at Bath (*Hat Bathu* – the Hot Baths) to a 'convent of holy virgins'. Osric's generosity was probably a political gesture intended to encourage the church authorities to provide a bishopric for his kingdom, which duly followed in 679.

It is usually assumed that the grant was to enable the *foundation* of the convent, and given Osric's foundation of a monastery at Gloucester, and the cathedral at Worcester at nearly the same time, this seems likely. The Abbess, Berta, was by her name almost certainly Frankish, and it has been plausibly argued that she was from one of a group of monastic houses around Paris, perhaps Chelles, which was active in spreading the monastic ideal. Her presence as a representative of the French missionary houses supports this view of her as the first Abbess of a new convent. However, it is also possible that this was a re-founding or re-organisation of an older religious establishment on the site, which would not perhaps be unlikely in the sub-Roman context. In either case, the Frankish connection is reinforced by the presence as a signatory of Leuthere, Bishop of Wessex, also a Frank. Theodore, Archbishop of Canterbury, originally from Asia Minor (modern Turkey), also signed. The international connections here are worth remarking on. These people were not toiling in insular darkness, however impenetrable it may appear to us.

Berta either died or returned to *Frankia* by 681, for in that year another charter refers to Abbess Bernguida, whose name indicates her nationality: it is a latinization of *Beornwyth*, a recognisably English name. Perhaps Berta, who would have been a very high-born lady, returned to the comforts of her homeland once her mission was accomplished, and an English abbess, certainly of equally aristocratic status, then took over. However, in the presence of the foreign-named Folcburg as the prioress, or second in command, do we see a supervising figure, left behind to advise and perhaps report back to the Frankish mother-house on the progress of the new girls?

The land granted to the new convent was 100 hides. This was probably the estate centred on Bath referred to in the last chapter, and the size of its constituent parts when identified in Domesday Book reaches a total very close to this, and probably forms the basis of the Foreign Hundred of Bath (**43**). Such an estate must have been a working entity, a functioning economic unit to support the new convent and to provide enough wealth to build and furnish the new house. We are not dealing with deserted land being brought back into cultivation by the monastic community, but a thriving estate of farms, flocks and crafts – indeed, it was a thriving estate in royal hands. Thus we see again the continuity in the countryside that archaeology still finds hard to confirm.

We can only speculate on how the new convent fitted into the town. In the last chapter we examined the decline of the city to the dramatic ruin of the poem, and asked what the eighth century town was like. The answer to this question, for the most part, must be based on possibilities and probabilities and the results are shown, perhaps overly boldly, in **10**. That the city walls and gates still stood and formed at least an enclosure, if not a fully defensible circuit, is fairly clear. The grant of Roman enclosed sites, such as forts and small towns, to monastic houses is a commonplace of early English ecclesiastical history. The ready-made enclosures fitted the requirements of monastic life, separated from the outside world, defined and different. However, it seems clear that the early church thought of itself as restoring a Christian organisation that had existed in late Roman times (and in this area had never completely vanished). It had claims to be no upstart culture, but one with roots going back to the days before the current political arrangements of the English. In other words the church, by associating itself with Roman sites and perhaps buildings, legitimised its position and enhanced its status.

There is as yet no archaeological evidence for Berta's nunnery and the written evidence has been entirely exhausted by the narrative above. Yet we can sensibly discuss what might have been. The Temple of Sulis Minerva can hardly have been standing, given the history of dilapidation we know from excavation, and its two-metre high podium was at least half buried by this time. The big public building found in recent excavations west of the baths was certainly demolished in large part by this time. The temple forecourt cobbles, including the blocks from the pagan religious buildings, were probably covered in earth, and there may have been timber buildings constructed in this region. The open areas at least may have been occupied by a farm or small holdings: one explanation for the dark earth found in parts of the town is that it was cultivation soil. The baths still largely stood, however, even if roofs were falling and walls tottering. The springs still flowed through the Roman courts, and both Bede and Nennius, using material dating from around this period, say that the baths were in use and well-known. It has been suggested that the King's Bath (the main spring, the *Fons Sulis* of the temple complex), may have been used by the new church as a baptistery, to Christianise and

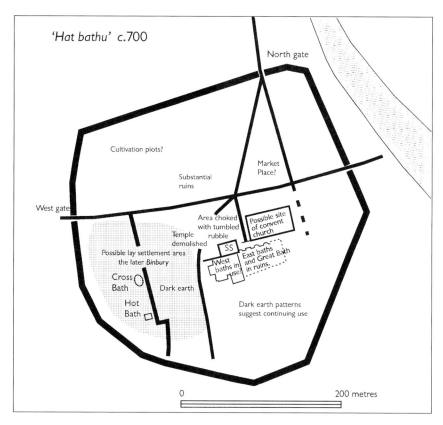

10 *Plan of Bath c.700, the town of* The Ruin. *Apart from the tumbled rubble there is little here that is certain. We have suggested that Binbury, 'the place within the walls', had its origin in this period*

exorcise the pagan spirits from this unnatural place. Yet it is curious that no patron saint or Christian mythology has ever been attached to the spring, and that the hot baths have never since had any kind of religious aspect.

The use of the rest of the walled area in this period is even less understood, but there does appear to be a massive concrete and rubble podium or platform under the present abbey church. This was seen and recorded by nineteenth-century antiquaries, and their descriptions have been confirmed by observations of tiny portions of it in recent years. It is of two phases, the first clearly Roman and probably a raised podium for a temple, the second of unknown date but obviously of both different construction and plan. It has sometimes been suggested that the later structure might be Saxon, but we simply cannot say at present. However, the very fact that it does exist under the abbey church, and that there is every reason to believe that the later Saxon abbey was sited here, makes it seem at least highly likely that Berta and her nuns chose this elevated and dry platform to build their church and conventual buildings.

It is tempting to think that such buildings must have been of timber, but other contemporary churches, such as St Peter's at Bradwell, and Wilfrid's church at

Hexham, were built of stone, largely recycled from Roman buildings, even (in the latter case) when the source of stone was some distance away. There is clear evidence in Bath of deliberate demolition of Roman buildings in order to re-use their materials in monastic structures. Unfortunately it is not possible to pinpoint precisely when this occurred, but the dating, such as it is, does make it possible that the early convent, a prestige-laden royal project, could well have been responsible. When the temple precinct under the Pump Room was excavated in 1981-3, the sequence of dark earths and stone and mortar floors referred to earlier was found to be buried by a massive scree formed of huge pieces of masonry from the Roman building around the spring (**1**). At first this was thought to be the result of the building's collapse, especially as there was clear evidence that the vaulted roof over the spring was unstable. However, close examination of the blocks made it clear that each block, some weighing half a ton, had been carefully moved from its seating, the iron and lead construction clamps removed as valuable scrap and the block then thrown on to the floors below. This incidentally shows that the use of the temple precinct as an open space leading to the spring had by now come to an end, as little attempt was then made to clear the blocks away.

No large-scale attempt to re-use these blocks appears to have been made, but smaller blocks, of which the rest of the spring building was made, were conspicuous by their absence. Were these taken away to rebuild the abbey? Possibly; they certainly appear in the only Saxon wall excavated so far in Bath. Curiously, this wall also contains re-used large Roman blocks. It runs under York Street, on the south side of the baths, at a level just above the highest Roman floors and smashes through the walls of the baths in a way and at a level that suggests the eastern part of the baths were by this stage already demolished to just above the latest floor levels, and covered in debris to this height. This wall was 6-8ft thick (1.83-2.4m), and was traced for over 60ft (20m). It was interpreted by its excavator, Robert Bell, as the precinct wall of the monastery, but it cannot be dated any more precisely than post-Roman and before the later Saxon period. It could belong either to Berta's convent or the later abbey. It has been suggested that this is the wall of the abbey church itself, but we know that no wall to the north can have escaped discovery in excavations in that area, and a building to the south of this wall seems too far south to make sense. The line of this wall continues towards the city wall to the east, and the suggestion is that these formed the south and east walls respectively of an inner precinct which lay south of the street or lane between the west and east gates. However, this wall survived to provide at least the foundation for the later medieval cloister, and may well belong to the later Saxon monastery. We may in that case imagine Berta's community, the nuns and the conventual buildings on the site of the present church and a supporting community of workers and servants, occupying a mix of new timber buildings and refurbished Roman ones occupying the 24 acres of the old town walls with no other subdivisions; and farming perhaps, or at least gardening, in the shadow of the surviving 'giants' work'.

This picture is perhaps the more likely, for one possible interpretation of the community at Bath in this period, for which there is not yet direct evidence, is that it was a *minster*: a church acting as a mother or head church to a small region of other churches (or more accurately, an area that had few if any actual structures to worship in at this early date), at a time when the parish system was not yet in use. These minsters usually held religious and spiritual as well as financial rights over the subordinate members (for example, burial rights). As the head of a spiritual and economic entity the minster often found it had created an urban focus in all but name, one of John Blair's 'monastic towns'.

We next hear of the community at Bath in 757, when a charter grants land south of the Avon to the 'brethren of the monastery of St Peter at Bath'. This is a little surprising as, quite suddenly it seems, the convent has become an all-male monastery – and it remains until the Dissolution as the monastery, later cathedral priory, of St Peter (SS Peter and Paul from the late twelfth century) at Bath. The best solution to this puzzle is to assume that Bath followed the pattern evident at Gloucester (not surprising when both were contemporary royal Hwiccian foundations), where the monastery had probably been a *double house*. This odd-sounding concept was not that unusual in early English monasticism. Two communities, one male and one female, lived under one rule and one leader, usually an abbess, on the same site but strictly segregated in different parts of the monastery. The less than formal layout, often with multiple churches, enabled such separation to exist alongside the normal requirements on all to work and worship according to the regulations of St Benedict. It is usually pointed out that Theodore, who signed the foundation charter, was known to be against double houses, but he may have been mollified by Osric's intention to found single houses (in the future?), as stated in the preamble to the charter, which may have led to the separation of men and women at a date before 757; and then perhaps the female house died out. We know that, coincidentally, Gloucester became a male house after the death of Abbess Eafe in 757.

As a result of King Osric's foundation arrangements, the abbey at Bath was probably held by the Bishop of Worcester. In 781 however, Offa, the powerful king of Mercia, over-king of the other kings in England under whom Osric's successors had dwindled to *ealdormen*, claimed 90 hides at Bath as his rightful property, wrongly held by the bishop. Offa was the most powerful king in England, and obtained papal support (or acquiescence) in his multiple holdings of monastic lands. The bishop, Heathored, was unable to resist the king's persuasive powers and a church synod at Brentford agreed the 'restoration' of the land to Offa, together with an additional 30 hides south of the river. The latter grant gives the clue as to why Offa was so keen to acquire the old Bath estate which Osric had given up. In the king's direct control, these lands were important in the continuing contest with Wessex: Bath was again playing its rôle as a border post. A curious feature of this story is that in the synod documents of 781 the abbey is described as *celeberrimus monasterium*. Why it was called 'a most famous monastery' we do not know; perhaps it was an empty rhetorical flourish, or perhaps it reflects a political or ecclesiastical importance of which we are unaware. Certainly, Offa claimed that the estates were rightfully those of his predecessor and kinsman, King Æthelbald, and it is possible that the city/estate was an important royal base for the defence of the kingdom during the earlier eighth century, and that this prestige rubbed off on the abbey.

The abbey was in any case firmly back in royal hands. The effect on the monks and abbot was probably minimal, except that they would have to do service or render pay to the king directly, and not the bishop. There is, however, a tradition recorded by William of Malmesbury, a generally careful and reliable historian of the early twelfth century, that Offa built St Peter's. This may be true, or it may be a record of his perceived involvement in re-founding it. A major rebuilding at this point under royal patronage is not unlikely, but we have as yet no other evidence for it. It is interesting, nonetheless, that Offa seems to have stayed in the monastery at Bath in 793, according to a much later medieval tradition, and his son and successor issued a charter here in 796, suggesting that Bath was firmly part of the Mercian administrative infrastructure.

The abbey disappears from documentary history for almost 100 years after this, but it is likely that it flourished for most of this time. A prospering abbey, royal interest, political and geographical significance and the continued flow of the springs mean that the economic and social basics were in place for the growth of a town again. Yet once more we have to say that there is little evidence to refute or support the notion. There is some indication that people were still visiting the hot springs, and throughout this period Bath is referred to as *æt baðan* 'at the bath'. Nennius, who put together a heap of facts and legends in the ninth century, gives an interesting description of the use of the Baths, classed as one of the wonders of Britain:

> In the land of the Hwicce [is a hot pool] . . . surrounded by a wall, made of brick and stone, and men may go there to bathe at any time, and every man may have the kind of bath he likes. If he wants, it will be a cold bath; if he wants a hot bath, it will be hot.

This seems to imply that some kind of organised use was still in place at the baths. The hot bath could have been had at any time by walking into one of the hot springs still contained within the Roman cisterns, but a choice of hot and cold seems to imply some kind of use of the Roman water supply and Roman pools. Cold springs are abundant in and around Bath, but cold baths were not available until the nineteenth-century 'scientific' expansion of water treatments. On the other hand, as Nennius himself says that he has not had the time nor skill to sort out all these fragments, this could just be a garbled traveller's tale. Still, his information is supported by Bede's statement in the early eighth century that 'warm springs . . . supply hot baths suitable for all ages and both sexes in separate places and adapted to the needs of each'.

Where might such eighth- and ninth-century bathing have taken place? One possibility is the western bathing complex of the Roman Baths. This is adjacent to the King's Bath, the main hot spring of Bath. The spring water was probably chan-nelled out into a new conduit running south and away to the river. This was its route in later medieval times, after the demolition and collapse of the vault over the spring had blocked the Roman outflow via the Great Bath, the hot swimming bath at the centre of the complex. The circular bath south of the spring may have filled with hot water from this conduit, (the circular pool in the land of the Hwicce?), but it is more likely that bathing in the hot spring waters had already taken on its medieval form of bathing directly in the Roman spring reservoir. West of the circular bath is a series of rooms still in good condition, and which were much more so when first uncovered in the mid-nineteenth century. In places they still survive to the original tops of the walls. The vaulted roofs over these buildings were much less ambitious and more stable than in other parts of the building, and probably stood intact for many centuries. The cold plunge bath and a small swimming bath still visible here are likely to have survived intact into the middle Saxon period, all close by the King's Bath. In particular, such continued use of the west baths might help to explain the outstanding survival of the Roman south wall of the King's Bath with its original openings and the piers of the corridor south of the Circular Bath, still standing to the springing of its vault. As this would all have been in the monks' control, it may have been a source of income or a way of extending a rather special form of monastic hospitality to visitors. One can well imagine Offa bathing *more Romanum*, especially as he aped other Roman customs, such as well-struck coinage.

The economy of eighth-century Anglo-Saxon England did not support or require towns, except for several large trading 'emporia', mostly involved in long-distance (and probably high-value) trade to the continent. These included London (*Lundenwic*), Southampton (*Hamwic*) and Ipswich, which flourished almost in isolation in the seventh and eighth centuries. But monastic settlements and estate headquarters probably acted as convenient and logical centres for whatever local trade was going on, and it is certain that the delivery of supplies from the abbey's lands to the monastery would have been the occasion for much trading. The medieval market place, while clearly in place by the late ninth century, might well have begun to be used on its present site during the eighth, conveniently sited as it is, just inside the north gate and north of the abbey church. The old Roman road leading to the north gate would still have been in use, as it seems never to have been abandoned, but inside we are ignorant of the street system (if that is not too formal a term to use for whatever arrangement of paths and lanes was in use). *Aquae Sulis* had never had a street grid, and indeed seems to have had a street system that changed from time to time, and does not appear to have formed the basis for later systems. But routes in this period would have to lead to and skirt the abbey itself, and provide access to and from the east, west and south gates as well. They would also have to take account of the standing Roman buildings and the piles of rubble marking those that no longer stood. An approximate straight line between the west gate and the original east gate (south of its present position) seems likely, but the route from north to south is hard to divine. Avoiding the abbey buildings, the route would move to the west, but then would have to negotiate the remains of the Baths. Perhaps the most likely route would be across the demolished temple podium and around the west end of the Baths. Remarkably, this is the line of Stall Street, generally otherwise attributed to the twelfth century. However, they would be little more than 'desire lines': these tracks were unlikely to be surfaced.

Given that Offa possibly stayed in Bath, and that his son certainly did, there ought to have been a royal residence in or very near the town. Somewhere in the abbey is the most likely location, but what in the later Saxon period was a royal holding, the Barton estate headquarters, probably in the fields just to the north of the town walls, is also a possibility. Here we might expect something like the early hall at Cheddar: a long, bow-sided timber hall with subsidiary buildings for the court and attendants. In the abbey, there could have been a *palatium* emulating those built by Charlemagne, or perhaps a refurbished Roman masonry building, the ancient prestige of which would suit the aspirations of a king like Offa.

There are a few archaeological finds from the area, but nothing very substantial. At Bathampton Meadow a silver *sceat* dating from the early eighth century was found near the settlement mentioned in chapter one. A spear head found there is a seventh century type. Both were simply stray losses, with little significance, except to show the existence of wealth at this time and place. The *sceat* is one of a rare group of coins strongly influenced by continental examples. This particular style seems to be related to the Friesian coinage (**15**).

The decades between the visit of King Cenwulf in 796 and the presence of King Burhred and his court in 864 were times of great political and social change in Anglo-Saxon England. At first, Cenwulf maintained Mercia's dominance. In the first few years of his reign he even tried to move the seat of the Archbishop of Canterbury to London as a punishment to the rebellious Kentishmen, indicating his continuing control of church affairs (the plan was later abandoned). Warfare against the Welsh continued (Offa had built the Dyke to mark the boundary of Mercia far into what had been Welsh lands), and Cenwulf died on campaign in 821. After his death Mercia's power waned. Ceolwulf lasted two years, and his successor Beornulf was defeated in battle by the resurgent Wessex dynasty led by Ecgbryht. In 829, Ecgbryht was recognised as over-king, *Bretwalda*, of England, and Wessex was the most powerful kingdom on the island.

The emergence of Wessex was to be very important for Bath in the long term, but these power plays were made largely irrelevant for the time being by the impact of a force none had foreseen, the arrival of the men from the north: the Vikings.

Further reading

The nature of the convent is best discussed in Sims-Williams 1974. There is not much easily accessible on the other areas discussed above. Cunliffe 1984 and 1986 and Manco 1998 are useful but less detailed summaries of the whole period. As usual, the VCH gives a good but dated local summary. Little archaeological material is available for this period locally and most of it is still unpublished. For the wider story, the Anglo-Saxon Chronicle is the basic (much disputed) source but the general Anglo-Saxon background is more easily approached through one of the general treatments, such as Welsh 1992 or Wilson 1971. For church organisation prior to 1200 see Blair and Sharpel 1992. A *detailed* study of Anglo-Saxon background would start with the magisterial Stenton 1971, but not for the faint-hearted. For *emporia* – the Saxon trading stations – see Hodges 1982 and for Saxon towns in the south see Haslam 1984. Bede is tangential to our story, but a fascinating insight into the lives and politics of the early English and their church.

3 After Offa:
Alfred and the town reborn

The first recorded visit of the Norsemen was a low key affair, except from the point of view of the Reeve (king's representative) of Dorchester. When he rode down to Portland Bay to enforce the rule that trading must take place in a port (i.e. a market town where it could be witnessed in case of disagreement, and tolls could be taken), he was killed by the three ship-loads of raiders that he had taken to be merchants. That was 789; in 793 at the other end of the country, the monks of Lindisfarne fled or were killed as Vikings pillaged the rich treasures of the holy spot. But this shocking event seemed isolated. The Norsemen did not return until 835, and this time they initiated a regular series of raids all around the coast. At first, they rarely headed inland and never stayed long. When they did offer battle they were often defeated as, in alliance with the Cornish, they were by Ecgbryht of Wessex in 838. Ecgbryht died in 839 and his sons succeeded him in Wessex and Kent. The Vikings came in larger numbers and defeated Saxon armies on several occasions: rather than three ships in 793, 350 sailed up the Thames in 851. In that year an army wintered in England for the first time. How seriously these raids were taken is not clear. The Chronicle entry for 855 couples an overwintering of Vikings in Kent with King Aethelwulf of Wessex spending a year in Rome as a pilgrim, while two years earlier Aethelwulf had assisted Burhred of Mercia in 'subduing the Welsh'. Aethelwulf died before the full force fell: Burhred bore it in full. In 864 he held court in Bath with his queen and a full retinue of councillors and bishops. The next year he began a ten-year fight for his kingdom.

In 865 a great army landed in East Anglia, and by 870 they had conquered most of northern and eastern England. It was during this campaign in particular that the Norsemen acquired their terrible reputation for barbarity. They destroyed not only lives and property, but works of art, literature and religion. During this campaign the young Alfred, then not yet king, led a contingent of troops in alliance with Burhred against the Vikings at Nottingham. The rulers of Mercia and Wessex had been close since Aethelwulf's reign: a Mercian was married to Alfred's sister, and Alfred's daughter was to marry into the Mercian royal family. The short term result of Nottingham was a truce, but in 874 Burhred was driven out of his kingdom by the Norse and died in Rome. Alfred had now become king of Wessex, but was under pressure from the invaders on all sides.

From the very beginning of Alfred's reign in 871 the Vikings, in this case the Danes, attacked Wessex but were held off. They attacked again in 876 and 878. In the latter campaign, after a defeat at Chippenham, only 10 miles from Bath, 'all Wessex capitulated' – except for Alfred. He retreated to the 'isle' of Athelney, an island in the marshes of the Somerset Levels. Here he built a fort and bided his time until, incredibly, he was able to raise an army and return to rout the Danes. The Treaty of Wedmore which followed effectively expelled the Danes from both Wessex and all England west of the Roman Watling Street.

It is hard to believe that Bath was not intensely involved in these events, but is not mentioned in the accounts. The surrounding estates and the monastery and settlement must have felt the effects if not the actual force of the Danes' presence in the months they were based at Chippenham, especially as the abbey and its lands were a royal possession. But as the town was part of Mercia, allied under a puppet king to the Danes, both financial and military service would have been at their service, not Alfred's. Perhaps, though, the monastery and its estates were already much reduced in wealth and importance. Alfred himself laments the collapse of monastic learning and proper religious observance in his time, and this is usually understood to have come about because of the turmoil and disruption caused by the continual raids and then the horribly destructive wars. Whether Bath even had monks or an abbot at this time is unknown, but later events do suggest that the abbey had lost most if not all of its lands during this period. This could have happened if Burhred's successor, Ceolwulf, the puppet king of the Vikings, had been compelled to distribute royal lands to his masters. Most likely the abbey did exist, but in a disorganised and impoverished state: what lands and property it might have retained were probably pillaged and harried during the 870s.

A new town

Alfred, however, was about to start a new chapter for Bath. It was a sign of his greatness that in the midst of the wars he was also planning to rebuild his kingdom, to strengthen or recreate all those facets he thought necessary for its future. Religion and education were foremost once the military security of the kingdom was assured. The first two would naturally be connected in contemporaries' minds with monasteries and other such centres. Alfred managed to found two, but could not secure enough interest for a more widespread revival (he had to bring in foreign monks to run Athelney and Winchester). It was not until the middle years of the next century that a full monastic revival became possible. Bath, as with other abbeys and convents, seems to have carried on in a probably less than satisfactory state, financially and liturgically. However, it is beyond belief that the monastery was not affected by the major event in Bath's history in these years: its incorporation in the system of defensive fortresses and refuges designed to ring Wessex and protect it and its population from further attack – the towns and forts of the *Burghal Hidage*.

These forts were set in a wide ring around Wessex, in strategic positions on frontiers, river crossings, and route centres (**11**). Others were founded in the interior of the kingdom. In this rôle they were strategic military centres; in another they were

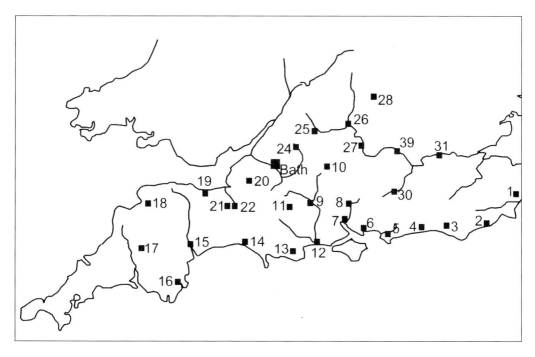

11 *The* burhs *of Wessex, Alfred's strongpoints, towns and refuges. The border distribution plus a heartland is evident. Nearby* burhs *include Axbridge (20), Malmesbury (24), Shaftesbury (11), Wilton (9), Cricklade (25) and Langport (22). Oxford (26) may be a later addition*

refuges for the population, and were generally positioned to be within a day's journey of the home of almost every one of Alfred's subjects. Some were new-built, earthwork and timber forts such as Wallingford and Wareham; some were small existing settlements completely replanned, such as Oxford; others, Roman fortified sites whose defences could be refurbished, such as Porchester, Exeter, or Bath. Malmesbury was an Iron Age hillfort with, like Bath, an ancient abbey within its highly-defensible circuit. What is astonishing is not so much the military thinking behind such a system of forts, which was successfully extended by Alfred's successors, and may have had origins in early fortified centres in Mercia, but that these centres were quite clearly meant to be centres of population, markets and production – towns. In other words, Alfred was setting up a new urban structure, not just restoring, but re-engineering the economic and social infrastructure. But there was another implication in this new beginning for Bath. Since Osric's day the town had been in Mercia; under Alfred and his successors it was now firmly a part of Wessex.

The document that tells us about these changes may have been put together after Alfred's death, although modern research suggests it dates from the 880s; no one doubts that it records Alfred's intentions and achievements. The document is called the *Burghal Hidage* because it details the allocation of land units (*hidage*) to the fortified centres (*burhs* – modern boroughs). Each hide (traditionally the amount of land needed to support a family, sometimes arbitrarily set at 20 acres or 8.33ha) allocated to a town had to supply one man to maintain and defend the town. Four men were required to defend one pole ($16\frac{1}{2}$ft or 5.03m) of the defences. So the hidage (number of hides allocated to a town) will tell us the Alfredian figure for the length of the town defences. This can usually be shown to be remarkably accurate. For example, Winchester is within 5.5 per cent of the given figure. For Bath, give or take a little, it indicates that the walls in use in Alfred's time followed the same line as when they were demolished and built over in the eighteenth century. In fact, the present known line of the walls is 1250 yards (1143.3m) long, and the length given by the Burghal Hidage formula is 1375 yards (1257.6m), which is a 9 per cent discrepancy. While various attempts have been made to account for the difference, the variation only reflects the round figure of 1000 men that was allocated to Bath, 91 over the linear theoretical requirement.

Nonetheless, it is not always the case that the walls of Alfred's *burhs* followed the line of available Roman predecessors. At Exeter only two sides of the old enclosure were used, and they were continued to the River Exe, which itself provided the other two sides of the defences, enclosing a larger area. It has sometimes been thought that this may have happened at Bath, as there is an enigmatic wall shown on early seventeenth-century maps running from the south-west corner of the city walls towards the river. This wall is called the Fosse Dyke on some nineteenth-century aps. However, it almost certainly pertains to the close of the post-conquest cathedral priory, as we shall see in a later chapter.

The Roman wall may have been in a poor condition, but we actually know little about how or if it was maintained after it was built. It is likely that repairs would be needed, and certain that the ditch would have to be scoured out, as defensive moats require constant attention if they are not to silt up. Excavation in front of the wall at Upper Borough Walls in 1980, though frustratingly limited by safety and practical constraints, revealed evidence of what may have been done in *c.*890. The large, late Roman ditch was silted up by this time, and it is not clear that it was cleared out for the Alfredian refurbishment. But it seems likely that some kind of timber revetment was carried out to the area at the lip of the ditch, probably in the form of a low timber palisade, a 'forework' to the main defences (**12**). Nothing similar was seen in excavations on the west side of town in 1990, nor under the Empire Hotel in 1995; but the latter made it clear that the Roman ditch had not been refurbished, and that a much smaller ditch, *possibly* originating at this time, was filled in by the twelfth century. The Roman gates may have been refurbished or rebuilt, a process easily within the abilities of Alfred's military engineers, as shown at Portchester, where the sea gate, at least, was rebuilt around this time.

The Saxon town plan

It is within the walls that the most astounding change was made, something all the more astonishing because it was repeated in all the new boroughs: the whole town was replanned. However the Roman street pattern had been altered and adapted for

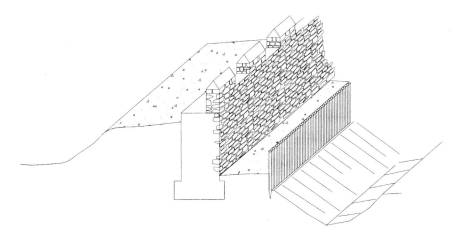

12 *Reconstruction of the Alfredian defences, based on excavations by T. O' Leary. The wall at this point, mostly Roman, is about 3m (10ft) thick. Compare figure* **55**

the various activities in the walled area, it was now completely replaced. No present street inside the walls of Bath follows a Roman line, with the possible exception of Westgate Street and some part, perhaps, of High Street, and these only because they lead from Roman gates. Most are directly descended from Alfred's layout. In fact, there seems to have been a standard system for this planning. A road ran around the town inside the defences, rather like that prescribed for forts by Roman military writers, to allow speedy access to the wall walks. The town itself was divided up into *insulae* or blocks, by a regular grid of streets, on either side of a main street which joined the main gates, again on the Roman pattern. Alfred or his architects clearly had a good understanding of Roman military and town planning practice, and had access to ancient writers like Vegetius. Alfred complained of the lack of learning in his day, but was a leader in trying to re-establish it. Of course, unlike the new foundations such as Wareham, there were existing constraints: the abbey, the three springs, standing Roman buildings or ruins. These meant that the plan at Bath was not so clear cut as at other towns; the ideal was modified by reality.

The plan reproduced as figure **14** was first recognised as of Saxon origin as late as 1976, but while the broad idea has gained acceptance, no attempt has been made to study the layout in any more detail. A main element was the market place, now High Street, just inside the north gate. This was probably laid out as a wide, open space from the beginning. It joined with the east-west street at its southern end, but there could be no central crossroads such as Carfax at Oxford, because the abbey stood athwart the line of any southern road. In fact this would have been an ideal place for a market, just inside the main entrance to the city and probably outside the gates of the abbey, and it has been suggested above that this may already have been a market place in earlier centuries. Whatever state it was in, the abbey would still have been the only major economic engine in the town at this point. It is hard to imagine the springs being much of an attraction in the conditions of the time.

Only the western part of the east-west street still exists, as Westgate Street and Cheap Street. Its eastward continuation was removed when the cathedral precinct was extended northwards after 1091, and the east gate repositioned in its present more northerly site. The extent of the abbey precinct at this time is unknown, but a lane which in the later Middle Ages ran southwards from the east of the King's Bath and divided the bishop's palace from the priory precincts may well have been an Alfredian street in origin, as it served the parish church of St James's (of near certain pre-Conquest date) until 1279. A short continuation north would pass the west front of the later abbey church, and provide a southern route in place of the direct one. The abbey precincts would then have been to the east.

The area north of Westgate Street and Cheap Street and west of the market place was laid out in four blocks divided by small lanes, which in the early Middle Ages were called twichens, Old English for a lane running 'between', indicating their function as dividers as much as thoroughfares. The southern area seems also to have been laid out notionally, but far less clearly, into four blocks, but these were nearly twice as long, and confused by the presence of the springs in this part of town. Stall Street may have been laid out at this time, but it has been thought by various writersc(including the present one) that Stall Street dates to the creation of the cathedral priory close after 1091. In any case the Roman temple of Sulis Minerva would need to have been completely demolished by the time this street was put through.

The lane parallel to the west now only survives in part, as Bilbury Lane. We shall come to *Binbury* later, but the interest here is that this lane is the only Saxon Street attested archaeologically. In excavations in 1986 north of Bath Street, on the site of the present BHS store, a short length of rough cobbled street was found running alongside the partly extant Roman temple precinct wall, on the line of the north-wards continuation of Bilbury Lane (**13**). It was not well-dated, but was considerably earlier than the mid-eleventh century and it was exactly where such a street was predicted to be in the 1970s. It is a little paradoxical that this archaeologically surviving street did not survive as a functioning street into the later Middle Ages.

It is natural to wonder how much the Roman street plan underlay the Saxon layout. As indicated above, the answer is hardly at all. The north gate is almost certainly on the Roman site, as are the original east and west gates. These and the walls acted as obvious constraints, but within them Alfred's planners seem to have started out afresh. The givens appear to have been the desire for an intramural street running around the inside of the ramparts, obviously to facilitate defence; an east-west route joining the gates; and the market place inside the north gate. In addition, the springs and the abbey had to be taken into account. It is possible to investigate how this planning might have been done by a careful study of the present layout, minus the late eighteenth and early nineteenth century 'improvements'.

The first thing that is needed in surveying is a baseline. The irregular route of the city wall does not offer an obvious datum, but a line between the east and west gates does. The present east gate is the only surviving medieval city gate in Bath, of thir-teenth and fourteenth century date. There are good reasons for believing that in Saxon and probably Roman times it was further south, on the line of Westgate

13 *The stone base layers of the short-lived Saxon Bilbury Lane as excavated in 1986. North is to the right, and the road has been truncated on north and south.* Bath Archaeological Trust

Street/Cheap Street, and was moved to its present position after 1091. Given this straight line across the town, we might expect to be able to detect some evidence of its rôle in the laying out of the town plan. A lot of assumptions have to be made and the picture that emerges is provisional: it is also convincing and highly probable .

As well as a baseline, a measuring unit is needed. We know that the city wall defences were measured in poles, units of $16\frac{1}{2}$ft or $5\frac{1}{2}$yards (5.03m). It is likely that the planning was done in these units, and looking at the town plan supports this theory. It seems as if groups of three and four poles were favoured. If we use the pre-improvement maps we can identify blocks which are certainly of medieval form and probably, given the conservatism of property boundaries, close to the Saxon shape and size (**14**). The intramural street seems to be two poles wide. Measuring along the north side of Westgate Street from the west gate the southern edge of the first block is 14 (which resolves into six and eight) poles. The 'twichens' are one pole, but are notionally included in the block or insula dimensions. The next blocks are 8, 12 and 12 poles respectively. The width of the southern end of High Street is six poles and the next block is nearer 12, the pre-existing city walls forming a fixed limit which was not amenable to the units used by the Saxons. The blocks were then laid out northwards on these base units, and again the city wall and gates required adjustments to the ideal. The blocks seem to have been laid out at right angles to the base line, but the northwest insula's west side sloped inwards. This and the northern edges of all the insulae, and therefore their length, was dictated by the city wall. The block alongside the market place was constrained by the shape of that open space, which

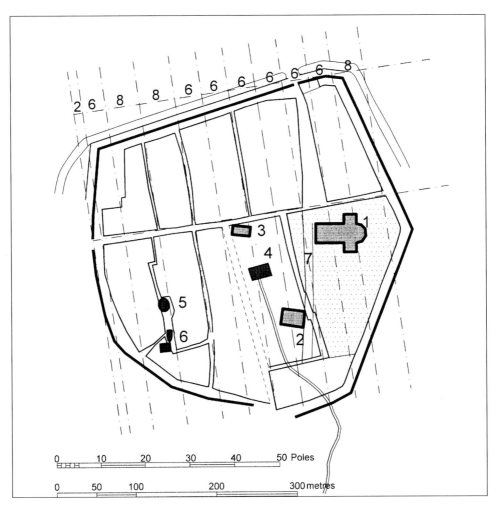

14 *Alfred's burh of Baðan and the possible units of survey. 1. The Abbey, 2. St James' Church pre-1279, 3. The chapel of St Mary (later St Mary de Stalls), 4. The King's Bath, 5. The Cross Bath, 6. The Hot Bath, 7. Hypothetical street*

itself shows signs of being planned carefully. It was laid out or perhaps preserved as a trapezoidal shape, two poles wide inside the north gate, four poles wide half way down and six poles at the southern end.

The main east-west street seems to have been set out as two poles wide, with the southern insulae again laid out from it. The layout was complicated by the springs, the abbey, and the possibility that some of the later medieval parish churches existed already in some form. The first two blocks are 12 and 11 poles wide, including the lane running down to the Cross and Hot Bath springs. The actual line was modified by the presence of the springs, and possibly St Michael's Within. Despite this, it follows the grid remarkably well. Stall Street is not considered here to have been part of the layout, as is indicated by the way it ignores the alignment of the grid. The next block might have been six poles, but from here on later alterations have obscured the layout – or perhaps the existence of the abbey prevented the application of the scheme, which would not be necessary in the abbey precinct. This area also contained the King's Bath Spring, and very probably St James' Church. This block is very uncertain as the lanes that define it are difficult to reconstruct, but its eastern boundary, running west of the abbey and east of the King's Bath, may be represented by Abbey Street, which could well have dog-legged to the site of the south gate along Abbey Gate Street. The next block east was for the abbey. This is likely to have been dictated by existing buildings and rights rather than surveyors' ideals, and is of no very clear whole dimensions. However, the broad Saxon wall mentioned in chapter 2 divided the abbey block neatly into equal northern and southern halves, measured along the lane to the west, of about 15 poles each. Further work is necessary, but there is little doubt that the new town was a planned one in most respects.

Churches

The springs and the abbey were clearly pre-existing constraints to the planning of the town, but it is much less obvious if the intramural churches existed at this time. In the Middle Ages there were four parish churches inside the walls apart from St Peter's, the abbey church, and some private chapels. St Michael's Without served the Broad Street/Walcot Street suburb. The parish status of these churches is unlikely to date before the twelfth century, when population growth and ecclesiastical reform led to a restructuring and expansion of the parochial system. They are, in fact, most likely to have originated as private chapels, founded by landowners within the town in late Saxon or Norman times to serve their tenants and households. At a similar date, the lords of country manors often founded a chapel for matching reasons (see St Mary Magdalen in chapter 6). On these grounds they are not likely to predate Alfred, and their dedications provide evidence (albeit weak) of a later date: dedications to St Michael and (especially) St Mary, while clearly in use earlier, were most popular in the twelfth century, and we shall see in chapter 6 that this is the probable date for St Michael's Within and St Mary de Stalls. An origin as private chapels for St Michael's and St Mary's by the North Gate is indicated by the later, lay ownership of *advowsons*, the right to appoint the incumbent. The pre-eminence of the Abbey as the mother church is also shown by its retention of burial rights (later taken over for the laity by St Mary de Stalls, which is significantly first mentioned as a chapel in the abbey's lay graveyard). However, St James' had a burial ground in pre-Norman times and its advowson was in royal hands later, suggesting a royal foundation in the royally-owned new town. St James was also a favourite twelfth century dedication, but this particular church may have been rededicated, given its pre-conquest cemetery. As Manco has pointed out, it could well have been founded by Alfred as a church and burial ground for the new citizens, distinct from the abbey.

An alternative view is possible. Early convents and monasteries sometimes have several churches, often set out on the same axial alignment. St Michael's Within, St Mary de Stalls and St Peter's are all on the same approximate alignment, raising at least the possibility that the two smaller churches originated as axial chapels, of the early foundation of the nunnery (which was hinted at in chapter 2). This would strengthen the argument that the early nunnery utilised all of the walled area, with conventual buildings and churches scattered throughout it. On balance however, it seems preferable to view these churches as originally being private chapels, as it seems unlikely either that the abbey would agree to the loss of such ancient chapels or, if it did, that there should be no ecclesiastical record of it.

The overall master plan, if such it is, also seems to have extended into laying out individual properties. Whether this implies an empty town, or one where the king had total freedom in dealing with the arrangement and awarding of properties, is not clear. That the town was royal property is certain, and several of the northern blocks do show evidence of rational subdivision into halves and so on, again implying a master plan (**26**).

This master layout also had to take people into account; the abstract town plan had to provide for the inhabitants. It is likely that the king, as landlord, provided some kind of inducement to tenants to take up property, above and beyond the provision of security and investment opportunity. This may have taken the form of exemptions from customary service, or advantageous rents (as some evidence suggests occurred at Oxford). It is likely that those who had obligations to the defence of the town under the hidage system would have been offered land inside the walls, and certainly major landlords had rights to service from properties in the town at Domesday. Of 178 burgesses (or property holders) in 1086, only 64 paid direct to the king, 24 to the abbey, and the rest to the king's barons.

Administration

This kind of town planning implies town administration, which Alfred also established. Bath was a royal estate, and such estates were run by *reeves*, royal appointees exercising the king's delegated powers. The town was probably at this time also a 'hundred', a judicial and administrative unit. The reeve's household would be his staff, and these people would dominate the hundred courts and meetings, as well as still having to administer the customary and bylaws in force (Alfred had also ordered the laws of his predecessors be drawn up and codified anew). We know little about these officials, but another Alfred, who was town reeve of Bath, and possibly King Alfred's appointee, died in 906, and his death was noted in the Anglo-Saxon Chronicle. Three years later the new see of Somerset was founded, with the bishop's seat at Wells. Bath's ecclesiastical status was linked for the first time to this small Somerset village.

In addition, Bath was the centre of the foreign hundred, the judicial, administrative and fiscal subdivision of the shire which was also part of the royal holding, and would have been run on behalf of the king by a bailiff. He would probably be based in the Barton farm just outside the northern walls, since this, the seat of the Barton estate in the twelfth century and later, was certainly by then synonymous (but not coterminous) with the foreign hundred. This hundred might have been the original estate granted to the abbey by Osric, but if so was now almost entirely in royal hands, the kings of Wessex clearly considering themselves Offa's successors in title by royal right.

Binbury

Bilbury Lane is a short length of road that runs from Lower Borough Walls to Beau Street, the Georgian replacement of Bell Tree Lane. While there was no continuation of the road north of Bell Tree Lane until the early nineteenth century, as mentioned above excavations have shown that it once did, and was of Saxon origin. Bilbury is a late corruption of Binbury (or sometimes Bimbery), which occurs in thirteenth-century documents, and probably comes from the Old English *Binnanburh*, 'within the fortified place'. Clearly the lane is within such a fortified place, the walls of Bath, but this is not very informative. We can learn more by plotting properties that in the thirteenth-century property documents are located in *Binbery* and *Binbury* (**10**) (these clearly refer to a nomenclature established long before, and the name largely disappears by 1250). This mapping shows that all these properties are in the south-west quarter of the walled area, west of Stall Street and south of Westgate Street. By 1335 there was a chapel of All Saints in Binbury, near the junction of Bimbery Lane with Bell Tree Lane, and St Michael's Within is on the northern edge of the area. Binbury also contained two of the three hot springs. Therefore Binbury is a well-defined quarter of Bath, and it is the only one with a name. What significance can we attach to this fact? The name must be significant. For it to be singled out as being 'within the fortifications' implies that it was there before Alfred's refounding, as the rest of the town was obviously and by definition 'within the walls' after that. It is likely that this area was the part occupied pre-Alfred, and distinct from the abbey. It may have serviced the abbey, or it may have grown up alongside it as the monastic town (or more realistically village) that was mentioned in chapter 2. If this is the case, then we have a valuable insight into the layout of the pre-Alfredian town. The abbey would occupy the eastern part of the enceinte, dominating the north gate and possible market place, and with the main hot spring, the King's Bath, in its probable ambit. The secular settlement contained the other two springs, and was convenient for both south and west gates. As Chapman and Holland have pointed out, such an established settlement might well have added to the difficulties of formal planning which are evident in this part of the Alfredian town. By contrast, the orderly northern part may have been laid out on the open, cultivated ground postulated in chapter 2.

A   B

C   D

15 *(A) Silver sceat from Denmark/Frisia dating 710-30, and therefore pre-Viking. Such coins are relatively uncommon and very rare this far west. Found in Bathampton, just east of Bath. (B) Silver long cross penny of Æthelræd the Unready minted in Bath. (C) Silver short cross penny of Cnut wearing a pointed helmet from the Bath mint. (D) Edward the Confessor on a Bath mint silver penny. The different look of the heads, despite their crudity, suggest the moneyers are attempting portraits.* Bath Archaeological Trust *(A) and* Roman Baths Museum, Bath *(B-D)*

The Bath mint

Early in the reign of Alfred's son, Edward the Elder (899-925), we know that a mint was functioning in the town. Coins based on a design from the Winchester mint were issued with Edward's name (although – oddly to our eyes – with no image) on the obverse, and 'BAÐ' on the reverse for *Baðan* or *Baðum* – 'at the Baths' (**15**). Coins from this period, and indeed from the whole first half of the century, are so rare that the lack of coins of Alfred does not make it impossible that Alfred himself set up the mint. Nonetheless, it remains true that no coins from the Bath mint are known from his reign. The mint grew, and was one of a large group of smaller mints providing coinage for Wessex, and later the rest of England, set up by Edward and his successors to supplement the output of the large mints at Winchester, Canterbury and London. Coin minting was a serious affair and a royal monopoly; moneyers were granted the privilege of manufacturing and issuing coins under very strict rules and supervision. King Athelstan (925-39) issued laws in 928 (probably restating the accepted position) stipulating that all mints had to be in a *burh*. This tied in with the rules that all financial business should be in the open and witnessed, and therefore in a centre of trade and population. The further stipulation that 'there shall be one coinage throughout the king's dominions' is an example of the highly effective governmental and administrative system that was developed by the Wessex monarchy in the course of the next 200 years. Coin metal was to be good quality, only approved dies were to be used, and those by approved moneyers, and coinage should be taken in and re-issued in a nation-wide quality check as often as every four years. Penalties for non-observance were draconian. Bath was now part of the efficient nation state of Late Saxon England.

Apart from Reeve Alfred, the moneyers are the first named individuals we know of in Bath since the nuns in the seventh century. We know little of them beyond their names, which were stamped on to the reverse of the coins along with the abbreviation for Bath. Herewis and Biorhtulf, the two earliest examples known to us, are English names. Biorthulf may have come from Kent, as the spelling of his name with an 'i' is typical of Kentish dialect. Herewis is probably the earliest name we have, from Athelstan's reign. Biorhtulf thrived under several kings, first appearing under Athelstan and last striking coin early in Edgar's reign, *c.*960. All the names up until the end of the tenth century and beyond are English: Æthelric, Æthelferth, Æthelsyge, Edstan, Wynstan, Wulfbald among others. They would have been wealthy craftsmen (the mint is referred to as 'a smithy' in the laws), able to stand the cost of, and provide the security for, holding quantities of silver. Only one mint existed in Bath (London, by contrast, had 10), so the moneyers must either have held the 'contract' for short periods in turn, or worked together from time to time. Under Edgar there were six moneyers in a reign of 16 years; under Æthelred Unræd (the 'Unready'), there were 20 in 34 years. Perhaps the wealthy burgesses of Bath took it in turns to provide the financial backing, and to spread both the risk and the rewards. The mint continued until the early twelfth century; and although its products have been found as far away as Scandinavia, not one has been found in or near Bath.

Archaeology

A few traces of this period have been found in excavation. The revetment of the town's defensive ditch (mentioned above) was seen in very limited excavations between Upper Borough Walls and New Bond Street. The interpretation of the excavator was that the silted-up ditch first dug by the Romans had been re-excavated, and its inner edge made vertical by a timber palisade projecting as a wall above the ground surface (**12**). This would have formed an outer defence around the wall which would have been quite effective. The dating is rather uncertain, but it is certainly post-Roman and pre-Norman, and Alfred's work provides by far the most likely context. Much more research is needed to confirm this interpretation, but it fits in with the rather more large-scale double walls on the north side of contemporary Oxford. Incidentally, if this outer revetment is used as the line of the defences, the Burghal Hidage figure of 250 poles (1375 yards) is rather close.

Inside the walls, the evidence uncovered to date has been both scarce and difficult to date accurately. The radiocarbon dates taken from three burials uncovered in excavations south of the abbey church in 1993 allow the possibility that some of the 20 monks and others buried there before 1091 were living in the community in the later ninth century. As the burials were in rows, they must have

16 *Saxon burials in the monks' graveyard at the Saxon abbey.* Bath Archaeological Trust

been marked above ground (**16**); and two elaborately carved stones, re-used in later medieval graves, may well have been employed for this purpose. Both are influenced by the Winchester style of manuscript illumination dating from the mid- to late tenth century, with its rich patterns of plant tendrils and flowers (**17**). One seems to have been an upright marker, the other part of a grave cover, probably set at ground level to provide a richly ornate, full-length grave slab. This apparent wealth is reflected both by the results of the physical analysis of the remains, and by a curious feature of the interment.

All the individuals were adult, aged from 17 to 45 or older at death. The five male examples whose height could be calculated revealed a range from 168.3cm (5ft 6½in) to 183.6cm (6ft¼in), suggesting a nutritious diet in youth. Caries were rare, but dental health in general was poor, with evidence of widespread tooth loss associated with plaque and infections. The incidence of osteo-arthritis suggested that these people worked quite hard, and at least one had a healed lower leg fracture which had left him crippled but still active. Two of the sample had extensive ankylosing of the bone, especially the vertebrae. This overgrowth with bony plates and extrusions is often associated with a fat-rich diet and being quite overweight. By adding the disarticulated bone from this later Saxon period, the total sample of recovered bone represented 33 individuals. Only four could be positively identified as women; of these one height determination was possible, which at 163.3cm (5ft 3in) again shows good nourishment in youth. This pattern matches well what we would expect from a Benedictine monastery – a well-nourished entry, plentiful food thereafter – but is rather more active than might be expected for a scholarly order like the Benedictines.

The curious feature of interment is one repeated in many high-status cemeteries of late Saxon times, or in groups that seem to be special in some way within a cemetery; the practice of laying the body on a bed of charcoal. These 'charcoal burials' are little understood, but seem to reflect status. Not all the Saxon inhumations in this cemetery were so treated, but it does have a remarkably high proportion, approaching 40% of a small sample. This becomes a bit less surprising when we remember that the excavated sample came from what was the most important area of the cemetery certainly after 1100, and possibly also in preconquest times. The women would be special guests or patronesses of the order, granted burial with the community. We are reminded of Eadgyvu, a tenth-century 'sister of the community,' whose coffin plaque was found in this cemetery in the 1890s (**17**).

Another cemetery, which despite being in the abbey precincts was probably lay, has been excavated under the abbey churchyard outside the Pump Room. The lower levels of this predate 1100, and some burials are certain to date from the tenth and eleventh century.

Nothing more of the abbey buildings has been found so far, but the monks' cemetery enables us to frame certain questions, and to narrow down some of the

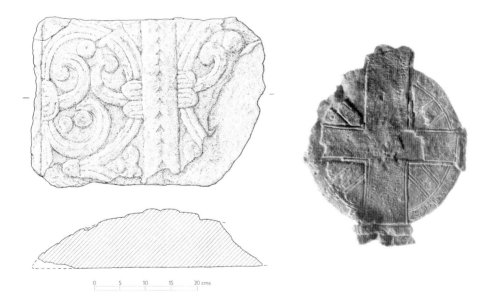

17 *The elaborate tenth-century grave slab found in the monks' graveyard in 1993, and the Eadgyvu plaque, a lead coffin fitting commemorating a 'sister of the community' of about the same time, found 100 years earlier. The lead disc is just over 10cm high.* Bath Archaeological Trust and Roman Baths Museum, Bath

possibilities. The burials were laid out in parallel rows north to south, aligned with the present abbey church. Seven such rows were found in the excavation area, and there could easily have been 15 or 20 across the cloister. This makes it extremely likely that the Saxon church was on the same alignment. The rest of the excavations south of the church make it fairly clear that the Saxon church could not have been to the south of the medieval abbey church; and the likely route of Cheap Street before 1091 leaves no room to the north, making it almost certain that we must look under the present church for the Saxon abbey church. While the sites of the Saxon predecessors of Wells and Winchester remind us that such an interpretation is not always applicable, other parallels such as Glastonbury or Romsey show that it is not unprecedented. The fact that no traces have yet been found is not surprising when we consider that the Saxon building would lie below the Norman church, whose floor is two metres below the present version; and the whole area in between is filled with post-medieval burial vaults.

Little is known of the rest of the buildings and activities in the town, and this has to be inferred from the results of excavation. We have already described one of Alfred's streets, found in 1986; and this is interesting because it did not survive in use for long. Dating evidence is not good, but we know it was blocked by an earthen bank some considerable time before the mid-eleventh century, but after a clay floor which had been laid out alongside the road was buried by rubbish (**18**). This bank was on the same alignment as a property boundary of the thirteenth century, and is

18 *The late Saxon bank excavated in 1986 blocking the Alfredian Bilbury Lane. The stones in the section behind are the metalling of the later 'Way to the Cross Bath' of about 1100. The scales are 2m long.* Bath Archaeological Trust

19 Finds from Saxon clothmaking from the excavations at Bath Street. 1. A fragment of a ring-shaped weight from an upright loom, originally about 16cm in diameter. 2. A glass "linen-smoother" for flattening out damp cloth (broken in half, c.8cm diameter). 3. A bone thread picker for lifting loose weft threads on a loom (c.8cm long). Bath Archaeological Trust

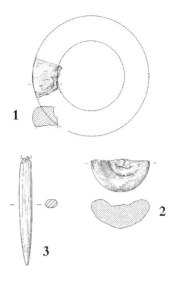

most likely to represent a change in Alfred's ideal street plan caused by property pressures. While encroachment of buildings on to the public highway is not uncommon in the medieval period, this kind of actual closure and new arrangement of property boundaries must have been agreed by the town elders. Quite what these property pressures would be is unclear, but they were most probably connected with commercial activity. Cloth-working, a traditional industry that had flourished in England since Roman times, become important again under Offa and went on to be a staple industry in the later Middle Ages, was apparently being practised in Bath at this time, based on the discovery of a glass 'linen-smoother' (which could be used for wool), a loom weight from a vertical loom, bone thread pickers, and evidence for the growing of teazel (used to 'tease' or raise the nap of cloth) (**19**). Iron-working is indicated by the presence of slags and charcoal in these layers, but what is most striking is the air of urban nastiness that comes from the area. The abandoned street and the blocking bank were buried by the continual dumping of organic rubbish, within which the evidence above was found. The limitations of excavation meant only a long, narrow strip of this area was excavated, but it appears to have essentially functioned as a combination of garden and rubbish dump. By the mid-eleventh century nearly a metre of rubbish had accumulated. At varying levels within it, flat surfaces had formed, sometimes with a firm clay floor, but more often just a spread of charcoal and stones. On these surfaces, as with fragmentary remains seen under the Pump Room, there is evidence of rushes having been used as a covering for the clay floors. Weeds and cereal grains show that the area was ecologically most like a bomb site or a neglected patch of disturbed ground, probably meaning the site comprised areas around urban workshops rather than tidy gardens: nettles and elder were a common feature. We can imagine timber workshops, shacks, hovels, and perhaps better-quality timber houses surrounded by a mire of organic rubbish. All this was probably taking place in the rear yards and open spaces behind the main buildings fronting the streets.

Within the refurbished defences and the sharp grid of Alfred's surveyors, and contrasting with an abbey church that was famed for its admirable workmanship, we can already see the busy commercial activity underpinning the wealth of the merchant-moneyers, the abbots and the king – as well as the urban filth and mess which resulted from it.

Further reading

For an overall background to the period, see Stenton 1971. This classic is now old-fashioned, but well written and very thorough on politics, and military and economic matters. See also Wilson 1971, Campbell 1991 and Welch 1992. For local archaeological details see Cunliffe 1979, O'Leary 1981, Cunliffe and Davenport 1985, Davenport 1991 and 1999. For a full discussion of the mint, see Grinsell 1973. On Saxon town plans see Biddle and Hill 1971, and for Bath itself, Greening 1971 and Cunliffe 1984. For the *Burghal Hidage* see Hill 1969 and Haslam 1984. For Alfred, Asser's life is essential if hagiographic (Keynes 1983).

4 Vikings, kings and abbots

Despite the rebirth of Bath under Alfred, and its growth under his successors, the abbey had suffered. It had probably lost much of its land in the anarchy of the Danish onslaught, and so set about acquiring new sources of wealth, not just out of greed, but because capital and income was necessary for an establishment of this nature. The main source was the king, although the church would solicit gifts from any person with wealth to spare. Alfred's successors seem to have considered Bath to be of special significance to the royal house. Edward had held a *Witan* or council meeting here in 901, possibly in the wake of his cousin Aethelwald's rebellion and flight to the Danes, and the mention of Reeve Alfred's death in the Anglo-Saxon Chronicle suggests the place had a certain standing in official eyes. The first record we have is a grant of land at Cold Ashton and Priston from King Athelstan, who also gave a book to the abbey. Edmund gave land at Tidenham, Bathford, Corston, Bathampton and Weston, all of which were close by and seem to have been parts of the estate that Offa had reclaimed all those years before.

Edward and Athelstan had enjoyed long reigns, in which war, while frequent and bloody (and mostly still against the Danes), was kept away from Wessex and West Mercia. Towns and country had time to recover and grow. It may be just coincidence, but it is in this period that the pottery industry, almost entirely absent in the west country after the fifth century, makes its appearance in Bath's archaeological record. The earliest pottery is identical to Cheddar fabric E, produced from the same kilns that supplied the royal palace there in the days of Alfred and Edward. Despite the royal connection, the sherds are from domestic cooking pots except for one, a handle from a pitcher. Pitchers, used for serving beer or even wine, represent a fairly sophisticated living standard and are better represented in Winchester ware, first identified in that city and probably made nearby. This pottery is the reflection of trading outside the local sphere, again suggesting relatively settled conditions. We are reminded of the sophisticated economics behind the mint system; and it is against this prosperous background that we can place the revival and restructuring of the monasteries in England, which although greatly desired by Alfred was only achieved under his successors.

The reformers themselves, notably the great trio of bishops, Dunstan of Canterbury, Oswald of York and Aethelwold of Winchester, tell of a sharp decline in the morals, finances and organisation of the monasteries, with some even collapsing into secular management. While we might expect these churchmen to exaggerate for political impact, it is clear from Alfred that this decline was real: buildings had been damaged or destroyed, manuscripts plundered, and monks replaced by laymen and secular clergy. The work of God was not being properly attended to. It took the first half of the tenth century to get the church as a whole, let alone monasteries, on some sort of even keel. After the confusion of the ninth century and the impact of many pagan settlers, the church had done well to get itself generally back into order, convert the Danes and so help assimilate them into English society. The luxury of monastic reform had to wait. But the reform gathered pace after the accession of Eadred (946-55), which ushered in a quarter century of peace in all parts of the country (954-81).

Dunstan was a well-connected nobleman, educated at Glastonbury, who became Eadred's chief minister. He was exiled under Eadwig (955-9) and, in travelling in Flanders, experienced first-hand the practice of the revived and reformed Benedictine Rule on the continent. Recalled under Edgar and made Archbishop of Canterbury, he was in a position to insist that all monasteries should be reformed and reorganised as Benedictine houses under a strict rule. He was aided in this by Oswald, Bishop of Worcester from 958 and Archbishop of York from 972, who had spent 18 years as a Benedictine monk at Fleury in France, a renowned centre for the reform movement on the continent. At Worcester, Oswald replaced the secular canons with Benedictine monks, effectively founding the monastery there (Osric's original foundation had dwindled to insignificance). Aethelwold at Winchester wrote, with continental help, the monastic rule book that all monks and nuns must follow: the *Regularis Concordia*.

While we have little direct evidence of what impact these reforms had on Bath, it is certain that the community there would have been reorganised, and the updated Benedictine rule enforced. That Bath was a model community by 973 is surely demonstrated by its choice as the venue for the coronation of Edgar in that year. The coronation was a sophisticated and carefully stage-managed spectacle, symbolic of the spiritual force of the renewed church and its rôle in validating the power of the monarchy. In this context, the abbey must have been deemed ideologically suitable, and the buildings of the monastery worthy. We have some hint of this from the description in a land charter from Eadwig dated 957, which describes the church as being *mira fabrica* or 'wonderfully wrought'; and we may actually have an illustration to refer to. A seal used on Abbey documents in the twelfth century is thought on stylistic grounds to date from the tenth century. It shows what appears to be one end of a church inside the Latin inscription SIGILUM ECCLESIE PETRI BATHONIS – the seal of the church of St Peter at Bath (**20**). If this is not just a generalised image – and it does look like an actual representation – then it seems to be showing us the east end of a church with three apses, decorated with strip pilasters. Further faint markings might suggest side chapels or porticoes. Unfortunately, while this gives us some idea of the church as being elaborate and probably quite large, the detail is too poor to allow us to decide between an eighth- or a tenth-century date, making it impossible to ascertain whether the building had remained from Offa's time (or earlier), or had been rebuilt in the wake of the founding of the *burh*. In either case the church would have been built in well-cut Bathstone ashlar (which is the most straightforward and likely meaning of *mira fabrica*), in large part taken from the Roman remains. Sculptural decoration would be rich, both figurative and decorative; the quality available can be seen from the tomb slab (**17**), and from the contemporary or slightly later carving at St Lawrence's, Bradford–on–Avon (**21**). Such visual richness would be becoming more common in

20 *A probably tenth-century sealing depicting the east end of Bath Abbey.*
Institute of Archaeology, Oxford

21 *A sculpture of an angel from St Lawrence's Church, Bradford-on-Avon, broadly contemporary with the decoration in the Saxon abbey at Bath*

people's lives, found (for example) in the carved crosses, several fragments of which are known from Bath, and to which we shall return. But still, why Bath for this national and indeed international occasion?

First, of course, both Bath and the abbey were royal possessions; and that the king controlled the use of the monastery is made clear by an odd story from the reign of Edmund. Monks fleeing from exactly the reform we have been discussing, at St Bertin in Omer, were granted (or given refuge in) the abbey at Bath, presumably on the king's say so. The land charters of Eadwig tell us that the king's chaplain, Wulfgar, was abbot (these charters also mention in passing the hot springs). Royal interest in the area was strong: the Barton estate all but surrounded the town and belonged to the king, and there were royal palaces at Cheddar and Pucklechurch. Bath may also have been felt to be politically significant in the relationship of Wessex and Mercia. The two had only formally been united in 918, and in the tense last two years of Eadwig's reign, his brother Edgar had ruled Mercia as a separate kingdom. On Eadwig's death in 959, Edgar reunited the kingdoms. Holding the coronation here, a town with important Mercian and Wessex royal connections, was symbolic of the unification of the two largest southern kingdoms. This was important; although Edward and Athelstan had been recognised as kings of all England (and over-kings of the Welsh and Scots), Edgar was to be the first *crowned* King of all England. It is likely that the grants of land to the abbey under Eadwig were related to reform (his exiling of Dunstan was based on personal dislike, not religious disagreement), and that the abbey, after 14 years of Edgar's enthusiastic encouragement of reform, would have been a beacon of the new monasticism.

The coronation itself was part of the reform of both the church, and the rôle of the monarchy within it. Dunstan and Oswald created a ceremony that likened the assumption of Christian kingship to the ordaining of a priest. Edgar was king because God had willed it. He was called to kingship as a priest is called to minister. The king swore an oath to perform his duty and uphold the church, and was anointed with chrism as God's chosen one. This correlation of being crowned king with being ordained to the priesthood almost certainly explains why the coronation was delayed. In 973, Edgar, who had come to the throne as a 16-year-old, reached 30, the canonical age for priesthood. If the king was a kind of priest, he could not be anointed king until that age. The ceremony included Edgar being led to the altar by two bishops chanting Psalm 88. He wore his crown, but laid it aside at the altar. Dunstan led a *Te Deum,* then the king made his oath to guard the church, forbid violence and wrong, and keep justice, judgement and mercy. After more prayers the monarch was anointed while the choirs sang. Dunstan then gave the king the regalia (including a ring, sword, sceptre and rod), and crowned him. The coronation was thus a propaganda statement about the enhancing power of the church in royal affairs, and the partnership of church and state in the land. As such, it was of fundamental importance to the future of church and state in medieval England, and still has significance to those who wish to celebrate 'a thousand years of monarchy'.

In the short term, the investment in Edgar was a poor one: just over two years later, he was dead. However, Edgar's second son Æthelræd became king in 978, and proved to be as much a creature of the church as his father. His reign might have been a disaster for his people (he is better known to us as Ethelred the Unready), but the Church retained all the gains in influence it had made.

A very important and influential figure in Æthelræd's reign was born at Weston near Bath in 953 or 954, apparently on his family estate. Ælfheah (St Alphege), 'while he was still very young', as his life puts it, ' . . . renounced the World and, notwithstanding the tears and entreaties of his widowed mother, retired into the monastery of Deerhurst, in Gloucestershire, where he served God with great devotion for many years.' He left to become prior at Glastonbury but, on finding the official duties interfered with his religious devotions, retired to a contemplative solitary life as a hermit 'near Bath'. St Alphege's Well on the hill slopes of Lansdown, above Bath, overlooking his home village, may mark the site of his hermitage. As late as the sixteenth century, the priory was making a payment of 10 bushels of wheat a year to its tenants at Weston, called 'St Alfege's gryst', which Manco has suggested may have originated in Ælfeah's time as a recognition of his origins or his time among them. Such was Alphege's reputation for holiness that his hermitage was turning into a rival abbey. His life says that he was persuaded by Dunstan to take on the task of reforming the secularised Bath Abbey after providing an ordered rule for the followers at his cell, but this sounds confused, and cannot have been literally true, as he was only 19 or 20 at the time of the coronation, and the abbey must have been reformed by then. Indeed, Æscwig was Abbot of Bath in the years including 965-70 and was probably Dunstan's appointee to do exactly that. But Ælfheah *was* Abbot of Bath before Dunstan appointed him Bishop of Winchester following Æthelwold's death in 984. He could not properly have been a bishop at a younger age, which indicates how much Dunstan prized Ælfheah's skills in administration and organization, as well as his religious zeal. Ælfheah became Archbishop of Canterbury in 1005, and is most famous now for his martyrdom at the hands of the resurgent Danes in 1012.

Ælfheah is the earliest non-regal figure in Bath's history about whom we know much more than a name. He was a nobleman but not of very high rank, one of the *thegns* who as a group occupied a major section of society, from the level of a free yeoman farmer with his own enclosed estate centre and a certain economic standing, to that of a major landowner, advisor and comrade to the king, just below an ealdorman. That Ælfheah went to Deerhurst in Gloucestershire as a young novice might suggest family influence in that area. However devout, a would-be monk needed connections to be accepted. He may have gone to the monastery as a boy of nine or ten, as Bede did. To have fled to Bath as a hermit dissatisfied by life at Glastonbury before he was 20 shows an independence of spirit and a fearsome determination. That he was dragged out of solitude to carry on the reforming work of Abbot Æscwig shows what an impression he had made on his seniors, for he was probably no more than about 25. At Winchester, Ælfheah became a powerful member of Æthelræd's court. In 994, he was part of an embassy to treat with the Danish king, Olaf Tryggvason, who had been waging war in southern England for three years. He succeeded in confirming Olaf's Christianity and successfully persuaded him to leave, never to return (although the payment of 16,000 pounds of *danegeld* to Olaf no doubt strengthened Ælfeah's persuasiveness). But other Danes moved in, and Ælfheah spent the rest of his life in the midst of Viking raids and negotiations. He was captured during a Danish raid on Canterbury and died, murdered by his drunken captors, after he refused to allow yet more ransom money to be paid to secure his own release. Unlike many of his contemporaries, he wrote little and no works survive to us. Clearly he was a man of action, and possessed of a great personal magnetism and power, which he put to great use in his faith, in church administration, in politics, and ultimately in his death.

The 25 years of peace came to an end in 981, with Viking attacks on the south coast and along the length of the Severn estuary. Unlike in previous years, the Norsemen came to raid and plunder, not settle, and consequently presented a moving target which the hapless Æthelræd was unable to counter. The king's men had local successes, but never enough to deter the raiding parties, which grew in size until Olaf Tryggvason's fleet comprised 91 ships. Olaf was the first to agree to be bought off with *danegeld*: an agreed sum which Æthelræd paid over and collected as a regular tax from his subjects. The results of such a policy are all too predictable: Olaf's £16,000 became £24,000 in 1002, and £48,000 by 1012. This out of an estimated annual circulation of coinage of £100,000 for the whole economy! Such payments show how desperate was England's plight, and the extent of the dynasty's military failure. Yet the nation that Alfred and his successors saved and united was so strong that it survived these military disasters as a social and political entity, remaining governable in the midst of crisis and, above all, wealthy, productive and disciplined enough to pay these huge ransoms.

Bath's citizens would have been affected by the demands for Danegeld, even though they appear to have been untroubled by the direct ministrations of the raiders (presumably kept safe by Alfred's walls). The regular demands for these payments, which were efficiently collected by the hundred and shire courts, must have been as financially painful as they were demeaning. The presence of the king and his *Witan* or council in Bath in 1009 was probably as much a symbol of defeat as pride. Yet Bath's standing as in some way symbolic of the Wessex monarchy, which we saw in the coronation of Edgar, led it to play a part in the final instalment of the Viking story.

Sweyn Forkbeard had been one of Olaf Tryggvason's comrades. Now King of Denmark, he decided that conquest would be a better way of acquiring the wealth of England and in 1013, after years of particularly vicious raiding, he conquered eastern England and was proclaimed King. Æthelræd fled to Normandy; London was cut off and surrounded, and rather than wait for it to fall, Sweyn

> went from there to Wallingford, over the Thames to Bath, and stayed there with his troops; ealdorman Æthelmær (the regional governor of Wessex) came and the western thanes with him. They all bowed to Sweyn and gave hostages.

Thus the Anglo-Saxon Chronicle describes the nadir of the house of Wessex. Bath might have been chosen both because it was easily reached by the Roman roads still in use, and because Sweyn's troops could live off the rich countryside surrounding it, which unlike the eastern counties had not been harried to exhaustion. In addition, neither Bath's status as a major royal estate, nor its symbolism as the site of Edgar's coronation could have escaped his attention. Was Sweyn's choice of Bath conditioned by a similar belief in a perceived imperial significance? Sweyn and his court probably stayed on the Barton estate, north of the walled town. If the Saxon estate head was where the later Barton Farm was, then the Danish conqueror would have kept his court on the site of Jolly's department store on Milsom Street.

We do not know whether there was any fighting around the town: the Chronicle entry suggests not. Yet the two archaeological finds that almost certainly reflect the event are somewhat warlike. The excavations at Upper Borough Walls were mentioned before in discussing the Saxon town wall. After the excavations were finished in 1980, a workman found a sword in what may have been the upper fills of the ditch (**22**). On examination this turned out to be of a fairly rare but well-known Scandinavian type datable to the tenth century, and probably made in England. While not as elaborate as some swords, it is a high-status weapon, forged from good-quality steel (still sharp when found) deliberately given a black patina to contrast with an inscription inlaid in bright iron on one side, and a decorative interlace motif and bars on the other. The pommel was inlaid in silver, and the sword was still in its fur-lined wood and leather scabbard. The context is uncertain and it may have been lost in the later Middle Ages after being

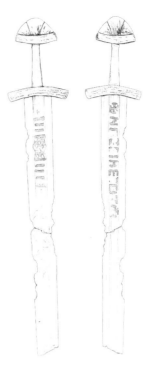

22 *The late tenth/early eleventh-century sword from Upper Borough Walls. In its broken state it is still 50cm long.* Institute of Archaeology, Oxford

kept as an heirloom, but it seems more likely (and certainly more romantic) that it was lost – by either side, since weapons in this period were not distinctively English or Danish – during some skirmishing in 1013.

The second find was uncovered far away from Bath. In southern Sweden (where many coins from Bath's mint have been found, taken there as Danegeld) an eleventh-century stone is inscribed in runes: 'Gunkel set this stone in memory of Gunnar, his father, Rode's son. Helgi laid him, his brother, in a stone coffin in England in Bath'. Gunnar Rodesson must have been one of Sweyn's men at Bath. Whether he died fighting, from illness or as the result of an accident on campaign is unknown. What is fascinating is that his brother had the opportunity and the desire to use a stone coffin, which would certainly have been a recycled Roman one. Was Helgi's choice of a Roman sarcophagus an echo of Sweyn's interest in the glories of Bath's ancient past?

London fell and Sweyn was in control. Early in 1014 he died and his son, Cnut, took over the Danish kingdom and army. Æthelræd returned, and there another two years of fighting followed. This time Somerset did not escape, and Cnut pillaged and ravaged Dorset, Wiltshire and Somerset in 1015. Æthelræd died in 1016, and his son

23 *Late Saxon carved cross heads. Dating from the tenth to eleventh century, these fragments are all that remain of the elaborate Saxon freestanding crosses that probably stood in churchyards. All but one were found close to the sites of parish churches within the walls, and at least one was demolished before 1100.* Institute of Archaeology, Oxford

Edmund Ironside fought Cnut to a standstill, repeating for a short while Alfred's success in retaining Wessex. But Edmund died late in 1016 and Cnut became King of all England, taking over the kingdom intact and ruling through the church and the (somewhat purged) English aristocracy in a firm, well-ordered and peaceful manner. *Danegeld* had become a normal if sporadic tax, and Cnut took it for himself in 1018 and used it to pay his fleet in later years. Apart from this, his reign was a much-needed respite from the terrible last days of Æthelræd. Bathonians, as did citizens elsewhere, resumed everyday life.

The main archaeological survivors from this period in Bath are rubbish pits, although some hearths have been found which seem to represent industrial activity. Money and time must have been channelled in the first place to reconstruct a ravaged country, but Bath had suffered less than many places and some wealth, at least, was directed to adornment and show. This is the interpretation of a small group of fragments of carved stone of late tenth- to eleventh-century date that have turned up in and around the city (**23**). These are parts of freestanding decorated stone crosses that probably stood in churchyards or (in the case of one smaller example) may have stood on an altar in a church. Most of the pieces have poorly-recorded find spots, but one was found built into the foundations of the Norman bishops' hall, suggesting it came from one of the abbey buildings, most probably the abbey church itself. The crosses are vigorously carved in the Viking-influenced interlaced style, and although not of the highest quality, the fact that they were commissioned at all is a remarkable indication of the resilience and wealth of Saxon England. Yet some individuals did retain substantial monetary wealth. Even in the turbulent last years of Æthelræd, Wulfan, as well as bequeathing land at Freshford to the abbey, was able to leave it 'certain mass robes, two gilt crosses and 60 gold marks'. Another high-ranking member of the community in the late tenth or early eleventh century was able to commission the carved coffin or cist cover (mentioned above) which was found re-used in a twelfth-century grave in 1993. This Bath stone slab was decorated with foliage and interlace in a style strongly influenced by the contemporary 'Winchester Style' of manuscript illumination, making it up-to-date, fashionable – and expensive (**17**).

It is also possible that the parish churches inside the walls at Bath began to crystallise at this time. St Mary's within Northgate may have been an early foundation, as it is situated in a favoured position in Saxon *burhs,* just inside the north gate. Its tower, while some 30ft (10m) inside the line of the walls, could have functioned as part of the defences, as can be seen at St Michael's at Oxford. St Michael's Within was situated near the west gate, but not so close as to appear part of the defences. Like St Mary's, it possessed no right of burial. The two churches vanished in the upheavals of the Reformation and little is known of them, even in their late medieval form. Both were small, neither being more than around 60ft (20m) long even at their greatest extent. For some idea of what they were like we can perhaps look to St Lawrence's at Bradford-on-Avon, or more likely the recently discovered little church of St Helen's at Malmesbury (now a cottage), which are both likely to be of late tenth or early eleventh century date. Even without burial rights, both were parish churches in the later Middle Ages, heads of tiny intramural parishes that probably started life as clusters of properties held by major landowners, with a private chapel serving its members needs.

By the twelfth century these private estates had been transformed by church initiative into organised parochial units (**26**). Apart from the church or chapel of All Saints, which was located somewhere along what is now Beau Street, and whose status is unclear, the other two churches in the walled area were proper parish churches with burial rights and a clear standing. Both have churchyards attached which go back into the Saxon period. St Mary de Stalls is probably first mentioned in documents around 1190, and Manco argues convincingly that it originated as the mortuary chapel in the lay cemetery of the abbey, which possessed the general burial rights of the town. These only passed fully to St Mary's after 1350, and its parishioners had to pay 32/- per annum for its use throughout the Middle Ages. The church stood in the south-east corner of the junction of Stall Street and Cheap Street, just north of the King's Bath, with the burial ground itself occupying the open space between church and bath. Part of this cemetery was dug in 1980, during preparations for the temple precinct excavation. While the bulk of the nearly 50 individual burials were from the twelfth to sixteenth centuries, (many more were represented only by stray bones from disturbed inhumations), 11 individuals were found beneath a building rubble horizon that dated to about 1100. These Saxon burials make it clear that the lay cemetery and possibly its mortuary chapel – St Mary's – was definitely in use in the eleventh century, and probably earlier. The dead were of both sexes and all ages, although the small numbers involved preclude any statistical analyses. The position of the burials and the lack of nails or fittings suggested that most were buried in shrouds only. One, however, the deepest and last to be excavated, was better preserved in waterlogged conditions, and lay in a timber coffin without any metal fixings or fittings, really a sort of plank lining to a tightly-dug grave, but with a base and a lid. This would have been extremely difficult to spot in the dry soils of the upper levels in less than ideal excavation conditions, so other such coffins may well have existed.

Another set of burials from a comparable archaeological level was excavated two years later on the pre-1279 site of St James's church (**26**). There was little direct dating here, but the stratigraphic context of the burials, documentary evidence and a curious anatomical feature strongly suggest that the 15 burials uncovered here were of pre-Conquest date. The anatomical feature is 'squatting facets', a polishing of the distal end of the tibia due to habitual squatting which also occurred on a small number of the St Mary's burials, and is often thought to be characteristic of pre-Conquest populations. As for the church itself, again we have no direct evidence. It was moved to a new location in 1279, and nothing except a small length of robbed-out wall footing survived the redevelopment of this site in the seventeenth century. However, it seems likely that we can outline the enclosure, the churchyard in which the building itself stood. The block or *insula* containing the church is an approximate rectangle, and the properties and building lines on it, as might be expected, follow the alignment of its sides – except for the plot which is now 2 Abbey Street (a fine, large, Georgian house owned by the Landmark Trust). This sits at a very odd angle to everything else, and is most simply explained as being the ghost or imprint of the orientated church and churchyard (**26**). When the church was removed in 1279 its nave remained as the bishop's private chapel, and thus the orientation of the old church survived until the Dissolution. The plot was shown empty on early seven-teenth-century maps and, by 1725, the Kingston map shows it built on almost as today (**31**). Property boundaries have changed somewhat since then, but the align-ments and boundaries on the Kingston map suggests that both 2 Abbey Street and the Crystal Palace public house next door to the south were originally part of the churchyard footprint. This should not surprise us, as the cemetery discussed above also spread under both sites, and may in earlier times have spread as far as Abbeygate Street, where excavations in 1964 famously revealed the skull of a young woman in a late Roman oven. Reconsideration of the evidence suggests that this was more likely part of a Saxon burial, which along with the oven had been displaced by seven-teenth- or eighteenth-century building work. Other displaced fragments of human bone were found nearby in excavations in 1984.

Bath and the abbey clearly flourished under Cnut, his short-lived sons, and Edward the Confessor, who was the son of Æthelræd, and had lived in exile in Normandy. Earl Godwin had risen to enormous power and influence under Cnut, and he and his sons not only engineered Edward's return but were the effective rulers during his reign. The great Earldoms of these years, effectively provinces ruled by Godwin and his sons, replaced the older system of shire-based ealdormen, reducing these men (who had been the king's direct representatives) to the position of admin-istrators for the earls. We know the names of a few of the Somerset ealdormen. In 826 there was Hun; in 845, Eanulf led the men of Somerset to a great victory over the invading Danes on the Parret estuary, while under Alfred, Somerset was ably held by Ethelnoth. In the mid-tenth century there were Ordgar and Edmund, and the last name we have is of Ethelweard, who presided over the county during the increasing chaos of the last years of Æthelræd. We know little of these characters beyond their names, but they would have been high-ranking noblemen and important local figures, intimately known and respected by the men of the shire. This personal system was replaced by the great Earldoms, Bath was in Wessex, ruled at first by Godwin himself, then passed to Swein Godwinsson, and finally his brother Harold, later King of England and the loser at the Battle of Hastings. The king's power was waning under the Godwin clan, but the abbey was once more receiving grants from Edward, the first since the Danish interlude. The house of Wessex was reasserting its interest in the area and in Bath: Edward's queen, Edith, held the Barton Estate which almost surrounded the city, as well as the nearby estate of Keynsham, while the king held the city itself.

The Abbot in 1061 was Wulfwold, who also held the abbacy at Chertsey. This is probably the explanation for the existence of several 'Abbots' at Bath at the same time, acting as his deputies. Edward granted land to Wulfwold in that year (although it was, in fact, a personal gift which Wulfwold later bequeathed to the brethren), yet we have references throughout the period of his abbacy to three other abbots. In the early 1060s, Ælfwig seems to have been replaced by Sæwold, who was one of the few churchmen to flee England after the Norman conquest, taking some of the precious stock of manuscripts with him. His place was taken by Ælfsige. Wulfwold was still abbot in 1084, but seems to have died soon after. Ælfsige survived him by three years.

Little is known of the other members of the community, but a document of 1077 does list the 17 monks at Bath, and the names are all English: Ælfric, Leofwig, Hiedewulf, Ælfwig, Ægelmær, Eadwig, Godwine, Ægelwine, Oswald, Ælmær, Theodwold, Eadric, Ægelmær (II), Sæwulf, Thured, Ægelric, Hærlewine. The first was clearly an educated and skilled man, as must also have been the other three anonymous monks who worked alongside him in the *scriptorium* (see below). Yet they or their English successors were considered ill-educated and unworthy of the new foundation by John of Tours in the 1090s (as we shall see in the next chapter). Given the generally high level of culture and education in late Saxon England, and the fact that these monks were themselves the elite of a much larger staff at the abbey, we may be justified in seeing merely foreign prejudice in John's dismissal of the monks as boorish.

The abbey was clearly rich and active at this time: the *scriptorium* was productive and we are fortunate that, despite Sæwold's theft of manuscripts, four gospel books written at the abbey survive from this period. They probably originate from about 1060, and the dedication to *Prior* Brihtwold has led to some suggesting the abbacy was vacant at the time they were written, a situation which only occurred at about this date. The gospels are written by four different monks, and we know the name of one, Ælfric, who was still a member of the community in 1077, and who tells us that the book was written at the monastery at Bath and for the Prior (**24**). The texts were unilluminated and so intended as everyday working books for use in services,

⁊fulligeað hig on naman. fæðep. ⁊runa. ⁊þey
halgan gaptep. ⁊læpað þhig henlðon ealle
þa ðing þe ic eop bebeoð. ⁊ic beo mið eop eal
lþ oaгap oð populðe ge enð un ge. finit
d   m   e   ꞃı :- Sic fic hoc hic Incerum:-
Ego ælfþucus scrupfi hunc librum inmona
fteno baðþomo   & dedi bphrpoloo prepofico:-
Qui fcrupfic uiuat inpace. inhoc munoo & in
fucuro fctó. & qui legic legacor inecernum:-

24 *The dedication page of the gospel of St Matthew, produced by Ælfric, a monk at Bath in the* scriptorium *of the abbey in about 1060.* Reproduced by permission of the Master and Fellows of Corpus Christi College, Cambridge

but blank pages were also used for recording events and decisions in the life of the abbey. One of these entries reminds us of the (to modern minds) brutal fact that the abbey owned slaves. Slaves, *servi* in the Latin of legal documents, *thræls* in English, were a regular part of Saxon society. Any substantial landowner might own them, and the church certainly did. The exploitation and trade in slaves went back centuries; and their acquisition was certainly one of the aims of the Viking raiders. The conversion of the Saxons to Christianity traditionally began when Pope Gregory saw Angles in the slave market at Rome around AD 590 and made his famous pun: 'not Angles, but Angels'. Nonetheless, to emancipate one's slaves or to arrange the freedom of those owned by others was a charitable act, a recognition of the essential evil of slavery. Typically, it would be dictated in a will (when, viewed cynically, the economic loss was no longer an issue), but often also was carried out during life; and such an act of *manumissio* is recorded for Abbot Sæwold.

Both *servi* and *coliberti* (freedmen) occur in the Bath sections of Domesday Book. This great census and tax return was carried out for William the Conqueror in 1086, but there is no reason to think Bath was so very different in 'the time of King Edward', as the phrase in the book constantly has it. Care must be taken, however, for Domesday is essentially an inventory of taxable assets, not a social or historical record. Nonetheless, much can be learnt from it. For example, Bath was part of the king's estate, but had been made over to Edward's queen, Edith. She held it as her dower until her death in 1075, when it reverted to William. Thus, all property in it was held eventually from the king. In fact, only 64 out of 178 burgesses (wealthy holders of property in the town) paid rent direct to the crown, with 90 doing so via baronial middlemen. The king made £4 a year out of his tenants, the barons, £3. The abbey had 24 properties leased out and made £2. In addition, the monks ran the town water-driven mill, positioned on the banks of the Avon and worth 20/- (£1) per annum. These figures make it possible to see the value of the mint although that at Bath was one of the smallest, it was still worth as much as the abbey's and barons' rental income combined.

The 178 burgesses represented the heads of landholding households, and the total population would obviously have been higher, but how much so is moot. The household of each burgess would be of several generations for a start, and would include servants and other 'employees' (*servi* and *coliberti*), as well as immediate family. A conservative multiplication factor of around six therefore seems appropriate. Adding the monastic community might make a population of about 1100. These numbers seem tiny to us (the present population of Bath is about 85,000), but the citizens in 1087 lived almost exclusively in the 24 acres inside the walls. The density this results in, of perhaps 46 per acre, would give a thriving, bustling city, with even more activity when people came to market or to the Baths. Bath was in the middle of a wealthy area. This is partly shown by the high number of royal estates in the area, but also by land values recorded in Domesday: Somerset in 1086 might only have been the twelfth richest county on average, but that position concealed huge variations, from the rich pastoral lands, such as those around Bath, to the waste moors of the Mendips.

There is little evidence of how the town looked. It still nestled behind Alfred's walls, and there is not as yet any sign that the roads leading from the city gates were settled. Stone churches rose above the houses, which were certainly all of wood, and even the wealth-iest of them would have been dwarfed by the abbey church. The abbey precinct, smaller than its successor, still occupied by far the largest plot in town, and would certainly have been walled off from the rest. The abbey's property interests would nonetheless ensure its active involvement in town life (and Sæwold's flight to France after the Norman Conquest implies some political involvement). This explains Abbot Ælfsig's apparent responsibility for refurbishing or rebuilding the Hot Bath, over the spring in the south-west corner of town. In the thirteenth and fourteenth centuries, this was referred to as Alsi's Bath in property deeds; and Manco has suggested that Ælfsig built or rebuilt it, leaving it his name. That the smallest bath was altered in this way suggests that all the springs were in use at this time, attracting visitors in the more settled times at the end of the Conqueror's reign. Access to the springs was important: it seems probable that if the Abbot was responsible for revitalising the springs (or at least maintaining them), he may have been the moving force behind a new street that was laid out between the King's Bath and the Cross and Hot Baths in the late eleventh century. This street, much later called White Hart Lane, ran west from the King's Bath, and then dog-legged to reach the Cross Bath. All through the Middle Ages it was the main link between the three springs. It was partly replaced by the grand colonnades of Bath Street in the 1790s, and finally disappeared as late as 1986. It was excavated during building works in 1986, and the earliest cobbled surface was dated by

25 *The late Saxon or early Norman street leading from the King's Bath to the Cross Bath. The cobbling was laid over the sites of earlier Saxon houses.* Bath Archaeological Trust

associated pottery to 'after 1050 and in use during the twelfth century' (**25**). In the excavation report it was attributed to the first Bishop of Bath, John of Tours (1090-1122), but there is equally good reason to think it was laid out by the last abbot. This new road gave the impression of cutting across some properties (several late Saxon hearths and occupation layers lay under it), and skirting others. It may be that the abbot took advantage of his holdings to rearrange some property boundaries while having to respect others; or he may have been able to use some of the six 'waste' properties mentioned in Domesday, which were without tenant or income.

However strange the centre of town would look to our eyes, we might find at least the pattern of villages and hamlets broadly familiar. Around Bath the villages of Batheaston (*Eston* – likewise part of Edith's dower and a royal estate), Bathwick (*Wica*), Bathampton (*Hamtona*), Combe Down (*Cuma*), and Bathford (*Forda*) were well-established, as were many others, such as Woodwick in the parish of Freshford. This was held in 1065 by 'a monk of the abbey' (curious for a Benedictine who was not meant to own property, though property was later attached to *offices* in the monastery, which is probably meant here), and in 1087 by one of the most powerful men in England, Ranulf Flambard, Keeper of the Conqueror's seal, Justiciar to William Rufus and eventually Bishop of Durham. This was indicative of the political changes that had hit the country after 1066. Of the holders of land in the area in 1066, only one maintained his grip in 1087: Alured, whose uniqueness is underlined by the epithet 'the English Thegn'.

Further reading

For the background, see the list for chapter 3. Although now out of print, Whitelock 1959 is a good general guide to Anglo-Saxon society. Local detail can be picked up in the *VCH* and Britton 1825.

5 Cathedral city

In 1075 the king and bishops met in the Council of London to promote the papal policy that sees should be based in towns. Even by the standards of the day, Wells, where the Somerset see had been based since 909, was a tiny place, not a town. Its days as the seat of the diocese were therefore clearly numbered. Then, opportunely, Abbot Ælfsig's death in 1087 was followed less than a year later by that of Bishop Giso. The deaths of these two prelates provided a (one is tempted to say heaven-sent) opportunity to bring the Somerset diocese into line by moving the seat of the bishop to the county's biggest town. What made more sense than to replace Giso and Ælfsige with a new abbot-bishop based in the illustrious abbey at Bath? In late 1088 John of Tours, William Rufus's physician, but also an ordained churchman, was made Bishop of Wells. He petitioned to move the see almost immediately, presumably in accordance with a plan agreed along with his preferment. In January 1091, he was granted the whole city of Bath, in the king's gift we recall, along with the abbey, 'that he may, with the greater honour, fix his pontifical seat there'. The Bishops of Wells, themselves successors to the Bishops of Sherbourne, became the Bishops of Bath. The bishop became the *ex officio* abbot, but the running of the abbey fell to the nominal second in command, the prior. Thus for the rest of the Middle Ages the abbey was officially a cathedral priory.

Rufus had no doubt been persuaded to grant the town (or more correctly now, the city) firstly by the money that John paid him, and secondly because it had been sacked and burnt in the rebellion of 1088, when Roger Mowbray and several other barons joined the king's uncle Odo in rising against Rufus in support of his older brother, Robert Curthose. The rebellion was short-lived and unsuccessful, but Bath had been attacked because it was the king's estate. How many of the citizens were killed, or had their livelihood destroyed, is unknown, but the town was devastated, making it, if not a clean slate for development, certainly ripe for it.

John of Tours shared the Normans' disdain for the English, and considered the monks, who were all English at this point, to be boorish and ignorant. He took all the abbey's lands and income for the see (they were notionally, at least, separate from those of the bishopric), and installed new Norman or French officers where he could, appointing a fellow Frenchman, also named John, as prior. He dealt equally imperiously with the canons at Wells. The church there was not monastic, but Giso had been attempting to create a quasi-monastic organisation during his long episcopate, requiring the canons to live in a community and indeed erecting conventual buildings there. John demolished these and sent the canons back to the wider community. He installed his brother, Hildebert, as Provost over them, perhaps foreseeing a possible focus of opposition to his new establishment. John was clearly a man of vision, albeit (like many such characters) not all that comfortable to be around. He planned a comprehensive redevelopment of the south-eastern quarter inside the city walls, involving a completely new monastic precinct, the laying out of a main street and the moving of one of the city gates (**26**). A new cathedral and associated buildings were planned, and he is also credited with rebuilding the King's Bath, the main hot spring, and with bringing it within the cathedral close. Almost incidentally, John also built himself a palace next to the priory.

What then was the impact on the city, on its fabric and on the population? If the Saxon abbey occupied the area hypothesised in **14**, of about 14.3 per cent of the walled area, then the new cathedral close took an extra 8 per cent of the area within the walls, with the bishop's new palace occupying an additional 4 per cent. The Norman cathedral priory had taken almost twice as much land again. The occupants of many Saxon towns, Oxford, Wallingford, Winchester, for example, lost large amounts of property to the imposition of castles by the new Norman overlords. The citizens of Bath had avoided this fate, only to fall victim to John of Tours' ambitions.

The extent of the alterations is shown on **26**, which can be compared to **14**. It is likely that Bishop John laid out Stall Street to replace the more easterly Saxon route to the south gate. This not only separated off the Bishop's palace and offices from the properties to the west of the street, but provided a large new area of frontage for lucrative lettings, at first occupied by market stalls and only later developed into proper buildings. These were an essential part of John's plan, as the money was all earmarked for the rebuilding programme. More street alterations were imposed to the north. An analysis of the pre-1700 street plan makes it clear that Cheap Street must originally have continued eastwards to a gate which provided access to the Monk's Mill and the riverside. This access needed to be maintained after the cathedral close was extended northwards, and so an east gate was cut through the wall further north, and a new lane was laid out skirting the edge of the extended close. This dropped back down alongside the outside of the city wall to meet up at a sharp right angle with the surviving short lane leading to the mill (**26**). This lane was called Lot Lane from the Lot Gate, the older name for the east gate. The current east gate, the only survivor of the city's gates, dates from the thirteenth century, but excavations under the Empire Hotel in 1995 revealed the latest nineteenth-century pavings of Lot Lane outside the wall, leading south from the east gate. The earliest cobbling underneath this contained pot sherds from the eleventh/twelfth centuries, supporting the view that the street was laid out in John of Tour's time.

Many properties must have been emptied of tenants to provide all this extra space, and it may be that this ruthless clearance gave some impetus to the evolution of suburbs outside the north and south gates. Both lay on important routes in and out of the city, and may have begun to be developed already. It does seem likely that at the very least John's action gave them a boost. As these words are being written there is the possibility of excavations in the southern suburb which may tell us whether this is true. The developments and redevelopments of the eighteenth, nineteenth and particularly the twentieth centuries leave little likelihood of anything surviving to be

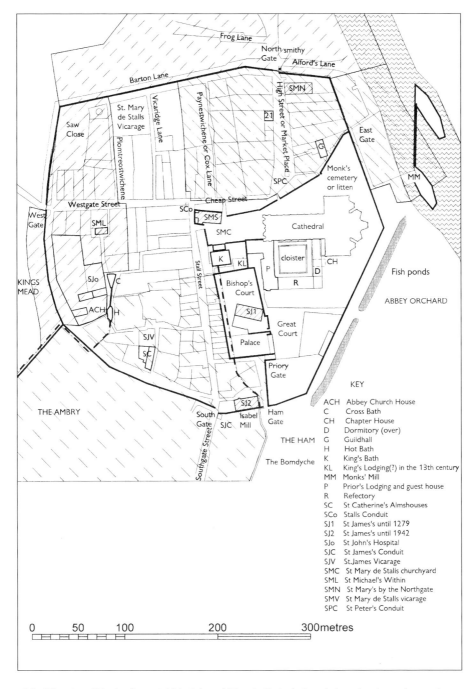

Frog Lane

North smithy
Gate   Alford's Lane

Barton Lane

SMN

High Street or Market Place

21

St. Mary
de Stalls
Vicarage

East
Gate

Saw
Close

G

Vicaridge Lane

Paynestwichene or Cox Lane

Plomtreostwichene

Monk's
cemetery
or litten

SPC

MM

Westgate Street

Cheap Street

SCo

West
Gate

SMS

SML

SMC

Cathedral

Stall Street

cloister

CH

K

KL

P

D

SJo

C

Bishop's
Court

R

Fish ponds

KINGS
MEAD

ACH

H

ABBEY ORCHARD

SJ1

SJV

Great
Court

SC

Palace

Priory
Gate

KEY

THE AMBRY

SJ2

South
Gate

Isabel
Mill

Ham
Gate

ACH   Abbey Church House
C   Cross Bath
CH   Chapter House
D   Dormitory (over)
G   Guildhall
H   Hot Bath
K   King's Bath
KL   King's Lodging(?) in the 13th century
MM   Monks' Mill
P   Prior's Lodging and guest house
R   Refectory
SC   St Catherine's Almshouses
SCo   Stalls Conduit
SJ1   St James's until 1279
SJ2   St James's until 1942
SJo   St John's Hospital
SJC   St James's Conduit
SJV   St.James Vicarage
SMC   St Mary de Stalls churchyard
SML   St Michael's Within
SMN   St Mary's by the Northgate
SMV   St Mary de Stalls vicarage
SPC   St Peter's Conduit

SJC

THE HAM

The Bomdyche

Southgate Street

0   50   100   200   300 metres

26 *The city of Bath after c.1100. John of Tours' Cathedral and close dominate the south-eastern quarter, which is further defined by his creation of Stall Street. The parishes (in various hatch patterns) and parish churches are shown, but seem to have come into being in the later twelfth century*

found close to the north gate, but pottery of the eleventh to twelfth centuries has recently been found a few hundred yards north of the gate at Beehive Yard, in association with the final removal of Roman ruins at that date. This suggests at least that some clearance – perhaps for horticulture, which is clearly attested in this area in the thirteenth century – might have taken place in connection with the spreading of the town beyond its walls.

Having acquired all this space, John set about building on a metropolitan scale. The starting date is not known, but allowing for the commissioning of a design, appointment of masons and the recruitment of the large workforce, not to say the opening of quarries and the transport of materials, a start date in the early to mid-1090s is probable. In 1106, John himself refers to the work that he had begun. A new wall to the cathedral close was erected, along with another which separated the close proper from the bishop's palace. Within them, the work included the construction of monastic quarters, a cloister, a palace and the main hot spring building, soon known as the King's Bath, as well as a new cathedral. No prelate would imagine that such a project could be completed in his tenure, but John clearly intended to have it all well under way. Writing in the early twelfth century, William of Malmesbury records the construction of 'a great and elaborate circuit of walls'. The completion of the church 'up to the lower vaultings' was recorded at John's death at the end of 1122.

Once he had ruthlessly amassed the financial wherewithal and got his programme both of institutional change and re-building well under way, John seemed to have started to soften his attitude to the monks at Bath. In 1106, he gave back all of the property he had taken from them, having in the meantime also managed to reclaim for the priory some estates which had been lost in the rebellions under William Rufus. This may be because by this time the English monks had all been replaced by ones more amenable to the bishop, and John felt he would be able to use the abbey's resources nonetheless. On the other hand, King Henry I stayed in the city in that year, during which time John obtained both a confirmation of his rights to its revenues and a right to hold a fair (which would produce more income from tolls and fines) on the feast of St Peter. In the light of this he may well have felt it was easier and more politic to return the abbey's income and, as he recorded in that year, devote the city income to 'the new work which he had begun'.

The bulk of the work was completed during the long incumbency of Bishop Robert of Lewes (1136-66), including the cloisters, infirmary, refectory, chapter house and the church. An impressive achievement, and yet no medieval cathedral priory can have vanished so completely as that at Bath. Not only can little be seen above ground, but even the ghostly traces that are often left in a town plan by the past existence of significant buildings are rarely recognisable. However, archaeology, documentary research and topographic study allow us to make very considerable strides towards rediscovering and reconstructing the buildings and layout of the cathedral close and bishop's palace.

We get our first record of John's church at the moment of its destruction. In the notes of his itinerary, King Henry VIII's antiquary, John Leland, confirms that the

27 *Drawing by F. Bligh Bond published in 1918, showing the surviving Norman fabric at the east end of the south choir aisle of the present church. Much of this can still be seen*

east end of John's church was still standing, apparently roofless, in the early 1540s. However, while archaeological excavations and observations started in the eighteenth century, proper records only began with the arrival of James Irvine, Clerk of Works during the restoration of the present 'Abbey Church' between 1864-73. Irvine was a well-respected builder, a serious-minded, hardworking Orcadian who nevertheless seems to have made and kept many friends as he travelled the country in his profession. Wherever he went, he kept meticulous records of archaeological finds made during the repair and rebuilding work he was supervising (**37 & 67**) and continued a correspondence with friends he had made during his sojourns. Irvine's records and letters allow us to recreate the basic plan of the Norman cathedral, along with some of its details. In addition, he made it possible for visitors to see some of this ancient stonework, and it can still be viewed today, inside and outside the church. In addition, he made some discoveries relating to the cloisters. The Glastonbury architect and antiquarian Francis Bligh Bond also recognised and recorded Norman stonework embedded in the east end of the present church, giving valuable clues to

28 *Excavations at Orange Grove, 1979: the remains of the north-eastern chapel of Bishop John's cathedral of 1092.* Bath Archaeological Trust

29 *The outer wall of the east cloister walk during excavations in the clergy vestry at Bath Abbey. The figure is standing on the medieval floor reaching up to the chamfered plinth which shows that this was originally an external wall. The cobbles behind him are part of one of the garden paths of the sixteenth-century residence created from the Prior's Lodging and the cloisters after the Dissolution.* Bath Archaeological Trust

30 *Excavations on the site of the bishop's palace. The broad walls in the centre are the corner and later extension of the Norman palace. The slighter walls to right and rear are part of the thirteenth-century rebuilding.* Bath Archaeological Trust

the appearance of the church above ground (**27**). Excavation in 1979 and 1993 (**28 & 29**) allowed tentative reconstruction of the plan of the east end and transepts, and fixed the position of the cloisters and another, rather puzzling building. The 1993 study also suggested the possibility of a crypt under the south transept. Other excavations in 1984-5 revealed the remains of the hall of John's palace (**30**).

By combining all this information it is possible to suggest the basic layout of the priory, and to offer some ideas about the appearance of several of the buildings as they may have looked in the mid-twelfth century. The cathedral close and the palace would have been separated from the rest of the town by a high wall, breached by gates. The position of only one is known, the 'Abbey Gate' of medieval and post-medieval documents, which stood at the end of Abbeygate Street, and was the main entrance to the priory. Demolished in 1733, with a chamber overhead and a porter's lodge to the north, it had an arched gateway for wheeled and animal traffic, and a smaller arch for pedestrians. St Peter's gate seems to have opened from Cheap Street past the east end of St Mary de Stalls, probably providing access to the burial ground in front of the cathedral's west end. It has already been suggested that St Mary de Stall may have started out as the cemetery chapel of the abbey, and then cathedral, lay cemetery. Another entrance may have been provided from Stall Street to the King's Bath. Certainly an alleyway existed here in the early fourteenth century. The palace would also have needed access, and while the sites of these gates are unknown, an entrance from Abbeygate Street into the south side of the bishop's palace seems a reasonable and logical site.

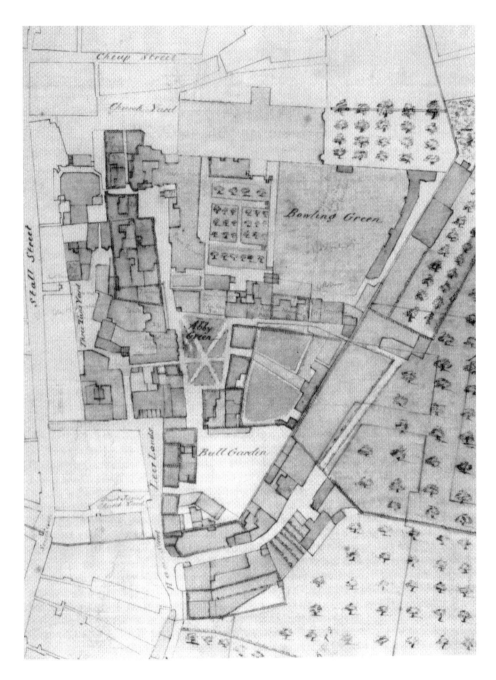

31 *The 1725 map of the Duke of Kingston's estates in Bath. The darker areas are the Duke's property. Abbey House, the prior's lodging can be seen south of the west end of the abbey church, with the cloisters, now a walled garden, to the east. Robert Sutton's chamber and garden may be the building on the city wall and attached enclosure just north of Bull Garden (see chapter 8).*
Bath Reference Library

The site of the bishop's palace enclosure can probably be quite closely mapped. It has been identified as an approximately rectangular area, south-west of the abbey church and south of the King's Bath, on property maps of the eighteenth century, and in particular the estate map indicating the Duke of Kingston's properties dating from 1725 (**31**). Writing shortly after the destruction of the monastery in 1539, Leland tells us that 'this John erectid a palace at Bath in the south west corner of the monasterie of St Peter's at Bath one great square tower of it yet appere.' A lease to one Miles Dennison in 1573 makes it clear that his property in Stall Street, a few doors up from the Abbeygate Street corner, backed on to the 'Old Pallace'. Other late sixteenth- and early seventeenth-century leases place 'the old pallace' and 'Old Palace Yard' south of the King's Bath and west of Abbey Green. A lease of 1310 shows that the bishop's enclosure reached as far as the King's Bath, while a fourteenth-century document gives measurements of the 'Bishop's Bower', the bishops private chambers, which match the lower part of the rectangle. Further details are only forthcoming from excavations. Fortunately, work in this area in 1984-5 revealed what is almost certainly the early twelfth-century chamber block, part of the bishop's private quarters (**32 & 33**). Archaeological dating can only suggest an early twelfth-century date, but as John entertained King Henry in 1106 it may have been completed by then. The excavated building was a rectangular hall roughly 19 x 10m, with walls 1.75m thick. The ground floor was paved with stone setts, and there were indications of an external stone stair to the north. There may have been a spiral stair

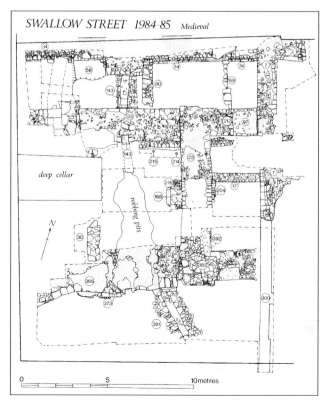

32 *Plan of the bishop's palace as excavated. The western end of the first palace is centre right. The thick walls running left from its corners are the twelfth-century extension, and the thirteenth-century rebuild is represented by the thinner walls at extreme right and top; cf. figure **30**.*
Bath Archaeological Trust

33 *Reconstruction drawing of the earliest Bishop's Palace, c.1100, seen from the north. This might have been the chamber block of the Bishop's Palace. It was certainly very close to the original St James' Church, which later became the bishop's chapel precisely because it was so close to his chamber*

in the thickness of the wall in the south-east corner, and thickening towards the west end of the south wall suggests a fireplace and chimney. There was a cobbled yard outside to the south, on the surface of which typically-medieval horseshoes were found. A contemporary culvert which ran close to the west end of the block had been filled in by 1150, when the building had been extended over it and further drains constructed. The filling included evidence of the very high-status diet enjoyed by those living there: game birds had been consumed, as had a very early example of a species probably introduced by the Normans, the fallow deer. In addition, the drain also contained remains of a large hunting dog. Only the aristocracy could aspire to such a diet and such activities and we are reminded that the bishop and his successors shared a deer park with the prior on Claverton Down, the modern day Prior Park. The possession of hunting dogs was only allowed by Royal Warrant; and Bishop Reginald gained (probably renewed) permission to keep sporting dogs throughout Somerset from Richard I. This was only a small part of the complex used by the bishop, but an attempt to indicate what this building might have looked like is shown in **33**.

There is no doubt that the lion's share of all resources went into the church itself. It seems likely that John sent home to Touraine for a master mason, as the closest parallels for the plan (especially its cramped east end) are from churches in that area. Using information from these churches, from the standing fragments of John's church in and under the present building and from the architectural fragments found in excavation, it has been possible to create the computer model from which the views in **34 & 35** have been taken. It was a grand structure in the high Romanesque tradition, which at approximately 350ft (107m) long and over 70ft (21.34m) wide proclaims its full cathedral status. The present church occupies merely the nave of the older building. Transepts, chancel and crossing tower all branched out east of it, and the remains extend under the road and traffic island of Orange Grove. A mid-twelfth-century reference to the 'principal' tower suggests

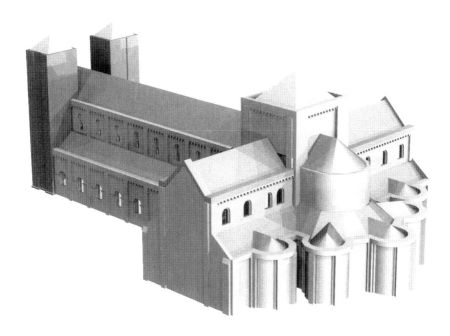

34 *A work in progress: a view of the east end of the computer model (still under construction) of John of Tours' Cathedral as it may have looked around 1160*

35 *Another view of the computer model of John of Tours' Cathedral. The nave interior looking towards the east end as it may have looked around 1160*

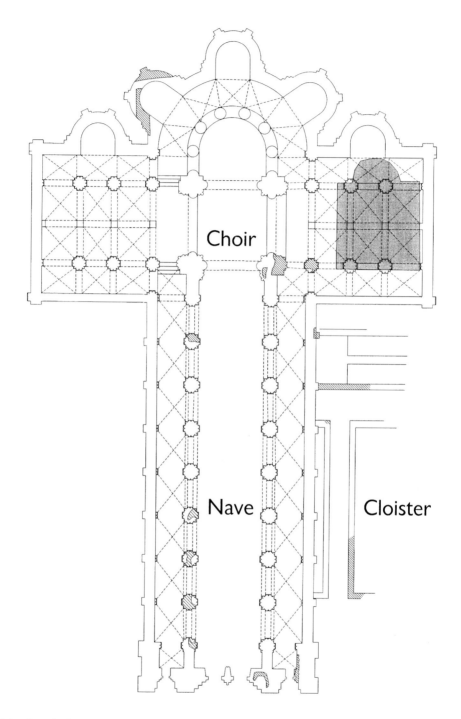

Choir

Nave

Cloister

36 *Plan of John of Tours' Cathedral. Despite there being so little known fabric, the plan is very likely in broad terms to be correct. The most uncertain areas are the western towers and the transepts, but even here we know that the latter were aisled* there were originally others, and it is usually assumed that there were western towers as well as the main one over the crossing. However, transeptal towers, which John would have been familiar with from Tours, are also a possibility, although because few were completed in Britain they have not been shown in the reconstruction. However, this acts as a reminder of how speculative the model is and further work will certainly change our views. It has, incidentally, been suggested that the eastern run of the city wall was rebuilt further east to make room for the new church. This is unlikely, as what appear to be Roman defensive works were recently found parallel to the existing wall; and in any case such a major undertaking would surely have taken place only if the church was to make full use of the space made available, which here it certainly did not.

A major feature of the church was the considerable variation in floor level, which is not simply due to the structure being built on a slight slope. The west doors must have been reached by steps, as inside the floor level was almost five feet above the nave floor of stone slabs. At the end of the nave, the floor in the choir under and beyond the crossing rose 18ins (45cm), while on the north the transept floor was 3ft 3ins (1m) higher again. The steps required to ascend the nearly 5ft (1.52m) from the nave aisles were seen by Irvine (**37**). The south transept was at the same level as the nave, and this implies that either the ambulatory at the east end behind the choir was

37 *The steps up to the north transept from the nave aisle of John of Tours' Church, as recorded by Irvine.* Society of Antiquaries of Scotland

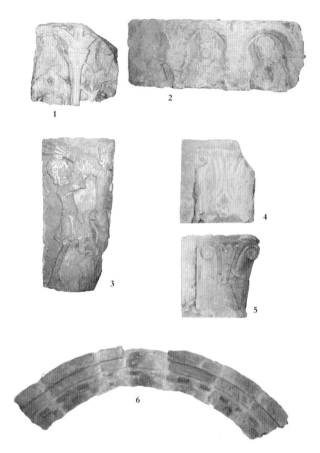

38 *Architectural and sculptural fragments from John of Tours' Cathedral. (1-2) Probably fragments of the altar reredos, perhaps showing apostles, c.1150. (3) One of a pair of capitals of nook shafts, probably from somewhere in the east end. It shows the martyrdom of either St Batholomew or St Vincent, again c.1150. (4-5) Two plainer nook shaft capitals, of c.1100. (6) A billet moulding from over an arched window, probably in the nave, early twelfth century*

at this level, descending immediately after the north transept, or that it stepped down from the north transept at some later point in its sweep (the former explanation seems more likely). The reasons for these variations are unknown, but they must at the very least have enabled, if they were not designed for, elaborate processional and choral effects during church services. This may have been the reason for the filling in of the transepts with a system of vaults supporting a first floor at gallery level, the most likely interpretation of fragmentary arches visible in early seventeenth-century prints. These sprang from the east end of the present church, which is still of Norman fabric at these points; and a single example is still visible in the fabric today, in the north-east corner buttress of the church. They are hard to interpret in any other way, but this feature, unusual in surviving Norman churches, is known from several contemporary or earlier examples, including Remigius's cathedral at Lincoln,

Lanfranc's at Canterbury and the Confessor's Westminster Abbey. The echoing chambers below and the high gallery above the vaults may well have been designed for grand choral effects.

The excavations in 1993 that clarified the floor levels of the south transept and nave also showed that what had earlier been interpreted as the junction of transept and nave aisle walls was in fact a free-standing pier. This implies a western aisle to the south transept, which in turn almost certainly means we have to have an eastern aisle (the reverse is almost unheard of). The church that John began was therefore not only large, but sophisticated. This is also shown in the geometry that underlies its plan. It is possible to deduce that the equilateral triangle was used to generate and control the planning of the cathedral. It may also employ the ratio of $1:\sqrt{2}$. This knowledge of geometry and proportion is not only one of the masons' craft mysteries, but is also at the heart of the intellectual concerns of twelfth-century scholars, and so could be seen as a reflection of the high level of academic endeavour in the priory in general. We know little in detail about either the members of the monastery, or John's episcopal curia. Bishop John was an intellectual, a physician, with an apparent interest in the spring waters. We do know of at least one contemporary Bathonian of the highest intellectual attainment, who was certainly educated at the priory if not a member of it: Adelard of Bath, who was born in the city in about 1080. We will come back to him later, but for the moment can note that even if he soared above the intellectual level of not only the monastery, but his times in general, his achievements show the high level of the academic environment around him.

The cloisters were built on the south side of the nave, but their eastern side was several bays down from the transept. This seems to have been because there was a pre-existing building projecting from the nave's south aisle, which prevented the extension of the cloister to the more traditional position further east. The west wall of this building was first noted by Irvine who thought, rather strangely, that it was the western wall of the cloister. Work in 1993 showed that this wall, much truncated in length, survived nearly 13ft (4m) high, built into a seventeenth-century vestry (**29**). Although it formed the eastern wall of the eastern cloister walk (the stone floor of which was also found in the excavation), the inside face was clearly originally built as an external wall, and so had formed part of a building to the east (**29**). When part of this was excavated it was seen to contain two deep but very narrow undercrofts or basements, parallel to each other. The excavator interpreted these as stairwells and thought they might have led originally to an eccentrically-placed crypt under the south transept, for which there was suggestive (but not conclusive) evidence. Whatever the truth of this, the building was important enough both to have been built first, and to have restricted the size and positioning of the cloister. The medieval church in Bath had relics. Could they have been kept in this putative crypt?

The southern run of the cloisters seems to have used as its external wall, the broad middle Saxon wall described in chapter 3. At any rate, that this wall's footings were robbed in the mid-sixteenth century, indicates that the wall, or a rebuild on the older foundations, was still standing then. The western walk ran inside the western range, which in later times was occupied by the prior's lodging and extended southwards in line with the west front of the cathedral. This slightly odd layout, especially in the position of the east walk of the cloisters, has led some to interpret this as a reduction of an earlier, larger cloister. There is no other support for this, and the archaeological evidence is against it – in particular, the building which dictates the position of the east walk is built of typologically twelfth-century masonry, especially the tooling, and similarly dated burials respecting its line lie under the paving of the walk. All the documents show is that in 1242, the monks had access to the cloister from the choir without passing through the nave. This could have been achieved via a slype or passage from the south transept, where normally access to the dormitory would also be made by way of the night stair.

Robert of Lewes is credited with finishing the cloisters, and built the infirmary, which some believe formed the large eleventh- to twelfth-century building found north of the King's Bath in the 1982-3 excavations. This was largely suggested because the building was constructed against the healing waters of the main spring, directly over the (now buried) Roman altar and temple courtyard. Against this attractive idea is the fact that infirmaries were usually placed in quiet backwaters of precincts, and generally conveniently close to the cemetery; and at Bath the monastic cemetery was south of the church in the cloister garth. The spot was also possibly noisy, although we know little of the use of the springs at this period. Three large wall foundations and a little piece of wall were excavated here, and form the base of a substantial rectangular building built barely inches away from the north wall of the King's Bath (**26**), and a simple reconstruction of a possible configuration is offered in **39**. The structure is so close to the King's Bath that it is hard to imagine it functioning in any way except specifically as part of the spring 'experience'. If it was not a monastic infirmary, perhaps it was built to offer some kind of accommodation for sick visitors to the springs, who came even in the troubled times of King Stephen, according to the *Gesta Stephani*. It would then be convenient for the lay cemetery of St Mary's, in whose graveyard it was effectively built. Unfortunately, we have no documentary record of such a structure.

It is certain, however, that the King's Bath, in the form in which we know it until the late eighteenth century, was built by 1138, as it is described by the author of the *Gesta Stephani,* or the *History of (King) Stephen.*

> Streamlets of water, warmed without human agency and from the very bowels of the earth flow into a receptacle beautifully enclosed with arched chambers. These form baths in the middle of the city, warm and wholesome and pleasing to the eye. Sick persons from all over England resort thither to bathe in these healing waters, and the fit also, to see the wonderful burstings out of warm water and to bathe in them.

It was almost certainly built by John of Tours, utilising the masonry of the Roman enclosure building as foundations, which dictated the rectangular form and the dimensions (**40**). It seems that this wall had remained as the hot spring enclosure all through post-Roman times, although the water level had risen three feet or more

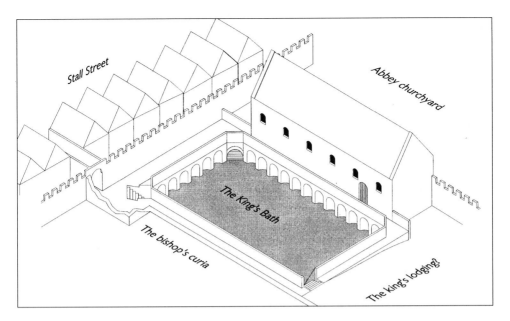

39 *A simple reconstruction of the King's Bath and the building to its north as it might have appeared c.1150*

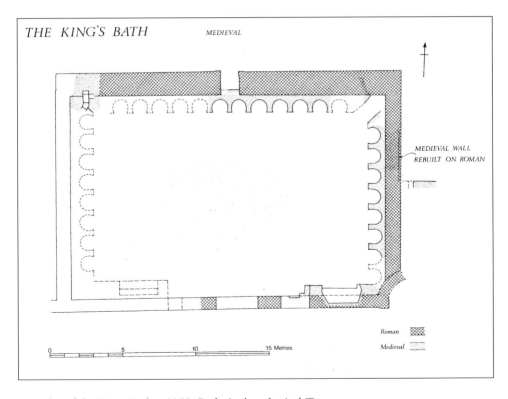

40 *Plan of the King's Bath c.1150.* Bath Archaeological Trust

(1m) as the bath was choked with collapsed Roman superstructure. The wall, 3ft 3in to 5ft (1-1.5m) thick, was still standing up to 6ft or so (roughly 2m), except to the south where it stood over 16ft (more than 5m) high. The lower walls were levelled to about 3ft 3in (1m), and on these sides a new wall lined with 24 arched niches was built inside and over the stump. On the south the Roman wall, with its two windows either side of the great arched opening still visible today, was simply incorporated wholesale. Access was via steps or 'slips' in the corners, an arrangement that continued until the late eighteenth century.

Therefore, by the end of the reign of Bishop Robert in 1166 the church and monastery had been completed and the bishop's quarters had also been finished – although not without incident. In 1137, the monastery suffered a major fire, in which most is said to have been destroyed, and the church was clearly affected too. This is presumably why Robert is credited with so much building work. He had arrived only the year before, and his long tenure meant the work of repair was completed under his oversight. Just how destructive the fire was is unclear. Any timber buildings would have been destroyed, but those masonry ones that had been completed probably only needed repair. Study of architectural fragments found in excavations in 1979, and dating from before 1137, showed that many had fire-reddening, which had been whitewashed over while the blocks were in place. This makes it clear that the buildings affected by the fire, including the cathedral, stood after the fire and were repaired. The church was probably completed by 1156, as in that year Bishop Robert obtained a confirmation from the Pope of the transfer of the see to Bath, and we know that there was a consecration of the building sometime between 1148 and 1161. By the time Robert was buried in front of the high altar in 1166, John's vision of a new cathedral priory had been realised.

The layout of the abbey can be broadly reconstructed from analogy, general Benedictine practice, and documentary sources, with archaeology able to add little directly outside of the church and the recognition of burial grounds, of which four are known in the priory precincts. The monks' cemetery was in the cloister garth (**26**), and important members of the community were buried under the cloister east walk. Not only monks were inhumed here: one of the twelfth- to thirteenth-century burials recovered in 1993, laid in a timber coffin, was of a middle-aged woman. This apparent anomaly is accounted for by the fact that an important patron or patroness could be received into the community, as an honorary monk as it were, and given burial with the religious. This is known to have happened in Bath, for example, with Isabella the widow of William the Goldsmith in 1200. Indeed, the skeleton uncovered in 1993 may even have been Isabella, but there is no way of knowing this.

Another cemetery, specifically called the monks' cemetery in 1296, was north of the choir (**26**). Excavations in the Orange Grove roundabout in 1979 revealed remains of 43 individuals at the southern end of this burial ground, close against the cathedral east end. This also contained women and children, probably indicating that it was available to servants and other connections of the monks. That they were of lower status is supported by the bone analysis. The children, in particular, were poorly nourished and had died at ages between 6 months and 13 years. Most of the adults died between the ages of 25 and 45, a normal medieval distribution of a lay population. Of the 18 individuals that could be sexed, only three or four were female, indicative of an artificial community. The monks tended to be better nourished and live longer.

The other two cemeteries, although within the cathedral priory boundaries at times, were the burial grounds not of the clergy, but of the Bathonians themselves. The lay cemetery was outside the west end of the cathedral under modern day Abbey Churchyard (**26**). We have seen that the cemetery was in use in Saxon times, and in *c*.1190 there is a reference to the chapel of St Mary in the Churchyard at Bath. This became the main cemetery for lay people when burials ceased in the fourth burial ground, that of St James, after its removal to a new site outside the priory walls in 1279 (**26**). While clearly under the control of the abbey at first, by the thirteenth century the churchyard had become that of St Mary de Stalls parish church. Excavations in 1980 uncovered 26 individual burials post-dating *c*.1100, and many more fragments from disturbed burials. In contrast to the cemetery excavated the year before in Orange Grove, these individuals were on average healthier, better nourished and longer-lived: perhaps being a monastic servant was not such a good career choice. The sex ratio was very nearly 50:50. One early burial, in emulation of the twelfth-century monks, was laid to rest in a stone cist. In fact, the medieval church of St Mary's became the parish church of the Corporation, and relatively affluent burgesses would favour this church and its burial ground, although the richest still sought inhumation in the church itself.

The dormitory of the monks was probably near the east range of the cloister or by the south transept, but like the refectory, we only have normal practice to guide us. Fragments of the footings and floors of a half-timbered building were found south of the south cloister walks, under the famous Sally Lunn restaurant in North Parade Passage, during excavations in 1984. It was in use from the twelfth to the fourteenth centuries, and other monastic foundations were mentioned alongside this alley in the early seventeenth century. Kitchen and refectory would be expected along here, and these remains confirm the existence of such structures, if not their function.

South again stood the great court around which the more workaday buildings of the priory would be set; and this is now represented by the shrunken open space of Abbey Green. Set just inside the abbey gate at the end of Abbeygate Street, this was convenient for all the comings and goings of trade and victuals necessary for the maintenance of the monastery and cathedral. The porter, a lay servant, would have little rest in his chamber on the north side of the gate (**26 & 51**). Stables, pigsties, fowl houses, bake- and brewhouse, stores and workshops would all cluster around or near this court.

Separated from the priory proper by a wall, and probably until 1279 by a lane leading to St James's Church from the abbey gate, was the bishop's court and palace. St James's church was enclosed by the palace and priory, and was adjacent to the bishop's chamber. We can only imagine the bishop's concern and displeasure at the parishioners jostling along the lane, almost under his windows, on their way to mass, christenings and 'weddings in church porch'. The problem was not solved until

1279, when the nave was converted into his private chapel, and the church moved to a new site by the south gate. The church/chapel must have occupied the site of 2 Abbey Street (as we saw in the last chapter), while the bishop's private palace was at the south end of the rectangular enclosure (**26 & 33**). When first laid out it must have taken over some of the churchyard of St James, as burials and disturbed human bones were found under the Crystal Palace public house and the site of the bishop's hall during excavations in the 1980s. North of the church were probably the more public or formal buildings with access to the King's Bath, and north again were the king's lodgings (or at least a likely site), on a property later known as Star Chamber, south-east of the bath (**26**). The king retained lodgings in the priory throughout the twelfth and early thirteenth centuries, and it is from this period that the name King's Bath becomes firmly attached to the main spring.

Adelard

Despite the cathedral's disappearance in modern times, the outlines of this great establishment can be discerned with varying degrees of clarity, with the help of archaeology and documentary studies. So too can be the outlines of the life and, much more, the achievements, of one of its greatest products. Adelard of Bath is renowned as one of the greatest scientists and philosophers of the Middle Ages. He is remembered as the first translator of Euclid's geometry into Latin, was instrumental in the introduction of Arabic numerals into northern Europe; he promoted the use of the astrolabe, and wrote a treatise on its use in navigation and astronomy. He also made contributions to the development of trigonometry, was an accomplished musician, and adept at falconry. Much of Adelard's contribution was made possible because of his knowledge of Arabic. To find and read the works which Arabic and particularly Moorish civilization had preserved from the ancient, especially Greek, world, he travelled widely and spent time in Spain, Sicily and probably further east (he describes being on a bridge during an earthquake in Syria). He was also a natural philosopher: his books *De Eodem et Diverso* ('Of Differences and Similarities') and *Quaestiones Naturales* ('Enquiries of Nature') show an awareness of philosophical questions, and an independent cast of thought. His discussion of moving bodies, though couched in thoroughly medieval terms, comes very close to a Newtonian view. On the other hand, we must also not make the mistake of assuming Adelard was a modern thinker, stranded in the Middle Ages. Although he was an early example of the scholars and artists of the twelfth-century 'renaissance', he was also a committed astrologer, casting horoscopes for the king in 1123. One wonders, though, if he was a little cynical about it. Apparently, he made no attempt to make the important corrections for the latitude of England, when using astrological tables that he had acquired in Toledo. Yet he had accurately calculated the latitude of Bath in his *Treatise on the Astrolabe*.

So who was this intellectual paragon? In the latter book, he tells us that he was born in Bath, and he claims citizenship of Bath in *Quaestiones Naturales*. Biographical inference from his education means he was probably born around 1080. His father, Fastrad, held land locally in 1087, a tenant of the bishop of Wells, and as Adelard was born in Bath it is likely that his father had some connection with the abbey. However that may be, it seems certain he was educated at the new cathedral school, which must have been set up by John of Tours early in his episcopate – indeed, it is hard to imagine where else an education such as he obviously received was possible. Adelard's period of study in Tours must imply patronage from John, and we know that they were together at the coronation of Henry I's queen, Matilda. He mentions in *De Eodem et Diverso* that he played the cithara for the Queen, so seems both to have had an introduction at court, and to have moved easily there. John, a powerful intimate of royalty and an important courtier as a senior churchman, seems to have provided the introduction (Fastrad, despite his land holdings and affluence, does not seem to be of high enough status to have such connections). Adelard must have been in Tours around 1100, and there he would have heard much of the new learning coming out of Spain, now more readily accessible since the Moorish capital of Toledo, a great centre of learning, had recently fallen to the *reconquista*. Whether he travelled further at this point is unknown. As a university student at Tours his life would be disciplined with little chance to travel. But his life's focus as a travelling scholar was set. He was certainly back in Bath in 1106 to witness a document for John, and as the King was in Bath at Easter that year this may have been when Adelard played for the queen. He had probably finished his formal studies several years before that and could already have started to travel. Given his ability to do this he was clearly not a monk despite his links with the monastery. He was probably in minor orders, but while this need not entail clerical duties and would be an almost automatic result of his education, we do hear that he is one of John's *ministri* or agents. He never seems to have married. But this paragon of academe was human. He was obviously a man of means, and tells us himself that he enjoyed fine clothes (being particularly proud of his green cloak). In 1130 Adelardus of Bath, by then about 50 years old, was excused a fine in a court in Wiltshire for an unrecorded transgression. He also clearly enjoyed and was a master of falconry. He was at court between 1135-9, as he witnessed documents for King Stephen.

The anarchy

The completion of John of Tours' plans for the abbey under Robert was a great achievement. It is all the more surprising when we realise that it took place during a civil war so disruptive that it is traditionally called 'The Anarchy'.

Stephen had come to the throne on the death of his uncle Henry in 1135, and almost 20 years of weak government and civil war ensued. Bishop Robert was the king's man, and Bath was a royal city. As Bristol was often in the hands of the supporters of Henry's daughter, Matilda, Bath was in the front line. In 1137 or 1138 Mathilda's half brother Robert of Gloucester sallied from Bristol, and somehow Bishop Robert was captured. The Bath garrison had, in turn, captured Geoffrey

Talbot (a prominent Matilda supporter) while he was reconnoitring the city, probably planning an assault. After a prisoner exchange had been agreed, Bishop Robert was released. Whatever the horrors of civil war for the general population, and we are told they were manifold, the upper classes, for many of whom war was a sort of sport, limited the damage they did to each other. Stephen, however, was furious about the loss of his prize prisoner, Geoffrey Talbot, which may tell us something about his relations with Bishop Robert. The king himself came briefly to Bath, to inspect the fortifications, and Bishop Robert met him at the gates and made his peace. The king gave orders to heighten the walls, mindful that an attack by Mathilda's men in 1138 had only been thwarted because the ladders they brought with them to storm the city were too short! No doubt the evil Bristolians were capable of returning with longer ones.

A chartered town

Other citizens of Bath in the twelfth century are in less sharp focus, and we only hear about the richer ones in any case. But the town must have been prosperous. We have already heard of Isabella, the widow of William the goldsmith, who had died before 1200. In the reign of Bishop Robert, Ralph, another citizen of the city, was rich enough to pay for not only most of the central tower, but also two great bells, and the timber and lead for the roof. It is clear that Bath had always had such rich and successful citizens, from the moneyers of the Bath mint onwards.

This was the status of the tradesmen and merchants, the wealthy burgesses of the town, who successfully petitioned King Richard the Lionheart in 1189 to grant the town a charter (**41**). Like all such men, their timing was impeccable. Richard was desperate for money for the Crusades, and would sign anything for an appropriate consideration – he said he would sell London for the right price. We do not know what the right price was for Bath, but we can assume it was not cheap. It was a bargain though: commissioned in haste, it gave the burgesses of Bath (recognised for the first time as a body – the Guild of merchants) the same rights to regulate and benefit from trade as the citizens of Winchester. Apart from the opportunity to make money through an effective monopoly, the significance of the charter is the recognition of a body of people in the town distinct from the control of rights by the church. The bishop still held the town at this time, though it was shortly to be returned to royal control. Richard's action was a snub to the church's predominance, though hardly deliberate: he just wanted the money. The cathedral priory continued to be the single most important element in Bath through the Middle Ages, but this charter marks the emergence of the other, and eventually longer-lasting, aspect of civic life: 'the mayor and commonality of Bath', the Guild and eventually, after 1590, the Corporation. In the next chapter we shall consider the governance and governors of medieval Bath and something of its commercial life, but for now we will complete the story of the conflict between Bath and Wells and its eventual resolution.

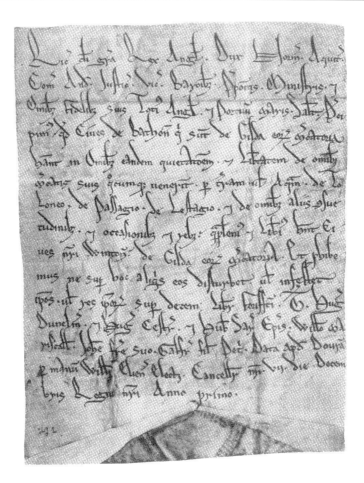

41 *The charter of 1189. It was granted by Richard I at Dover, just days before he left for the Crusades.* Courtesy of Bath and North East Somerset Council Archives

When Bishop Robert died in 1166, the see was left empty for eight years – a common ploy, as it allowed the king to receive the income from the see during the vacancy. In this case, though, procedures were complicated by the feud between King Henry and Archbishop Thomas à Becket, and when Becket was murdered in 1170 church appointments came to a halt. The conflict with the pope meant that no new bishops could be consecrated until matters between king and pontiff were resolved. Reginald Fitzjoscelin was the king's man, and played an important part in the resolution: the bishopric was his reward. Even so he had to travel to Rome to be consecrated and tidy up concerns about both his involvement in the conflict with Becket, and his parentage (his father had been Bishop of Salisbury).

The position of Wells in the election and its episcopal status had been made clear by John of Tours: it had none. This did not stop the canons at Wells nursing a huge and growing sense of outrage at the loss of the *cathedra*. Robert had gone some way to granting the canons a rôle in the election of a bishop, but in the rush of great events it is hardly surprising that they were not consulted when Reginald was appointed. The canons of Wells seem to have appealed to the Pope after being again ignored, and in 1176 the Pope decreed that both churches were to be the seat of the bishop. He was to be enthroned first at Bath and then at Wells, and the canons were confirmed in their right to take part in the election. This was the origin of the double title of the Bishop of Bath and Wells. That this was the outcome of a long and well-planned campaign by the canons of Wells is clear when we consider the building history of Wells Cathedral. The canons had commissioned major works, in or just before 1174, on a new and state-of-the-art building, whose style and size clearly said 'cathedral', but which was officially still only a minor collegiate church. Work on its completion was pushed ahead during those precise years until 1245, when the affair was finally settled.

The path to resolution was long and confused, however. Reginald was translated to Canterbury, but died on the journey. On his death bed he asked Prior Walter to support Savaric, Archdeacon of Northampton, to take over from him at Bath. As his successor is likely to have been already chosen, or at least recommended to the king (who had in effect the final choice), Reginald's dying recommendation suggests an awareness that Savaric might be a controversial candidate: and so he proved to be. The Bath monks duly voted for Savaric, but the Wells canons were once again excluded from the election. Immediately on his elevation, Savaric started a complex and obviously carefully planned 'reform'. He surrendered the town to the king (John of Tours, we remember, held it from King William II) in exchange for Glastonbury Abbey, the richest monastery in the diocese and indeed the west, and proudly independent. In addition, he restyled the see into that of 'Bath and Glastonbury', bypassing Wells altogether.

Savaric had two motives for carrying out this odd manoeuvre. The first was to bolster his authority as bishop over the monasteries in his see. Glastonbury was, and continued to be, resistant to the regulatory visitations of their bishop, proudly asserting its ancient status and independence. Even Bath on occasion refused the absolute right of its bishop to visit, even though he was titular abbot! If Glastonbury gave in, who else could refuse? Thus it was a question of power and church politics. The second motive was to get his hands on the huge wealth of the abbey; again, a question of power and church politics. It was during his reign that the abbey acquired lands and dependent houses in Ireland. No doubt this was seen as another investment, but in fact this holdings only ever cost the community money. Savaric was good to the monks, paying the monastery's share of King Richard's ransom from the see's income (thanks to Glastonbury), but nonetheless appears to have been unable to win their favour.

Savaric died in 1205, and his actions seem to have brought Wells and Bath together. They *jointly* elected Joscelin of Wells (called Trotman), the archdeacon of Wells, and the monks and canons all signed a statement in 1206 bearing witness – anything other than that man again, we seem to hear. Incidentally, the document shows that there were 41 monks at Bath in 1206, the medieval high point in numbers. Joscelin was to be Bishop of Bath and Wells. However, times were still difficult and dangerous. King John's quarrel with the Pope led to Joscelin being in exile from 1208-13, and even before that he probably felt safer in Wells, Bath being now the king's town. The king was in Bath in 1209, 1212 and 1213 and while there he forced the monks to pay for his keep, as well as that of his servants and retinue. This was so ruinous that the monks had to borrow from the canons at Wells to buy corn. The Bishop returned after John was forced to make peace with the Pope, but was the first holder of the see to prefer Wells. He started the palace there, and the ruins of his impressive great hall are still visible. It was not until 1219 that the name of the diocese officially reverted to Bath and Wells; and it was also in this period that the abbey church and cathedral at Bath settled down to its dedication to SS Peter and Paul, rather than just St Peter.

Despite the apparent amity between the two houses, scheming was clearly still under way. Joscelin died in Wells in 1242 and was buried there hastily, when he should have been interred at Bath, and the canons invited the monks to join them in electing a new bishop. The monks, rightly smelling a procedural rat, refused. Yet another appeal to the Pope led to the final settlement, essentially repeating the decision of 1176 and confirming the dual name. In 1245, Roger of Salisbury became the first bishop under the final agreement. He and his successors through the thirteenth century seem to have kept an even hand between Bath and Wells, building churches and episcopal palaces at both places.

Further reading

For general background on post-conquest medieval England, King 1988 is good for an attractively-illustrated introduction, while Platt 1978 and Steane 1984 are especially good on how the archaeology of the period works with the history. For Adelard, the biography by Cochrane 1991 is the best and only recent source. For the ins and outs of diocesan politics the *VCH* is still good, as is Britton 1825. The individual entries in the Dictionary of National Biography are well worth perusing for the bishops' wider careers (but see appendix 2). For archaeological and architectural details on the cathedral see Davenport 1991 and 1996 and Bell 1996. Information on the medieval burials and the King's Bath can be found in Cunliffe and Davenport 1985 and Davenport 1991. The material from the cloister cemetery has not yet been published, except in passing in Bell 1996. For further delving the Somerset Record Society volumes (SRS), especially Hunt 1893, provide much information. A detailed and reliable history of the abbey/priory has been commissioned in connection with the quincentenary of King's Church, and should appear in 2003 or 2004.

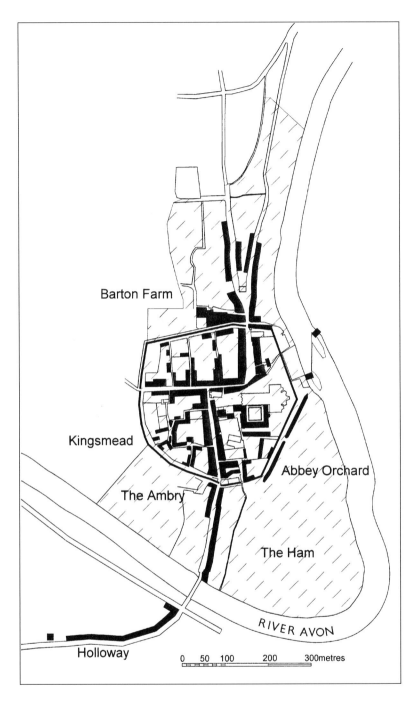

Barton Farm

Kingsmead

Abbey Orchard

The Ambry

The Ham

RIVER AVON

0 50 100 200 300metres

Holloway

42 *The Bath Hundred, the administrative unit from which the Guild of Merchants was distinguished by the granting of the charter of 1189. Until 1590, when the new charter extended the Corporation's jurisdiction, the hatched area was effectively the city limits. It contained five parishes, but predated their creation*

6 City and Guilds

We have seen in chapter 4 that the late Saxon city would have been administered for the king as his property, so Alfred the Town Reeve was directly responsible to the king. Nonetheless, even the king's property was a part of the administrative entity of the *hundred*, and came under its hundred court. This adjudicated the laws and obligations in regard to land grants, tax, inheritance, and suits criminal and civil. All free men were obliged to bring their suits and requests to the court. The lord of the manor, in this case the king, received the profits from such cases, as well as the rightful render from his property. The later medieval city boundaries seem to reflect this Bath Hundred, called *The Hundred of Le Buri,* and the hundred court probably met in the walled area (**42**). A much larger area, including the parishes around Bath that probably made up the original royal estate of the early Saxon period, formed the Bath Foreign Hundred or *Forinsecum,* and the caput of this was the royal manor of the Barton based just north of the town itself (**43**). Medieval references mention the courthouse in the bailiff's farmhouse at the Barton, and this legal framework continued into the seventeenth century, with its last vestiges not being extinguished until the nineteenth century. The Barton Farmhouse was a few hundred yards north of the city walls, and like the legal framework it represented, it too survived until the nineteenth century. Its position can still be seen as a Jacobean-style façade in the rear of Jolly's department store.

This system was essentially rural, traditional and inflexible, and must have been ever more irksome to the increasingly wealthy and influential burgesses of Bath, who had no obvious status in the eyes of such a system. Their activities created much of the wealth of the town, yet it was, for example, to the bishop that King Henry I granted the right to hold a fair (and therefore make much profit) around the feast of St Peter (29 June) each year. This was in 1106, and seems to have been held in the High Street. It was probably merely confirmation of a much older fair, as was definitely the case with the twice-weekly High Street market, also granted to the bishop in the fourteenth century. The powerful men of Bath, however much they leave or grant large sums to the church for the good of their souls all through the Middle Ages, would have chafed under such a lack of recognition.

Thus the opportunity at Dover to extract a definition of status from a hurried and impecunious King Richard was well taken. The merchants of Bath were organised into a body with rights and privileges which were essentially commercial, but structured in such a way that it was inevitable that its power and influence would grow in other ways. As early as the first half of the thirteenth century, perhaps as early as 1220, David, son of Goldriana, bought a parcel of land. The purchase was made, as

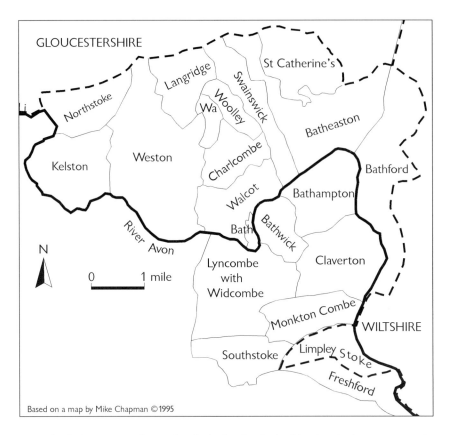

43 *The* forinsecum *or foreign hundred of Bath, the local legal and administrative unit before the creation of the parish. This is probably the estate of 100* manentes *given to Abbess Berta in 675, and may be of Roman or even earlier origin. It continued as a legal entity into the nineteenth century.* After A. Keevil

would be normal, 'in full hundred', witnessed and approved by the traditional hundred court. In addition, however, the purchase was also witnessed by 'our guildsmen of Bath'; and even more revealing, the deed was sealed with the seal of the Guild. This deed also gives a hint of the Guild's structure, as one of the witnesses is Reiner the Goldsmith, scrivener (secretary) of the Guild. At about the same time we also have the first reference to the Mayor: 'John of the Gate, at that time, Mayor of Bath', again in a property deed. References to the Mayor and his officers remain sparse until the last 20 years of the century, when we have the names of 10 or 11, though we hear of Walter de Falc in about 1249 and Henry the Tailor in 1262 and 1277. After Reiner the Scrivener we next find reference to the officers of the Guild in the 1280s or so, when John de Dover and Walter Ring, as 'cofferers', were nominated to receive payment due under a property transaction.

The charter was confirmed in 1246, and by this time the Guild of Merchants was well on the way to becoming the ruling body of the city. This process was helped by the continued absence of episcopal control. The city was not restored to the bishop until 1275, when Robert Burnell became bishop and re-acquired Bath and the Barton from the king in exchange for Glastonbury and £20 per annum. Church control of the city and land surrounding it might have slowed the growth of the influence of the Guild, but Bishop Robert was not only Chancellor of England and friend to Edward I (and therefore more often out of the diocese than in it), but also the last to spend much time in the palace at Bath when he was here. It was he who moved the parishioners of St James to a new church outside the monastic precincts and converted part of the old one to his private chapel, demolishing the rest. He or his immediate predecessors probably rebuilt or refurbished the palace, but none of his successors used it, or at least very seldomly, staying at Wells or, when in Bath, residing at their manor at Bathampton. By the early fourteenth century the palace was in ruins.

Opportunities for the Guild to take over more and more of the running of the city were obvious. Craft guilds, such as the cordwainers, or shoe and leather workers, appeared later in Bath's history, but this original Guild was a society of the major merchants, entrepreneurs, traders and money men. The basis of their commerce would indeed have been the cloth trade, based on the wool flocks of the Cotswolds and the Somerset highlands, but it was wealth and power that mattered, and that gave an entry into the club as it were, not merely the trade itself. Thus the Guild easily transformed into the 'mayor and commonality', the ruling body of later medieval Bath, membership of which was essentially based on wealth and mutual advantage.

That the citizens of Bath were not cowed by the church is shown perhaps by the independent spirit of a jury that, in a Royal enquiry in 1274-6, reported the prior for unlawfully acting as patron of Walcot Church and for pulling down part of the city wall to repair the monastery; as well as (a politically astute charge) for allowing the king's lodging in the priory to fall into disrepair. Earlier, in 1256, David de Berewyk and his son William successfully challenged the prior's denial of pasture rights on land south of the city. The *Commonality* or citizens together challenged the Bishop in 1260 over common pasture rights on Kingsmead.

Yet city and church worked together. By the mid-fifteenth century the Guild held the fee farm of Bath from the Bishop (and had probably held it from the early fourteenth), which means that they effectively held administrative control as tax collectors and enforcers. Even before this, active men still looked to the advantage they could gain by working the system. Richard of [Bath]Ford paid the large sum of £42 16s 10^d to the prior for the farm of the Barton in *c.*1180 – that is, for the right to collect all the dues. He would hope to make a handsome profit, and the prior would be absolved from the bother of collection. He was also recompensed by the grant of the manor of Shockerwick a few miles east of Bath, and close to Bathford, but had to act as bailiff of the Barton in return, again relieving the prior of the administrative burden.

The Guildhall

The business of the guildsmen needed premises. These would not only serve for meetings, both for business and pleasure, but also provide somewhere to store the increasing number of records of civil transactions. While such a building must have been available from early days, it is equally true that meetings could have been held in the leading citizens' houses. There are no remaining merchants' houses from this early period in Bath, but there are likely to have been a number of substantial timber or stone built ones. The richer of these, at least, will have had secure storage and strong rooms, as well as comfortable halls for council meetings; and one fragment of such a house, which could date back to this time, does exist in the basement of Abbey Church House. One end of the oldest part of this, which seems likely to predate *c.*1400, represents the undercroft, or stone, semi-subterranean cellar of a large house, a *capital messuage* fronting on to the street inside the city walls. It was later owned by St John's Hospital. But such arrangements would only ever be temporary. The need for a purpose-built or at least dedicated guildhall would soon be felt, and that we do not hear of one until 1355 is probably due to the paucity of records before the fourteenth century.

The 'Gyldehall' is clearly well established by this time but, more importantly, had a clear symbolic rôle. The Mayor was to be 'appointed' in the Guildhall, and it is clear that the ritual was also well-established: the various rules and agreements in the Guild's archives were read out ceremoniously at the Mayor-making so that all should remember them. The 'Mayor and Commonality', as the Guild was regularly referred to from the thirteenth century, by its very name implied its representative capacity – and not only in the material world. The Guild received money and maintained the chapel of St Catherine in St Mary de Stalls Church as early as 1249. That particular grant was to pay for the saying of masses for the souls of the faithful citizens departed.

The work of Elizabeth Holland has shown where the medieval guildhall was. A deed of 1359 places it in the lane going towards the Lot Gate (the east gate), and later documentation fixes it quite clearly. Unfortunately, we have no archaeological evidence for this building, and little is likely to survive the redevelopment of the area in the nineteenth century, but from the dimensions of the plot of land, and later post-medieval information about the building, which was not finally demolished until the eighteenth century, some picture of the medieval Guildhall can be attempted. Miss Holland provides a tentative plan of the Guildhall in around 1400, and this has been used to create the impression, rather than reconstruction, shown in **44**. It has been assumed that the detached kitchen is timber-framed, and the main hall constructed from masonry under a wooden roof. The gallery is documented and would have overlooked the main hall, which had a dais at the south end. It underwent many alterations before its final demolition.

An object that neatly brings together the legal status of the Guild and its physical expression, the Guildhall, is the seal of the Guild, or as it says around the edge 'The Seal of the Citizens of the City of Bath'. Probably dating from the early fourteenth century, the centre of the seal shows the town, represented by its walls, with a single low building in the centre, with three doors or windows, no doubt the Guildhall itself (**45**).

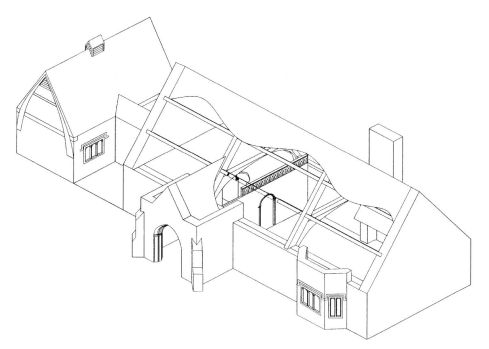

44 *An impression of the medieval Guildhall c.1400, based on property boundaries and later descriptions*

45 *The early fourteenth-century seal impression of the Guild Merchant of Bath.*
Courtesy of Bath and North East Somerset Council Archives

Men and women of Bath

From about 1220 onwards we can begin to get a clearer idea of the men (no women, of course) who were elected (or perhaps more accurately, selected) by their peers to lead them: the Mayors of Bath (appendix I). Many are mere names, but even these can be informative. Among the earliest we have Henry the Tailor and John the Innkeeper (*tabernarius* – taverner). John Le Veniur, Mayor in *c.*1300 appears, from his name, to be a hunter, although by this period surnames were beginning to stick. For example, Richard Whyteson alternates with Adam in the mayoral list. They may have been father and son, Adam surviving longer, but Richard was a miller, as his name suggests. John Pistor is a baker; Robert a Draper. Others are incomers from their names: Stephen de Devizes; John de Combe. Some Mayors have left a little more of their circumstances to us. Alexander the Dyer was Mayor nine times between 1332 and 1347. He owned property in both suburbs, and according to tax returns in 1340 (see below) he was the second richest man in Bath. His son, Thomas Saundres, gave several properties to the Guild in 1387 in return for an annuity – a pension arrangement to give him a worry-free old age, and an example of a process that left the Guild the biggest landowner in central Bath. William Phillips, whom we shall meet again, was a wealthy merchant who, apart from being Mayor many times in the early fifteenth century, also represented Bath in Parliament. All the Mayors would have been men of substance, property owners and merchants, or at least big time businessmen. We may strongly suspect that Adam Whyteson's rank as third poorest taxpayer in the town in 1340 (see below) was not quite so definite as he may have wished the tax collectors to think; while Henry the Tailor is unlikely to have spent the time between council meetings sitting cross-legged on a bench. The aim of most of these men will have been to earn enough money to buy sufficient land to be able to cease business altogether. An example is John Wyssy, who was a big land-holder in Bath and Bristol in the mid-thirteenth century, owning areas in High Street, Vicaridge Lane, Southgate Street and south of the town in Berewyk (Bear Flat and *The Bear* public house are reminders of this vanished rural community). A member of Bath and Bristol councils and Mayor of Bristol in 1272, he seems to have traded generally, but cloth was his mainstay. In 1270, he gave all his land in Berewyk to the Hospital of St Mary Magdalen 'for his parents' souls'.

Prosperity could be a transitory achievement, but certain families did seem to keep their wealth intact over several generations. So the de Berewyks appear in documents as major landholders in Weston and Berewyk from 1219 to 1379 and one of them, John, was prior in the late 1370s. The de Westons dominated that village west of Bath in the thirteenth century.

It was not just commercial failure that destroyed prosperity, however. Robert Little was outlawed in about 1229, apparently for his wife's murder (or at least being involved with her death). He must have sought sanctuary, perhaps in the cathedral, and would have got away with the penalty of outlawry if he could contrive to escape the kingdom. The charge took with it, however, the forfeiture of possessions to the Crown.

Someone else had got into less serious, but obviously worrying, debt with the king at about the same time. In 1249, Henry Peytevin sold property at the west end of Stalls Churchyard to raise money 'because I was charged with money due to the king and was heavily indebted for my Ransom'. The sale raised four silver marks and a blue woollen cloth. Whether this cleared Henry's debt is not recorded; neither, unfortunately, is the reason why the king ransomed him. It is tempting to suggest that he had gone on the sixth crusade, and been one of the prisoners held by the Sultan of Egypt in 1239-40. The King's, brother Richard of Cornwall, had secured their release in the latter year, a transaction that no doubt involved the payment of a substantial ransom. A less interesting possibility is that he had fallen foul of the king's somewhat arbitrary forest laws, and received a fine, which would have been owed to the king directly. We shall never know, but this does make us aware of the complexities and excitements that lie behind the dry legal documents that survive to us.

Men held most of the power in medieval England. Women had no right to be Guild members and when married, all their property came under the husband's control. Property held as a dower or marriage portion could not be alienated, but was still under male domination. Yet women could still be influential: widowhood was one status that gave women the right to both own and control property. A clear and lusty example of this is Chaucer's fictional Wife of Bath, who achieved her freedom and control precisely through judicious widowhood: 'Thonked be God that is eterne on lyve, Housbondes at chirche dorre I have had five'. This reminds us of the fact that medieval marriages were not solemnised in church, but usually at the church door or porch. In about 1250, Juliana Jay 'in her free widowhood' quitclaimed (gave up any rights to) land in Southgate Street which her husband Henry Gervase 'gave me at the door of the monastery'. In other words, this was part of her marriage settlement, which, in fact, she was selling. She and Henry were married outside the door, probably the great west portal, of the cathedral.

Women's names appear regularly in property deeds. We have already met Mathilda of Champfleur, who made advantageous property deals for the priory, as well as Isabella, who was welcomed into the priory because she had wealth to bestow. Another widow who made an impact posthumously was Odierna, who flourished in the early thirteenth century. Her great-grandson made a claim on the property of John de Berewyk in 1280, based on his inheritance of her property rights; Thomas Roberd took the case to the hundred court, but lost.

Margaret Little was an interesting case. Her father, Robert, was outlawed, as we have seen above, and his property was forfeit to the king – it was granted out to one Geoffrey of Bath for 1^d (0.4p; see appendix III for translations into current money) and feudal service. His wife's dower and any property not directly held would not normally be at risk, but especial care has been suspected in the range and quality of the witnesses to the deeds both documenting and then confirming Margaret's rights to property in Southgate Street. Her brothers and uncles continued to flourish in the area throughout the century. This paternal concern for (rich) women's welfare can be seen in Richard de Forde's grant of land to his daughter Edelina (*c.*1220) 'with the consent of his heirs', the point being that their male rights would otherwise override hers. Thus, women did have rights and wealth but their control of them was limited while husbands and fathers lived, and might sometimes be at risk after their deaths.

Despite this, women continued to hold property. In about 1300 Sir Richard Junior was left a stone house by his mother; and at the same time Ellen de Bathon (who may have been the daughter of Walter Brian, a fuller, who held land in Southgate Street) granted land outside the north gate in Slippery Lane. Her mother, Gunnilda, was given the rent from a house in Southgate Street around 1280, and she may have been the Lady Gundreda mentioned as owning a house there earlier in the century. At the same time, Betriche (Beatrice) Marleward sold *her* tenement. At the beginning of the century four sisters (Amicia, Ymma, Agnes and Alice) together sold a piece of land by Alron's (possibly the Cross) Bath, witnessed in full hundred.

Death and taxes

It is 1340 before we first get anything approaching a picture of a wider cross-section of the citizens – but still only those wealthy enough to be assessed for tax. In that year Adam le Muleward (mill keeper, not muleherd!) and William Cubbell, who had been Mayor in the year before, were sworn in as returning officers for a subsidy or tax of one ninth of movable property (i.e. everything except land). The list of tax payers included all males and unmarried women over 15 years old (this probably meant having reached 16), 106 people in all, and also showed the tax they paid. As it was a fixed proportion, this tells us something of the relative wealth of the taxable inhabitants (remembering that land was not included). Some of the inhabitants have names that clearly tell us what their professions were. Ralph the Taylor for instance, who shared the distinction of third poorest taxpayer with Adam Whiteson – they both paid 6ᵈ. Adam was Mayor on several occasions in the first half of the fourteenth century and, as we have observed above, one must suspect that rather than being a relatively poor man he was a clever accountant. The word is 'relative', however: Roger the Tanner paid only four times as much, and was a burgess as well as a trader. The largest taxpayer was Henry Hurel, who paid 20s. Alexander the Dyer, many times Mayor of Bath, was the second most wealthy, and he paid 13s 4ᵈ. The poorest men in town were Nicholas de Dyer, rendering 4ᵈ, who may have been an apprentice or journeyman to one of the big dyers, and Ralph le Hoper or barrel maker, who paid 3ᵈ. The nicely-rounded figures, by the way, are clearly an agreed approximation, not exactly one ninth of taxable property.

The returns do not specifically give occupations, but names of the form 'x the x', such as 'Thomas the mason' do provide this information. Thus we have some idea of trades and businesses in town. The aforementioned Thomas was taxed at 2s: a fairly average amount. He would have been a prosperous building tradesman. Richard le Vingour was probably a vintner or wine merchant, and his tax dues at 7s

6[d] reflect the greater profits available from exploiting both human weakness, and also possibly poor Ralph, who was probably working with William the Cooper (worth 18[d]). Henry the smith was worth 2s to the king, and Elias the grocer, 5s. Adam the Barber seems not to have made a fortune out of his practice, which included surgery and treatment of injuries as well as personal grooming. He was rated to pay just 6[d]. The town also supported at least one shoemaker and a baker, but the largest number of references was, as we might expect, to the cloth industry. Five dyers are mentioned, none paying less than 2s. Two 'of dyer's are mentioned, but these may already be simply surnames. This reminds us that the numbers in occupations are the minimum. We have no idea what most people with non-occupational surnames did. There are three weavers, but no spinners are mentioned, and only one fuller. There are six brewers in town in 1379, and there can hardly have been fewer in 1340, but none are identifiable here. One tailor and one linen draper represent the retail side of things. So the 1340 document gives some idea of occupations, albeit a very incomplete one. It gives us only a hint of the probable population range for the city, but a very clear statement of the spread of wealth. On these figures the richest lay member of the citizenry was worth 80 times as much as the poorest taxpayer. Of course, others, non-taxpayers, were poorer: 'true mendicants' were excluded from the tax, as presumably were any who had no taxable wealth, or were able to hide it. Clergy were taxed separately, if at all.

A broadly comparable set of figures is also available from 1379. In the second regnal year of Richard II a Poll Tax was set. Every man and unmarried woman of 16 and over was to pay a set amount based on their status. A *laborar* (broadly translated as working man or woman) paid 4[d], and a Duke 10 marks or £6 13s 4[d], with a graduated set of rates between. The highest payer was the Mayor, John Natton, at 10s. This listing explicitly gives the occupations on which the tax rate was broadly based; and since it also gives the street that people lived in, we can map the distribution of occupations. The table overleaf is taken from the publication of this information in 1889, with one correction of an arithmetical mistake.

As might be expected, the biggest group are the unskilled or semi-skilled working men and women. Seventy-three are servants, and 118 are workers in other trades. Artificers are unclassified skilled craftsmen, engaged in hand manufacture of a variety of objects. 'Sons' and 'daughters' are probably adult but dependent children of wealthy individuals, not otherwise engaged in trade but with property that brought them within the tax bracket. The meaning of the reference 'nil' is unclear. The cloth trade clearly dominates, but other trades are represented in the kind of proportion one might expect.

Nine years after the 'tax of the ninth' the Black Death struck. This epidemic had been raging across Europe since 1347, and reached England in late 1348. Nationally, a third or a quarter of the population may have died. There is no account of the detailed impact of the Death in Bath, but the snatches of evidence suggest that the impact was broadly in line with the national picture. In the winter and spring months of 1348-9, the death rate of priests in the diocese (the only indicators of mortality we have) was two per week. Nine parishes immediately around Bath lost their priests in January 1349.

	Stall Street	Walcot Street	Broad Street	N'gate Street	Souter Street	Westgate Street	S'gate Street	By the Bathe Street	Bynburi Street	Total
Artificers	5	16	7	10	3					41
Brewers	4			1	1					6
Butchers	2			1						3
Daughters	1	1		1						3
Spinners	3		1	2	3	1	1			11
Fullers	3	1	1				1			6
Goldsmith				1						1
Hostlers					2					2
Labourers	21	17	15	10	11	12	11	13	8	118
Peddlers	4	3		2	5					14
Petty merchants	1				1					2
Servants		3		8	5					16
Serviens	19	3	7		5	1				35
Famulus		12	8	3						23
Shoemakers	1	2	1	1	1	1				8
Skinners	2									2
Smiths	2			1	1					4
Sons		1	1							2
Tailors	5			1	1				1	8
Tanners							1			1
Weavers			1	1		1				3
Nil	3	6	5	1		1				16
Illegible							4			4
Total	**77**	**65**	**47**	**42**	**39**	**18**	**18**	**13**	**9**	**329**

Table of occupations as given in the Poll Tax of 1379

Batheaston's replacement died in February. The number of monks in Bath Priory fell by more than half, and never again reached its earlier strength. If the better nourished and more comfortable clergy suffered so much, it may be that the less well-recorded citizens of Bath suffered at least as severely, losing up to a third of the population. There may be a hint, though inconclusive, in the mayoral lists: only one Mayor in the lists in the 20 or so years before 1349 reappears later. Most notable is the powerful and influential figure of Alexander the Dyer, who completely vanishes from all records after 1349.

Later in the chapter, we make an attempt at estimating the population in 1379. Even allowing for recovery (though the years after 1349 were still heavily plague-ridden), the late thirteenth- and early fourteenth-century population, whatever the actual numbers were, must have been considerably larger.

Wool and cloth

By the fourteenth century, the cloth trade was clearly thriving. There are few references to the wool trade before this, but we do know that the diocese of Bath and Wells owned a fulling mill at Dunster in north Somerset in 1259, showing that the area was producing not just wool, but cloth in industrial quantities at that date, and surely earlier. Bath mill, on the Avon below Pulteney Bridge, is mentioned in Domesday and was owned by the priory, and called Monk's Mill until it burned down in 1883. It was both a tucking or fulling mill and a grist mill; and we hear of Walter Brian the Fuller in Southgate Street in the mid- to late thirteenth century. The priory would, of course, be a leader in the industry and its local development. In the fourteenth century we find it purchasing wool in industrial quantities, which can only have been for spinning and weaving into cloth (although by third parties, not the monks themselves).

In 1337, 219 sacks of Somerset wool were exported to Italy through Bristol, and in 1341 the county's wool tax quota was over 601 sacks. The quality, judging by price, was good but not the best. In 1343 Somerset wool cost 11 marks ($£7$ 4s 8^d) per sack: the most expensive, from the Cotswolds, cost 14 marks. Prior Thomas Crist had to source a large order from Wiltshire in 1334, over 900 sacks, suggesting demand outstripping local supply, although Wiltshire is very close by. Such a trade clearly needed organisation, middle men to match (and manipulate) supply and demand. The holding of stocks, possibly speculative, is shown by bequests of wool, common in medieval wills, as is woad, a valuable dyestuff. Men like Alexander and Robert, dyers, and Mayors of Bath in the mid-fourteenth century, grew rich in this fashion. Prior Crist also had a relative, Roger Crist, twice Mayor of Bath in this time, and a few years later the de Berewyks also straddled the divide. One wonders how much cornering of markets might have gone on. We should remember that Guilds were first and foremost about protecting members' interests. The public might suffer from this, but not gladly. Legislation was passed in 1389 forbidding the sale of unwrapped bolts of Somerset cloth. This seems to have been as much to protect the merchants as the purchaser, as one of the reasons stated for the law was to prevent the physical assault of merchants by purchasers who found their cloth sub-standard (generally in length) when it was opened! It was not until 1489 that an act was passed 'for the maintenance of drapery and making of cloth in Somerset' that provided for standard lengths and widths, qualities and weights.

This purchase of wool and the holding of dyestuffs confirms that both Abbey and townspeople were engaged in cloth manufacture. The tucking mill owned by the monks in what is now Parade Gardens, just outside the city walls (and possibly Isabel Mill outside the Ham Gate, driven by the outflow from the King's Bath), also suggests the monks' involvement in cloth manufacture. Isabel Mill is first mentioned in 1279, and the Monks' Mill was probably converted to driving fulling stocks in that century. Probably the earliest references to cloth manufacture in Bath is Aylmer the Weaver who had died by 1290, and William the Clothmonger in 1292, although we should remember that archaeological evidence for cloth manufacture in Bath goes back to late Saxon times. Another weaver, Edward, had property outside the North Gate in Broad Street in 1290. Serlo the Tailor flourished before 1230. It may have been his land near the north gate mentioned in a deed of about that date. He also owned land near the Cross Bath, and must have been a well-known local character: an early name for St Michael's Passage, which leads from Westgate Street to the Cross Bath, was Serlo's Lane.

Cloth manufacture remained the mainstay of Bath's wealth until the early sixteenth century, and was at its peak in the fourteenth and fifteen centuries. Chaucer's fictional character, the Wife of Bath, shows that Bath's cloth traders were widely known and known to be wealthy. 'Of clooth-making she hadde swich an haunt/She passed hem of Ypres and of Gaunt.' Both were Bath's continental competitors.

Important though wool was to Bath, and Bath to the local economy, we might pause to remember how small the city was on the national scene. Three times during King Richard II's reign (1377-99) forced loans were taken from various corporate bodies. Bath gave £20; Bristol, a wealthy, nationally significant port and city: £800.

Wool and other agricultural products obviously supplied the basic wealth of the area, and this provided for the purchase of both necessities and luxury items. The latter are shown by three references to goldsmiths: Reiner (whose name looks German, but could be a version of Reynaud) and William, who both flourished before 1250; and another William, who had died by 1200. Both were clearly wealthy and influential citizens. In addition, in 1379 there were Henry and William, goldsmiths (and earlier we must recall Ralph who paid huge sums towards the completion of the cathedral in the mid-twelfth century, although we know nothing about the source of his wealth).

One business is missing completely. There is nothing that makes us think there might have been any kind of trade exploiting the hot springs that, regardless of human interest, had never ceased to flow. We have seen that Bede refers to the Baths in the eighth century, and that they were refurbished by John of Tours and merited an admiring mention in the *Gesta Stephani* in the twelfth, but there is a remarkable lack of comment on the use of the hot springs for the rest of the Middle Ages, and nobody appears in the Poll Tax returns or any other records as anything to do with the Baths. As far as we can tell, no one was making money from visitors, and the priory had not obviously capitalised on them, for example by claiming they possessed any kind of miraculous qualities. Yet the priory continued to maintain the king's and the other baths. When the Hospital of St John was founded in the late twelfth century (see below), it was at first referred to as the 'hospital of the Baths' and we hear of the unfortunate leprous monk, Elias, who came from Reading and bathed for 40 days in the hot springs in 1170, but to no avail. The baths were certainly in use in the mid-fifteenth century, when Bishop Beckington issued a decree banning naked bathing; and moreover they were clearly a part of everyone's experience of the town. Deeds, from the earliest examples in the thirteenth century, regularly and casually refer to them as topographical markers: 'the way to the Cross Bath'; 'Alron's Bath' (of uncertain meaning, but possibly the Cross Bath); 'by the bathe streete'. It also seems that the priory contained its own hot baths. Leland, writing in the 1540s says that 'Ther goith a sluse out of this Bath [the King's Bath], and served in Tymes past with water derived out of it 2 Places in Bath Priorie usid for Bathes: els voide; for in them be no springes'. It would be perfectly in keeping with Benedictine practice for Bishop John to have provided bathing facilities for the brethren, but there is no other evidence for this. However, later traditions of a Prior's Bath and an Abbot's Bath (the bishop was the abbot, we remember) might suggest that the prior's lodging and the bishop's palace were provided with private hot baths. While these have never been found, the palace was provided with well-built stone culverts; and another has been recorded, dated to the thirteenth or fourteenth century, which passes through the city wall south of the priory, and shows clear signs of having channelled thermal spring water.

Wealth, we are told, trickles down. These wealth creators, both lay and clerical (for the church was, and remained throughout the Middle Ages, a major engine in the economy) provided the basis for the smaller, everyday economy of the region. Food supply was obviously a basic industry for the city, occupying the majority of people in the surrounding area. Supply and purchase of food and everyday domestic needs took place in the twice-weekly market in High Street. This was first mentioned in a charter of 1371, but as existing 'from time immemorial'; and it was also where cloth was sold. The market presumably very soon divided up into specialised areas, but the only evidence of this is that the area around the junction of Stall Street and Cheap Street came to be referred to as Corn Street and Cornmarket in the early years of the fourteenth century. Presumably the buying and selling of this basic product involved so many traders that it had expanded from the market place proper to a new or extra space around the corner.

Less regular and more expensive purchases, and larger-scale or seasonal agricultural trading, took place at the (generally) annual fairs. The Bishop's Fair was held in the High Street market place and lasted about ten days. It must have been cramped, but it is not known whether it spilled out beyond the walls, although in much later years the sheep fair took place outside the Northgate, along Walcot Street. The fair was a valuable addition to the see's income. With the bishops' declining influence in Bath after *c.*1300, the priors obtained two fairs from the king, both in 1304 and outside Bath, at Lansdown and at Lyncombe.

Other than clothmaking, manufacturing was on a small, domestic scale. Horn and bone were the plastic of the Middle Ages, and all sorts of objects were made from them: accordingly, rubbish pits excavated north of Bath Street in 1986 produced thick layers of horn dust from the preparation of artefacts. Leather was the other all-purpose material; Adam the Tanner appears in a deed of *c.*1250 and Roger the Tanner appears influential in the town in the 1340s. Another tanner is mentioned in the Poll Tax returns, and it appears his tannery was at the bottom of the Southgate Street suburb, next to the river. He may have been the son or grandson of Roger, as the latter held land in Southgate Street. This noxious process was best kept as far as possible from the rest of town, and the river no doubt received the bulk of the waste. Apart from two more wealthy occupants, the Southgate suburb was one of the poorer parts of town, which might further explain the siting of the tannery. The leather produced was worked in the town: various skinners in the records were more likely to be leather workers than butchers, for example, Serlo the Skinner in *c.*1225. In 1331, Benedict Hercy bought four pounds' worth of hides in Bristol, but whether this was for trading or to bring into Bath is not known. A deed of 1359 suggests the former, as it informs us that Benedict had failed to pay his bill and had lost his property in Stall Street to his creditors. Fragments of leather have been found in rubbish pits in excavations, but no leather artefacts have survived. Yet straps, belts, shoes, aprons, sheaths, hats, harnesses, even writing 'paper' (parchment) were made from leather, as, of course, was all manner of weatherproof clothing. Richard Glover may have been a glovemaker in the late fourteenth century, he was an 'artificer' in the Poll Tax returns.

Pottery was mostly imported from north Somerset and north Wiltshire. Even pottery from the Laverstock kilns near Salisbury is extremely rare, although a fine example of a face jug was excavated from the priory in 1984. Curiously, Bristol's pottery products made little inroad into Bath, although ware from Ham Green near Portishead is found occasionally. Imports from abroad were limited, but French pottery, presumably along with wine, was reaching the town in the fifteenth century. This would have come via the huge port of Bristol, but exactly how it was transported from there presents a difficult problem. An eighteenth-century antiquarian made the oft-since repeated claims that the river was navigable as late as the early fifteenth century, and that wine and cloth were sent up it. The river *was* ordered to be cleared of obstacles in 1327, but this only shows it was obstructed: such instructions were notorious for not being carried out in this period. Little else is known from excavations or documents of trade contacts with Bristol in the Middle Ages, and no other Bristol connections can be made. It is much more likely that mill and fish weirs, fords and braided channels will have generally made the river impassable from early days, and this is probably reflected in the paucity of contact with Bristol goods. We may remember that the river was only made navigable in the post-medieval period by substantial engineering works in the early eighteenth century.

Carpenters and masons figure little in the earlier records, yet must have been in constant demand. The fortunate survival of the accounts of the churchwardens of St Michael's Without from *c.*1460 to the mid-sixteenth century (albeit with gaps) shows an almost constant expenditure on masons, plasterers and carpenters repairing the church's investment properties. Quarrying was carried on *ad hoc* as needed, and old workings are known, if poorly dated, on most of the hillsides around Bath. They sometimes reveal themselves as field names such as Quarr Ground and Upper and Lower Pitts in Berewick, alongside the present Wellsway on land owned by St Mary Magdalen (**46**).

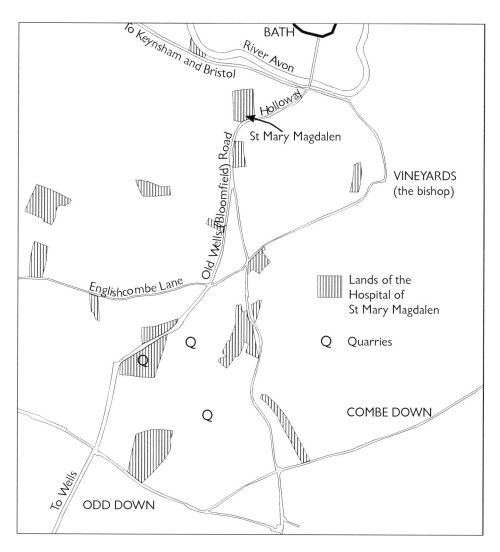

46 *The lands of St Mary Magdalen, stone quarries and vineyards south of Bath.*
After Mike Chapman

Labels within the map:

To Keynsham and Bristol

BATH

River Avon

Holloway

St Mary Magdalen

VINEYARDS
(the bishop)

Old Wells (Bloomfield) Road

Englishcombe Lane

Lands of the
Hospital of
St Mary Magdalen

Q Quarries

Q

Q

Q

COMBE DOWN

To Wells

ODD DOWN

Irvine noted that the fragments of vaulting from the Norman cathedral he discovered during the restoration works of 1863-71 came from St Catherine's Valley, several miles east of Bath: the priory owned large parts of this area. The quarries on Bathampton Down must have been in use throughout the Middle Ages, but references are only available for the end of our period. In 1479-80, the churchwardens of St Michael's paid 10s 8^d *pro viij lodys de Hamptonys quarra pro ij^{bus} cameris dicto ten^o in Bradestrete cum cariacione ejusdem x^s viij^d* ('for eight loads of stone from the Bathampton quarries for the second room in the said tenement in Broad Street, including carriage: 10s 8^d'). These accounts also show that stone is being increasingly used even in smaller buildings by this period, alongside timber construction.

Another source of stone would be the various Roman ruins that still dotted the area. It is common in excavating Roman buildings outside the walls, along Walcot Street for example, to find that they still stood above ground level as late as the thirteenth century, before they were finally grubbed up and even the foundations removed at around our period. Not only stone would be required: there is some suggestion from excavations into Roman buildings near Walcot church that lime mortar rather than stone blocks was being taken, probably for reburning and slaking for new mortar. Other quarries would have provided fuller's earth, the special absorbent clay present in large quantities in the hillsides around Bath, and used for degreasing woollen cloth in fulling. The centre of woodworking seems to have been Saw Close, an open area inside the north-west corner of the walls (**26 & 51**). Excavations in Seven Dials just outside the walls revealed what were probably saw pits, still with sawdust in them, dating from the twelfth century (**47**). Accounts from 1569 (just after our period) show city money being spent on clearing out the saw dust from the pits in Saw Close. The area seems to have been used for shaping large, structural timbers. Walter le Carpenter was a fourteenth-century Mayor of Bath, who was probably a large-scale contractor.

As suggested earlier, most craftsmen and manual workers would have been of a lower status. The poll tax returns of 1379 show about one third of the taxable population as workers (*laborari*) paying the minimum 4^d due. Artificers, or craftsmen, could cover a wide range (for example one tailor paid 6^d tax, barely above a *laborar*). In the thirteenth century Adam the Blacksmith held property in Westgate Street, handy for traffic coming into town from the west gate. Another smithy existed from before 1206 just outside the north gate on a tiny site next to the city wall (excavations next to this site in 2002 produced large quantities of iron slag from medieval layers). Another may have existed, just inside the north gate, as a messuage was granted by Alexander the Dyer to Henry Marshall (a smith) in 1325. While the largest part of the smiths' work involved farriery, many other objects would be made of iron, including knives and tools of all kinds, door and window fittings, locks, latches and keys (several of which were found lost on the medieval road surface of 'the way to the Cross Bath' or Pillory Lane, as it was also called, during the 1986 excavations). Many of the deeds and leases that survive in increasing numbers from the thirteenth century onwards contain references to 'a shop' and by the fourteenth century they would have lined the main streets, as the naming of Stall Street indicates. Bath was not large enough to develop concentrations of specialist or similar

47 *Twelfth-century saw pit at Saw Close excavated in 1990. The collapsed timber and wattle lining kept the soft sides in place.* Bath Archaeological Trust

trades, but there is a suggestion of a grouping of shoe makers in Souter Street (Shoemakers' Street), officially renamed Cheap Street in 1399.

The day-to-day work of the smaller tradespeople can be glimpsed in the accounts that were kept in ever more detail in the later Middle Ages, especially those of the parish churches. We have already looked at those from St Michael's Without, just outside the north gate. In 1460/1 local craftsmen were paid, *inter alia,* for repairing books, fixing a pulley for the altar canopy, fixing stained glass in the church, mending and oiling the bells, replacing the bell rope and providing candle wax. Locks and chains for the vestment chest were purchased, and the accounts also refer to fees paid for bookkeeping, and to the custodians of the church clocktower. Thus we have references to bookbinders, candle makers, joiners, locksmiths, stained glass makers and a ropemaker; and we must not forget the accountant. These would all be the artificers not further distinguished in the earlier records, individuals too lowly to appear in the deeds and wills recording the doings of the richer citizens. This is particularly striking in the case of William Galwyne, who was paid 12^d for digging and weeding the garden of William Abingdon, and a further 3^d for planting 700 teazels (we noted earlier that teazel seeds have been discovered in excavations in Bath). The spiky heads of these plants were an important element in clothworking, used to raise the nap of cloth and to comb wool before spinning, and their cultivation must have been an important minor industry in any cloth town.

Much building work in the church's property is recorded. In succeeding years there are references to oak and elm planks for doors, shutters, floors and gutters; lead for roof and gutter work; beams for repairing walls; clay and stone tiles for roofs, including decorative ridge tiles (*crestis*), recorded along with the sums dispersed to the small builders, the plumbers, joiners, plasterers, masons and thatchers. In fact, the churchwardens at St Michael's seem to have spent a large proportion of their rents on building maintenance. A curious note also emerges from these records: in 1550 Thomas the Tyler's house was thatched.

Life is never all work and amid the payments made by St Michael's in 1481-2 we suddenly find evidence of what must have been a great day or two off. Fourpence was spent on drinks 'for the players acting in the various different plays'. Two bushels of frumenty were also acquired 'for the same'. A book box or chest seems to have been needed, and bread and flowers were also provided. Richard Tanner provided skins (parchment?) and 'William' painted various tools (props?). Cheese was ordered to the value of 13^d, which must represent quite a substantial quantity. This happy event might have been an Easter mummers' play, as John Fowler was paid to carry the 'tomb' to the cemetery 'at the time of the said play'.

The social distance from top to bottom of the scale is again illustrated by the taxes paid in1379. At 10s the mayor's contribution was 30 times that paid by the working man, and just about one thirteenth the top rate paid by a Duke. In earlier years, workers frequently might not be free men; Wulfrich was given both his freedom and a lodging by the prior, in return for becoming the priory's plumber and glazier in 1316. In a different league of the trade is John the plumber, who is mentioned in a deed of 1337. Of the professional classes we hear little: most of their functions would be provided by the church. Master Roger seems to have been Bishop Reginald's doctor or *medicus,* possibly in orders but possibly not. Arnold is the monks' physician in 1206, and may well have been a monk himself. John de Bathon, the monks physician in 1328, was clearly not, but was given a *corrody*, a pension and lodging in the priory, in return for his medical services. It is possible, from his name, that Thomas Leche was a physician, living in Walcot Street in 1379. It is interesting that the very few book titles known to us from the cathedral library include several of the medical text books of Galen, the Roman physician whose thought and practice dominated medieval medicine.

The priory ran sheep and cattle on its farm lands, and was largely self-sufficient. Vegetables and fruit were grown on the land between the city walls and the Avon in the Abbey Orchard, and the Ham was used mostly for sheep. These plots had been given to the priory by the bishop in the 1270s, but they also had the use of land along Walcot Street, north of the suburb and south of the hamlet of Walcot, where an area in the possession of the Prior's Kitchen [possibly a kitchen garden] is recorded in the fourteenth century, and where to this day 'Old Orchard' can still be found. Archaeological excavations along the northern half of Walcot Street regularly find a buried stratum of rich cultivation soil dating to the Middle Ages. More surprising to modern prejudices is the fact that vines were grown. The bishop refers to his vineyards along the lower slopes of Lansdown and Beacon Hill in the twelfth century (modern 'Vinyards', along the west side of the Paragon, continues the name), and the prior had others in Lyncombe and Widcombe which were mentioned as not being included in the grazing rights conceded in 1260 to Richard de Berewyk (**46**).

In 1204, the prior had leased the Barton estate from the king. Later, Bishop Burnell acquired it and continued to let it to the prior. The estate was large and wealthy and was farmed both by tenants and in demesne, which more than covered the £20 annual rent. The estate was run, at least notionally and at the beginning, as a traditional co-operative open field system, with rights to commons by the free citizens of Bath. The land was cultivated in a standard mix of arable and pasture, with carefully graded rights to graze on stubble after the harvest for various 'eweflocks'. Income came from rents and fees as well as the direct profits of the demesne, but the church also received tithes from all produce: one tenth of all agricultural produce flowed into the church, from wheat, barley and meat animals to dairy products and fowl. Fish was also an important part of the diet, with specially constructed fishponds common on estates in the Middle Ages: and accordingly Bishop Burnell granted land and £10 in cash for the monks to build themselves a fishpond. This may have been dug in the city ditch by the south east run of city walls, where water could be easily tapped from the river. An interesting question is whether the monks used warm spring water to feed the ponds. Fish have occasionally been kept in the hot water of the Roman Baths in the twentieth century, and flourished exceedingly well. Spa water was certainly available from outflows on the south and east of the walls, but whether in sufficient quantity is uncertain.

We have mentioned individuals, processes and institutions, but it is legitimate to ask how big was Bath, how many real people were involved in all these legal, administrative and commercial frameworks? The answer, of course, is that the population varied. We saw in the last chapter that Domesday suggests there were 178 taxable properties in the town in 1087. The Poll Tax returns of 300 years later (although on a different basis) imply a maximum of only 20 more inside the walls but another 130 outside; the town must have nearly doubled in population and spilled over into the suburbs. Estimating population from heads of households is inaccurate at best, but if we could find an appropriate multiplier we might suggest a figure. If each burgage plot at Domesday represented six people, which seems conservative to this author, then the population in 1087 would be very approximately 1068. Adding in the monks gives around 1100. In 1377 the figures represent all unmarried adult women, and males aged 16 and over. The multiplier here is going to be different, but if we say four to allow for what ought to be a lower relative number of households, we end up with a figure in the region of 1316; and adding the monks we get around 1350. We might bear in mind, however, that the latter figure represents the period after the Black Death. The 1340 tax returns (see above) are even more difficult to use to estimate population, but do not suggest a lower figure.

Hospitals, almshouses, the rich and the poor

We have seen that the priory and the bishop both held considerable amounts of property in and around the city, and 'owned' the fairs and markets, bringing the church into a close relationship with the commercial and administrative life of the town and its citizens. The hospitals founded in the city, within the walls and without, formed another link. St John's Hospital was the richest and largest. It was founded by Bishop Reginald Fitzjoscelin between 1174-80 for the 'support of the poor of Bath' and still exists today, albeit in much altered form, carrying out essentially the same purpose. Land was given in 1180 by Roger, son of Algar, although whether to provide a site for a hospital to be built or as gift to generate income we do not know. The hospital gave support to those who through poverty could not look after themselves. As sickness easily resulted in poverty in the Middle Ages, the hospital evolved into an infirmary (a hospital in our sense of the word). Nevertheless, it never ceased to provide sanctuary for other deserving poor, both men and women. Numbers are not stated but there were never likely to be more than 10 or 15 inhabitants, and there were definitely fewer in later times. Both men and women were provided for.

The hospital was founded on land just west of the two smaller hot springs, the Hot and Cross Baths, and indeed, as we have seen, was first referred to as the 'hospital of the Baths'. Its layout in the early days is unknown, but it is likely that the chapel was on the site of the present early eighteenth-century chapel with the accommodation for the poor inmates to the west. Other parts of the hospital probably spread to the south, bounded by the now-vanished Nowhere Lane. The hospital later extended to the north, having acquired land here in the early thirteenth century, and included provision for gardens as well as its own cemetery, which was consecrated by Bishop Ralph in 1336 (burials were uncovered here during alterations in 1954). We do not know if the hot water was any part of a therapy (care, not cure was the norm for a medieval infirmary), but the hospital certainly had a bath in the sixteenth century, which it was claimed had existed 'time out of mind'. As the sixteenth-century bath was claimed to have been for the use of the master of St John's, perhaps it was a product of later, more decadent times, when senior ecclesiastics enjoyed their comforts. At any rate, bathing was available for inmates only a few steps from the front door.

Fitzjoscelin's foundation was an ecclesiastical one, under the control and supervision of the monastery. The hospital was to be run by a Master (in early days the title prior was also used, but this was soon abandoned), who would be a cleric, and in 1270 there is a reference to a small number of brethren and sisters 'serving God there' (both sexes were necessary if men and women were to be looked after). It is clear from other sources that the community was essentially monastic; but curiously, the style and order of the community remains unknown. Manco has made a convincing case that the brethren were Augustinian, as was quite common for hospital 'staff' elsewhere.

The first grant of land was followed by others, with large areas of both rural and urban land acquired for farming income and rental in the first hundred years after the foundation. Specific, additional sources of income were arranged by Bishop Reginald. The details are fascinating, if only because they are typical of that age when cash was rather rare. Reginald arranged a sheaf of corn to be donated yearly from each acre of his demesne land, and the same amount from the priory lands (later bishops commuted this to an annual payment of £5). The monks donated a tithe of their bread and salt meat; and the bishop also arranged, *inter alia,* a payment of four silver marks or £2 13s 4ᵈ a year; a weekly shipment of dead wood from his parks; and the right to pasture 100 sheep on Lansdown, the high pastures north of the town.

Thus the physical needs of the infirm would be met. But spiritual needs were also not to be neglected, and the chapel was as important (if not more so) as the infirmary and kitchen. The ministrations of the staff were not reserved for the souls of the inmates; many of the grants of land were conditional on masses being said for the souls of the benefactor. Richard of Combe and his wife Alice gave a field near Frome with this intent; William, vicar of Locking bought land specifically to make over to the hospital in return for a chaplain praying for his soul, while a canon of Wells gave the large bequest of £35 8s 8ᵈ to have daily prayers said for him. He must have had a strong sense of guilt to feel the need to pay such a sum, especially since he also made provision for all the members of the community to be paid 2s to attend the annual service of remembrance that he stipulated. Prayers were also said for the bishop in return for his largesse. Thus the community was to be a powerhouse of prayer, as well as a house of cure.

St John's may have been the largest hospital, but it was not the oldest. Between 1088 and 1100, and perhaps in 1094, when he became Sheriff of Wiltshire, Walter Hussey gave his house and private chapel of St Mary Magdalen to the see of Bath. The chapel was situated just across the river from the south gate of the city on the Holloway, the main Wells road. Walter stipulated that the chapel was to be rebuilt and 'exalted'. By this he seems to have meant that what was clearly his private chapel should become a small monastic foundation: this was certainly the meaning of the same phrase used of a chapel at Dunster, given to Bath Priory some time later. Nothing further is heard of the chapel until 1212, when the 'house of lepers in the suburb of Bath' is mentioned in Hugh of Lincoln's will (Hugh had started his distinguished ecclesiastical career in Reginald Fitzjoscelin's retinue), and it seems more than likely that Bishop John of Tours took the gift as an opportunity to set up a hospital for lepers. Leprosy was a terrible and feared disease in the Middle Ages, dealt with by the strict seclusion and separation of its sufferers from society. Little was more meritorious than working with them; and for those unable to face this, supporting a hospital was the next best thing. Again, benefactors left money and property so that the brothers and sisters would pray for their souls because, as St John's was to be, the lepers' hospital was established and run as a small monastery. Walter's wishes had clearly been respected. What the hospital-priory was like in the earliest days we do not know, but the monks and nuns must at first have simply moved into Walter's house and chapel and, as well as looking after the inmates, taken over the farmland he left with it. The lepers, as long as they were fit, would help with looking after the four cows, six oxen and 90 sheep that came with the endowment.

The Hospital of St Mary Magdalen was never rich, although it seems to have attracted a slow but steady stream of small bequests and endowments through the

48 *St Mary Magdalen Chapel on Holloway. The body of the chapel and the porch is Prior Cantlow's work, refurbished in the eighteenth century, when the tiny tower was also rebuilt. The far end, the chancel, was rebuilt in the early nineteenth century*

49 *Philips' St Catherine's Hospital, the Black Alms: a view of 1825, just before its demolition. Manco (1998) has suggested that only the furthest four cottages are the original 1430s versions, which may have been extended southwards in the sixteenth century.*
Bath and North East Somerset Library Service

Middle Ages. One of these reminds us that private chapels were not uncommon in the city: John Wissy left money in 1270 on condition that prayers were said for his soul in his private chapel in Bath. After the Black Death the community seems to have been reduced to just the Master, one Edward, although it seems that patients were still being cared for. In 1486 it was reported as ruinous, and likely to default on its debts. Prior Cantlow undertook to rebuild the hospital and pay its debts (**48**). Some of his work survives in the substantial rebuilding of the house and chapel in the eighteenth and nineteenth centuries. The lepers left in the sixteenth century, but in this rebuilt form the house and chapel still occupy the site given by Walter 900 years ago.

The last medieval hospital founded in Bath was symptomatic of the social changes in the later part of the period. St Catherine's was founded as almshouses, not by the church or with its assistance, but by a wealthy individual, six times Mayor of Bath and twice its MP, William Phelippes, or Phillips. In 1435 Phillips bought property on Bimbury Lane and built a row of four almshouses (**49**) (at some point in the fifteenth or early sixteenth century a further three cottages were added). These houses had access to a garden at the rear, and the eight poor people who were to occupy them included a bedsman to act as warden. One of this man's duties was to pray in the chapel of the foundation, and it seems that the chapel of St Catherine in Stalls Church was intended for the fulfilment of this function.

This chapel played a significant rôle in the charitable trust that Phillips set up. In his 1444 will he urges the completion of the rebuilding of the chapel that he has paid for. He also stipulates that this is to be the scene for the usual prayers for himself and his wife, and institutes a further charitable bequest, again to be enacted there, which demands that at the Easter time he sets down for the intercessory prayers (5s 1^d being set aside for this) there is also to be bread and a peck of beans to be distributed to 100 poor people. To administer the almshouses, their endowment of property and these other complex arrangements, Phillips set up a trust. This was run by his executors initially, but was almost immediately put into the hands of the 'Mayor and commonality' of Bath, i.e. the Guild or the later Corporation; no longer a church affair, Phillips' final charity saw the city and its citizens taking the initiative. This self-assertiveness had been growing as the church's influence had been waning; and the chapel of St Catherine's was a case in point. As we have seen, having prayers said for one's soul to reduce the time spent in Purgatory was a central concern of Christians in the Middle Ages. But paying for the time of a priest in perpetuity was expensive. In the later medieval period, groups of people banded together to have prayers said for them. The burgesses of Bath belonged to the Guild of St Catherine (the patron saint of the city and of weavers), and corporately supported prayers for all the commonality of Bath. This increased their sense of independence from the Church, represented here, of course, by the cathedral priory.

Another illustration of this desire for independence took place a few years before. The bell in the cathedral tower had always sounded out both the official start of day (at dawn), and the curfew, the end of the day when business came to an end and the city gates were closed. In 1408, the townsmen started ringing their own bells (apparently those of the parish churches) later than that of the cathedral in the evening, and earlier in the morning. A farcical yet serious battle for precedence between the town and the priory ensued, and the case actually went to law in 1412, and was dragged through the courts until the church won judgement from the king in 1421 (by appealing to *Magna Carta*). The case was farcical as it seems so petty, yet serious because it was symbolic of the desire to reduce church authority and rights over lay matters.

This itself was part of the social unrest that followed (and in parts preceded) the Black Death. The church had seen the refusal of dues and services by tenants and even the unfree across the diocese in the later fourteenth century. Religious indiscipline was also rife: an unofficial priest 'without orders', Henry Wells, was flogged for preaching in Batheaston in the early fifteenth century, while Agnes Cold of Norton St Philip, south east of Bath, denounced the representation of the Trinity in the cathedral in the 1420s, and had to recant in front of the Chancellor of the diocese. This was the time of Lollardy, a dangerous heresy from the church's point of view. Henry was lucky to get off with a flogging, and Agnes did well to recant.

The citizens of Bath, unlike the barons of the humorous *1066 and All That,* did not know that the Middle Ages were coming to an end. But there was a sense of change, crisis and dissatisfaction in society, and the city and church were moving in different ways.

Further reading.

For a wider background see Keen 1990; for the Black Death see Ziegler 1998. The Somerset volumes of the *Victoria County History* (*VCH*), though written many years ago, are still a good introduction to the period locally. The relevant chapters in Cunliffe 1986 form an intelligent synopsis, if read critically. Various papers by the Survey of Old Bath are good at teasing out the individuals of medieval Bath and their properties: these include Chapman and Holland 2000, Chapman 2000 and Holland and Chapman 2000. Much detail on the Hundreds and questions of medieval tenure can be garnered from the comprehensive studies in Keevil, 1996 and 2000. Davenport 1991 and 1999 are useful for archaeological detail. On the Guildhall see Holland 1988. Manco 1998 is a very attractive study of St John's Hospital and the other foundations in Bath, and gives a useful exposition of medieval background. The major source for the commercial activities of the wealthier people of Bath is *Ancient Deeds of Bath* (Shickle 1921). The deeds and some other documents kept by the Guild and its successors were translated and arranged by this Master of St John's, and while there are mistakes and mistranslations the book is invaluable. For those who want to delve deeper, the Somerset Record Society (SRS) have published most of the official medieval documentation. The Poll Tax and Lay Subsidy figures are most easily accessible in Green 1889. St Michael's accounts are published in Bush 1877-80, but not in translation. However, it is very easy Latin that keeps breaking into English; and the post-Dissolution accounts are entirely in English.

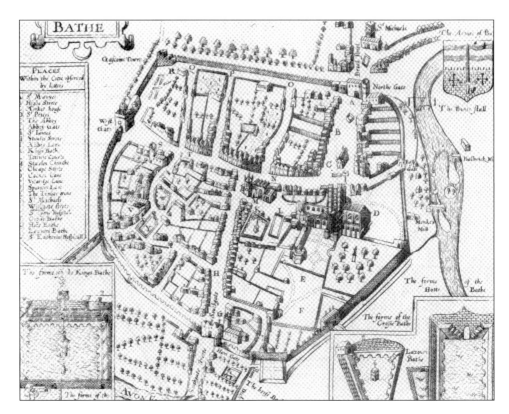

50 *(above) Speed's map of Bath, published 1610. Speed implies this is not his own survey, but borrowed from an unknown original: compare* **51**. *Both this and Savile's map give a vivid impression of the early post-medieval town, our only – albeit distorted – representation of the medieval city*

51 *(right) Savile's map of Bath, after 1603. This may be Speed's source, especially as it is more detailed, but there is some reason to believe it may be later.* Private collection

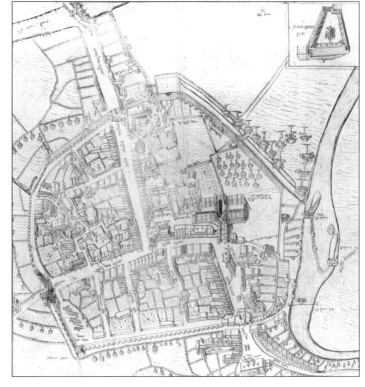

7 Topography and townscape: the shape of the later medieval city

So little of the medieval city remains today that any attempt to map and study its physical form demands an imaginative exercise of some magnitude. To control that imagination we have to depend on documents, which were not intended to give us the information we need; topographical study, which is interpretative to a high degree; and on archaeology, of which, in Bath, there is very little. What follows is my own interpretation of this difficult material, necessarily building on the work of many before me. The resultant maps and descriptions are a mix of known facts, inference and some guesswork. They are obviously provisional, but are highly probable. A few words on methodology are, therefore, advisable (although these may be skipped).

The earliest useful maps date from the beginning of the seventeenth century. Speed produced his version as an inset to his county map of Somerset, in his atlas of Britain published in 1610 (**50**). For various reasons it has always been accepted that this map was copied from someone else's original, which some identify as the Savile Map of *c*.1600-4, although other researchers are loath to accept its authenticity, pointing out topographical details that do not seem to fit with the early date. The Savile map is more detailed, and has more circumstantial information (**51**). Neither is surveyed to modern standards, and both are represented as bird's eye views, but this does mean that they also give a pictorial impression of the town at the time and, allowing for the changes since the Dissolution, some impression of the late medieval city. No other independent surveys exist until Gilmore's of 1694 (**52**). This too is a bird's eye view, and is based on a measured survey. In addition, it has little drawings of individual buildings around the border of the map. We have to be aware that a great deal has changed in the intervening decades, and the map is essentially of a late seventeenth-century town. The next and (for our purposes) the last really useful map is that of the Kingston Estates in Bath, dated to 1725 (**31**). This is the only reliable map in our sense of the word, and is useful as it shows both the design of streets and properties before the 'Improvements' of the later Georgian period and, particularly, the layout of the area of the priory before the redevelopments of the mid-eighteenth century. More information is provided by the many artists' depictions of Bath, none of which date to before 1600, but which will contain images of medieval structures and

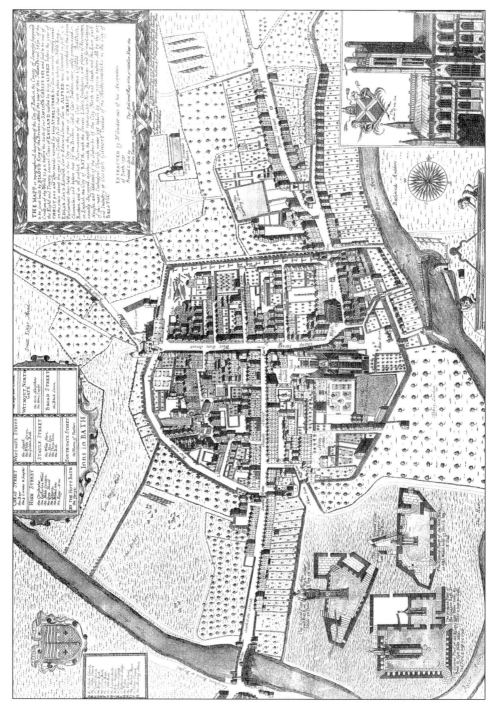

52 *Gilmore's map of Bath of 1694: the city just before its major rebuilding during the eighteenth century. This gives a clear impression of both how rural the city's setting was, and how it was contained by the walls.* Victoria Art Gallery, Bath

53 *Johnson's view of the King's Bath, 1672. This lively drawing shows the Bath approaching its fashionable height, and already all the buildings around it have been rebuilt. The small gabled building near the centre beyond the Bath represents the kind of construction along Stall Street that would have overlooked the spring in the later Middle Ages. However, both the arches around the spring and the slips are essentially twelfth century.* © Copyright The British Museum

layouts which survived up to the time of the view. The most famous of these is the Johnson drawing of 1672 (**53**).

These maps can be studied to provide an idea of the topographical framework of the medieval town, assuming no major changes in street pattern took place in the sixteenth century. Property boundaries are generally very conservative in our old towns, so later maps and documentation can be carefully used to work out older dispositions, and often illuminate medieval documents that are uninformative in themselves. They can and do change, nonetheless, so caution is necessary. Medieval deeds and leases, wills and other legal documents survive in varying degrees (Bath is not so well-served in this respect as some other medieval towns, such as Winchester). As they often refer to the neighbouring properties as a way of identifying themselves, a map of sorts, of relationships rather than absolute positions, can be worked out. Some properties, such as St Catherine's Almshouses, for example, and the cottages that preceded them, can be positioned exactly and we can begin to piece the sites together in absolute terms. Using the early maps as frameworks, real topographies can be recreated. Such work has been predominantly the labour of the Survey of Old Bath (now the Survey of Bath and District), which has produced topographical and property histories of several parts of the town. The seventeenth-century town is fairly well understood; the high and late medieval periods can be fragmentarily reconstituted. To go back further is possible, but the more detail that is pursued, the more the results will be open to revision, and therefore become mere hypothesis, albeit controlled.

The physical aspects of such hypothesis can be checked by archaeological investigation. The existence of a thirteenth-century wall under a later property boundary is usually good evidence that the boundary is at least that old (though a later subdivision may make use of an internal division of a property). A road found running over or under properties obviously indicates major changes in land use. Care has to be taken to avoid circular arguments when comparing archaeological to historical evidence, but clearly the finding of medieval streets and buildings in archaeological investigations is as direct a line as we are going to get to the topography of the period.

With all this in mind, what can we say about medieval Bath as it developed between about 1100 and 1550?

The city walls

As was the case with nearly all medieval cities, Bath was defended, and in part defined, by its walls. Visitors arriving would know that they had reached their destination when the remarkably compact bulk of the walls presented the parcelled-up city to view. Despite the suburbs, it was not until the early eighteenth century that the town started to ignore its walls, and that was when they started to be dismantled.

Alfred's refoundation of the city provided the basic framework of streets and properties, but the walls remained the most restrictive constant of all pre-eighteenth-century planning. Thus although John of Tours' plan for the city involved new streets and property boundaries, the best he could do with the defences was to move a minor gate. Until after the Civil War of the seventeenth century, walls were essential for the security of the city and the kingdom. We have seen how King Stephen came to inspect the walls; we saw the prior reported in the thirteenth century for damaging the walls; twice in the fourteenth century the city was ordered by successive kings to put the defences in order.

The walled area of Bath is actually very limited: at 24 acres it is one of the smallest of all medieval circuits (**26**). It seems to have been based directly on the Roman circuit (although, strictly speaking, this has not been proved). Roman ditches are known on the later alignment on the north and east of the town, suggesting a Roman enclosure, while a length of metalled track with a drainage gully (not a moat) ran just outside the western wall at Seven Dials, suggesting a Roman enclosure on this alignment here too. Roman-*looking* wall has been noted along the south-eastern run, and near the south gate, but nowhere is the date strictly proven. Nonetheless, it seems most likely that the walls, 10ft (3.03m) wide at their base and over 20ft (6.06m) high, were the much-patched inheritance from Roman and Saxon times (**54 & 55**). Little can be seen above ground, but more survives than had until recently been

54 *The City wall during excavations in 1959 on the south-east corner of the walls in Orchard Street. The upper part has been rebuilt but the lower, neater elements are probably Roman. A fragment of the upper part of this wall can still be seen in the modern car park and loading bay on the corner of Orchard and Henry Streets*

55 *Upper Borough Walls. A view of the white-washed outer face of the city wall. It survived because the eighteenth-century Mineral Water Hospital's paupers' cemetery occupies the small patch of land in front which would otherwise have been developed. The parapet was remodelled in the later nineteenth century, but the evidence supports the restoration*

thought. The most easily seen is the much-restored length complete with its crenel-lations (which, though heavily restored, are not so false as often claimed) in Upper Borough Walls. The eighteenth-century burial ground against its outer edge has precluded development, and some idea of the difference between the inside and outside levels at the end of the medieval period can be seen here (**55**). This is what Leland saw in the 1530s: 'The toune waulle within the toune is of no great highth to theyes: but without it is *a fundamentis* of a reasonable highth.' A more dramatic illustration can be achieved by looking down into Parade Gardens from Terrace Walk. At balustrade level, more or less at wall-top height, the pavement is over 20 ft (6.06m) above the gardens: the medieval surface there was even lower than the present one. When John Wood came to build the Parades in the 1730s, just outside the walls and south of the gardens, he had to raise the new houses on tall, vaulted platforms to bring them to the internal level. The vaults now form the southern boundary to the 'sunken' gardens.

Another fragment of wall can be seen behind Marks and Spencer in Little Orchard Street (the name being a reminder of the Abbey Orchard). A large length of wall was destroyed here in 1959 when the store was constructed, but much was left in place under the floors of the new building (**54**). The most impressive sections of wall were only discovered in the mid-1990s, yet they stand almost to full height. One section was incorporated into an eighteenth-century house, the cellars of which were then built into the Empire Hotel in 1900 (which otherwise was destructive of a particularly impressive length of wall). This surviving fragment reached from the buried paving of Lot Lane to just below the modern pavement level, a length of over 20 ft (6.06m). It was revealed during conversion work in 1995. Curiously, the oldest photographs taken in Bath, dating from the 1840s, actually show this section of wall (**56**). A similar but longer section of wall survives, but cannot be easily visited, built into vaults under the covered markets. Even the crenellations seem to exist at the top of the walls, but more study is needed of these sections, which again were only discovered in 1995.

From the limited observations possible it does seem that the city walls are of two distinct designs. Along the north and east sections the wall appears to be vertical on both inner and outer faces (although at Terrace Walk, the inner face was stepped or rebated slightly every few courses). The south and west sections of wall seem to be built on a base that steps out on both inner and outer faces to a considerably greater width than the wall proper. This was associated in the excavations of 1951 with a late thirteenth/early fourteenth century date. An undated, but certainly post-Roman (and probably medieval) bank was seen piled up against the inside face of this wall during observations of a utilities trench at Seven Dials in 1991. It is known that a new gate, the Ham Gate, was built in this section of wall, east of the South Gate. Its construction is mentioned in the bishop's grant to the priory in 1279 of the Ham and Ambry, outside this part of the circuit. It is possible that the whole section was rebuilt at this time, when the Bishop had regained the city from the king (a section of wall seen in 1996 just west of the south gate seemed to be of the vertical fronted type, but this might be connected to the rebuilding of the south gate in 1363). This

56 *One of the earliest photographs of Bath, the Rev Lockey's c.1848 image of the wall by the east gate, looking along Lot Lane. Note how the windows of the eighteenth-century houses above slot into the crenellations*

might also be the context for the building of the wall shown in early seventeenth-century maps running from the city walls to the river, along the western boundary of the Ham (**51**). Little is known about this wall. It was crenellated, but this does not mean it was defensive – the cathedral close wall for instance was a similar structure. It is more likely to have been built to mark off the new limits of the priory after the grant of 1279. The outflow from the Hot Bath and the Cross Bath ran to the river along the outside of the wall, probably marking it out as an existing boundary before the wall was built, as implied by the grant of the land. What is clear is that the parish boundary of St James ran along this line, and this is still the boundary of its post-war successor, St Peter's.

The city gates were of tremendous importance to the town. As late as the eighteenth century important visitors were met at this point, continuing a tradition we have seen observed when Bishop Robert of Lewes received King Stephen at the gates. Conversely, to close the gates would be a symbolic act of defiance; and they formed a useful stopping-point for collecting tolls and dues. The only evidence for their appearance in this period are the tiny images seen in the Savile and Speed maps, which tell us little more than the eighteenth-century descriptions by John Wood. They seem to have had round arched openings, which were about 10 ft (3.03m) wide. The north gate had a small separate pedestrian arch. The narrowness of these was not really a problem until the eighteenth century, but their existence clearly constrained all traffic routes and street layout. They were closed at dusk, and at night a sort of bypass, Barton Lane, passing along the narrow strip between wall and ditch from the north gate to the west gate, joined the London to the Bristol Roads (**26**).

57 *The East Gate. A watercolour of the same stretch of wall as* **56** *at about the same time as Lockey's picture. The buildings in the foreground have been conveniently 'removed'*

This became redundant in the mid-eighteenth century, when the gates were demolished, and was built on, although its position can still be seen in the narrow plots of the Georgian houses along the north wall, built exactly over its line. Like the streets in the northern part of the town, Barton Lane seems to have been laid out under Alfred. A metalled track in this position, and assigned to the Saxon period, was found during excavations further to the east in 1980 (**12**). A much later surface was uncovered under Broadley's Vaults Public House in 1987, near the northwest corner of the walls and probably dating to the late 1600s.

One naturally wonders whether the gates might have been the Roman originals;,but this is unlikely, chiefly because Roman ground surface was so far below the seventeenth-century street level that the arch would have been too low to use. The most likely date for the gates in use in this period would be Alfredian. At only about 6ft 6in wide (2m), the East Gate was even narrower than the others, and very much a subsidiary opening in the walls. Its medieval name was Lot Gate, derived from *ludgeat*, Old English for postern. We have seen that it was probably moved to its present position by John of Tours, but if so it was rebuilt in the thirteenth or fourteenth centuries (**57**). Unlike the other gates, which gave on to main routes away from town, and in two cases important suburbs, the east gate simply gave access to the Monks Mill and the ferry to Bathwick. This subsidiary status is why it alone of the city gates survives to the present day, and why it is little more than a hole in the wall.

The South Gate was rebuilt in 1363, and had a statue of Edward III over the arch. The West Gate was also rebuilt, possibly in 1572, but the main gates all seem to have had single, low towers over them, which, in later years, were certainly occupied. Part of the North Gate served as a gaol in the post-medieval period. The West Gate, as rebuilt, faired somewhat better, housing several distinguished visitors, including monarchs, in the sixteenth and seventeenth centuries. There were no other towers in the circuit of walls, despite their appearance in an eccentric view of Bath dated to 1568, but two towers are referred to in the post medieval period. Gascoine's tower was the north-west corner of the circuit built a little higher by William Gascoigne 'as for a fine for a faught that he had committid in the cite' in living memory of the 1530s. The north-east tower was called Counter's Tower. We know little of it, but post-medieval property boundaries strongly suggest a complication in the walls here which might be explicable as some sort of low tower-like outwork. This might make sense as overlooking an approach from the river.

The other gates through the wall were simply access points from the priory to the new ground given them in 1279. The Ham Gate was 50 yards east of the south gate and was made to allow the monks to drive their sheep to pasture (implying that they were kept in pens within the priory in the winter or overnight). A lane was made from the priory gate at the end of Abbeygate Street to provide access (**26**). Another smaller gate was built, a few yards west again, to give access from the Shury (Shoe-ry) stables to a small enclosure outside and against the walls. This could indicate the use of this part of the priory close, with stables and farriers' shops on the south side of the great court. The gate was excavated in 1951, but misinterpreted as the Ham Gate. It was built over a ditch, probably part of the priory drainage system, which was later replaced by a stone culvert, built into the wall; and it certainly carried spa water away, perhaps to the fishponds (as speculated in the previous chapter).

The walls were supplemented by a ditch or moat. Walls were bad enough to maintain, but ditches not only slip and erode, they are wonderfully convenient rubbish bins, and consequently in times of peace they soon silted up. It seems that the northern run was filled in by the fourteenth century, at least by the north gate, as houses were built over it by that time. To the east, the ditch was certainly filled up by the fourteenth or fifteenth century, if not earlier: medieval house floors have recently been found overlying it. On the side toward the river, a short length had been re-dug, perhaps in late Saxon times, but was filling in by the early to mid-twelfth century, while in the late fourteenth century the city was commanded by Edward III and then Richard II to clear trees and debris from the ditch. Despite this, Bath was still seen as a place of refuge and safety. In an early thirteenth-century lease, Walter Hussey granted away property with the proviso that he should receive lodging in the house 'in time of war'. No doubt the recent horrors of the Barons' Wars against King John were fresh in the memory.

The defences had done more than keep enemies out and the citizens in. The ground level in Saxon times had risen over three feet (1m) above the area outside (in addition to the Roman levels), and it was to rise another 3ft 3in to 6ft 6in (1-2m) by the end of the period, in places even more. The walls were like a dam, keeping the accumulations of urban living in one place.

Inside the walls – and out

Into this restricted area were crammed the schemes of John of Tours; the expanded abbey (now the cathedral priory), the new bishop's palace, and three new streets all had to be fitted inside the walls (**26**). It is an obvious hypothesis that this resulted in a displacement of population, which resulted in the creation of the suburbs. We have no knowledge of suburbs before *c*.1100, and the Domesday account makes no mention of suburbs (although such distinctions were not relevant to its intentions). There is not yet any archaeological evidence for Saxon suburbs, and although some occupation along the main roads out of town might yet be found, the suggestion that the suburbs were really established after the arrival of the see in 1092 is attractive. In chapter 5 we suggested that in that year a further 12 per cent or so (nearly three acres) of the walled area had been taken for the new cathedral priory, and on this hypothesis, the displaced burgesses would have set up shop on new premises outside. The city limits, or the Hundred of Bath, incorporated the northern suburbs (the parish of St Michael Without) and the southern suburbs as far as the river (in the form of St James') (**42**). It is quite possible that these parishes grew out of the needs of the new communities. St Michael's is first mentioned in the early thirteenth century.

Archaeological evidence suggests that properties several hundred yards north of the north gate, along Walcot Street, were occupied by the twelfth century, but we do not know what form this occupation took, or whether it was part of a continuous strip of development. Pottery of the period was found in the demolition layers of Roman buildings, which at least suggests clearance at this time. In the thirteenth century, deeds show that properties were occupied along Slippery Lane (Alford's Lane in medieval references: this ran against the outside of the city walls from the north gate to the riverside where there was a ferry to Bathwick), as well as more generally outside the north gate. As early as 1206 a smithy is mentioned just outside the north gate, apparently run by the prior's smith; and this appears regularly in deeds until the end of the medieval period. A small property survived on this site until the mid–eighteenth century, and is now amalgamated with 14 Northgate Street. Frogge Lane appears in the fourteenth century as a short street running west from Broad Street, just outside the North Gate. Properties are described as running 'from the lane to the borough walls', which shows that the city ditch here had already been filled in. Barton Lane must have been diverted via Frogge Lane, which took its name from Froggmere, apparently referring to the silted-up and boggy terminal of the city ditch west of the north gate, which the lane seems to have skirted to its south. Investigations here in 1980 indeed found a broad and thick deposit of silt that had formed under just such conditions.

While the 'suburb of Bath' is mentioned in documents from the thirteenth century, only one or two properties in medieval deeds which are clearly urban (and not paddocks and tofts) can be shown to be more than a few tens of yards north of the city walls. This is not to say that the suburb was not substantial, it is just that surviving deeds and references to tenements are clustered near the city gate. Broad Street is mentioned often, and was probably the centre of clothworking in the town: one etymology for the name is that it contained the looms for weaving broadcloth. However, in 1377and 1381 there is only one weaver in *Brade* Street, suggesting the street name is in fact descriptive: it was broad in comparison with both the streets inside the city and also in relation to Walcot Street, the other main arm of the suburb, which was only 18ft wide before being widened in the eighteenth century. In the fourteenth century Walcot Street had shops along the frontages, and a large proportion of the artificers of the Poll Tax returns lived there. The lower part of the street must have been quite heavily built up.

Outside the west gate, the road led to Keynsham and Bristol, but nothing earlier than the later eleventh century has been found there. What was found is rather interesting. The city ditch had been allowed to silt up, and roughly rectangular pits had been dug across it and to either side. The pits were waterlogged and had remnants of wattle panelling in them – probably a lining, as they were dug through soft material. Some also had thick layers of what appeared to be sawdust (**47**), and were probably saw pits. As the site was adjacent to Saw Close, it is possible that the traditional function of this area went back as far as *c*.1100. There is no clear sign of occupation otherwise, and it seems that there was no western suburb.

On the south, Southgate Street or South Street led to the river crossing. Observations and excavations at the southern end suggest that before the thirteenth century the river bank was further north, and the road sloped down to a ford at or near the site of the later Old Bridge (**60**) When the river was first bridged is unknown, but a *Nigel pontarius* (bridgekeeper) was recorded as having owned land in Southgate Street before 1230. At about the same time we hear about the *fontem*, literally 'spring', but in fact the outlet of the piped water supply that was brought across the river from springs in Beechen Cliff via the bridge. In 1263, the prior *rebuilt* the cistern connected to this spring. We can be sure, therefore, that there was a bridge by the early thirteenth century. Given that the bridge carried the road to Wells, and that the Wells connection had become important again in the late twelfth and early thirteenth centuries, perhaps a date of around 1200 would not be far wrong. The gradual silting of the north side of the river during the thirteenth century was probably due to the bridge construction changing the river current pattern; again this suggests an early thirteenth century date. The bridge survived until 1755 when it was replaced with a Georgian version, itself demolished in 1966. The original was stone built, with five arches. It was quite wide, around 20-25ft (6-8m) and was around 100ft long (30m).

On the south side there seems to have been a causeway connecting to Holloway, the Wells Road. Money was left for its repair in a will. The best record of it was made by Bernard Lens in 1718 (**58**), but the other illustrations from Speed, Savile and Gilmore all concur (**50, 51 & 52**). The bridge was typical of its kind, with double rows of voussoirs, no obvious keystones and stone cutwaters. It rose to a high point over the central arch. Lens' view is ambiguous on whether the arches were pointed or rounded, but a date of around 1200 would certainly not be amiss for the style. On the town side of the central arch was a stone-built oratory to St Lawrence. This little building jutted out over the water from the parapet on the east side, and was supported on a stone-corbelled base resting on a semicircular cutwater. Above the southern-most pier two stone turrets or towers rose above the bridge, providing the sides of a defensive gate that could be used to close it off. The arrangements are

58 *The medieval bridge from the east as depicted by Bernard Lens in 1718. The gate was part of the city defences. The small overhanging building was the chapel of St Lawrence. The bridge, probably built in the late twelfth or early thirteenth century, was cleared away in 1754.* Victoria Art Gallery, Bath

unclear because of Lens' viewpoint; Gilmore, 24 years earlier, shows the gate consisting of merely a timber framework between the towers. The drawings of Savile and Speed from the first decade of the seventeenth century show, albeit rather crudely, a stone arch with a crenellated parapet above. This agrees well with Leland's description in 1534-40 of 'a great gate with a stone arch.' This must be the medieval arrangement, and immediately begs comparison with the well-preserved example at Monmouth, the Monnow Bridge. The arch was probably damaged during, or dismantled after, the Civil War, when Bath suffered a siege.

After the alterations related to the flood prevention scheme of 1966-8, no vestige of either this bridge or its Georgian successor remains to be seen. Its position can be worked out today by standing at the bottom of Southgate Street and looking towards the twin turrets, flanking a pointed arch in Bath stone, that embellish the railway viaduct. This was built by Brunel to close the vista across the bridge. The old bridge, medieval and Georgian, stood in the line of sight.

The probable layout of the walled city in the medieval period is shown in **26**. It is an average picture, and jumbles together features of various times between 1092 and 1539: not all of them would be there at all times. For example, parishes have been indicated, but they would probably not all have been fully organised until well into the thirteenth century. Until then, and even after, it is likely that the nave of the cathedral served the majority of the citizens inside the walls, with St James' taking all those south of the priory. St James, of course, was rebuilt on its new site in 1279 (**51 & 59**). In 1190, St Mary de Stalls, which became both the premier parish church in

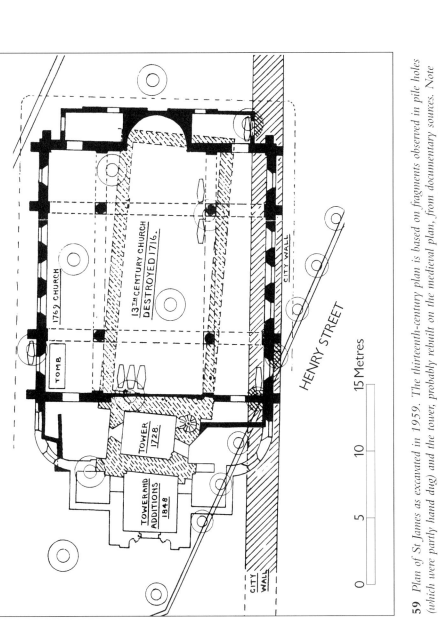

59 *Plan of St James as excavated in 1959. The thirteenth-century plan is based on fragments observed in pile holes (which were partly hand dug) and the tower, probably rebuilt on the medieval plan, from documentary sources. Note the burials within the church. There will be many more, for the site was not destroyed when the new building went up. The late Georgian church is shown in solid black. It was destroyed in the blitz of 1942. After Wedlake 1966*

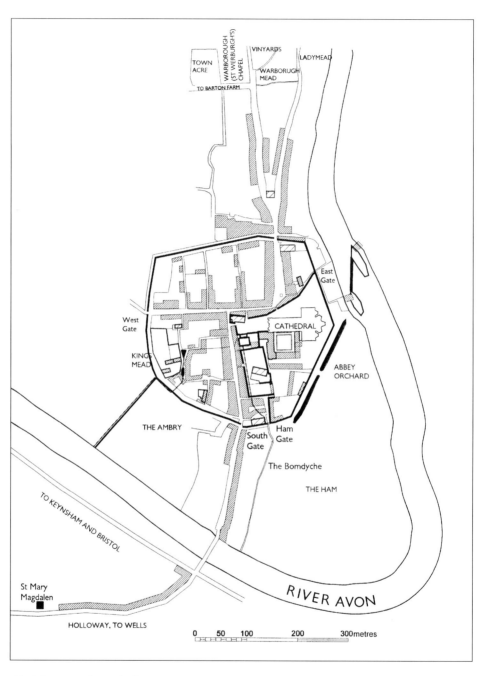

60 *The city and its suburbs; some attempt is made here to show the extent of built-up areas in the high Middle Ages*

later years, and the church of the Corporation, was still only the chapel in the (lay) graveyard of the cathedral. The first clear reference to the church of the Blessed Mary of Stalls is in 1249, by which time masses were already being said for the commonality. St Michael's Within may be the parochial chapel first mentioned in 1210, but is not clearly attested before 1285. Manco suggests convincingly that it originated as a private chapel, and was part of a bequest of property to the priory in the 1180s. St Mary's by the north gate or *intra muros* is first mentioned in 1190, when the bishop paid for repairs. It is a poorly documented church and is next mentioned, apart from passing references in deeds etc., when its Rector, despite being an appointee of the priory, sided with the citizens and the Rector of Stalls over the bells dispute in the early fifteenth century. St Michael's Without served the northern suburb (**60**). It is clear from these references that the parishes were being established in the years after 1200. The position of the Guildhall is shown, but may not have been built here until the fourteenth century. Stall Street had been laid out by Bishop John with properties along its eastern side backing on to the wall of the palace. Traces of the planning of the western side are possibly visible in later properties but are less tidy, because that side had to tie in with existing property boundaries.

Bravely (or foolishly), property boundaries have been indicated within the street pattern. The recreation of property holdings on the ground is an academic minefield, and what is presented here is both hugely optimistic and, in much detail, certainly wrong, based as it is on eighteenth-century pre-Improvement plans. On the other hand, many of the properties of this period can be shown to be the same as the medieval ones. However, the broad picture of holdings of various sizes, with its hints of division and amalgamation, is not too misleading. The map shows the huddle of small properties along Stall Street, deliberately laid out for commercial use. Properties along the older streets tend to be larger, but were often subdivided for rental (as we shall see below). This is not indicated on the map because of lack of detailed information, but a hint of the process is shown at 21 High Street (see below). While it is not possible in most cases, it is not uncommon to be able to trace back a property from a clear eighteenth-century lease to its position in the fourteenth or even thirteenth century. Occasionally the topographic descriptions in an old lease will tell us immediately where it was, with such references as 'outside the north gate', or 'the King's Bath [is to the] south'. The map shows property boundaries: actual buildings, a very few of which are shown, will have occupied a very variable proportion of a site. The earliest maps of the seventeenth century show large areas unbuilt, but significantly they show that the street frontages were fully built up, indeed crowded, and what evidence we have certainly suggests this will have been the case in earlier times. The only exceptions are the *Rampires,* as the ways inside the city walls were called in later years. These frontages remain open, and seem to have been regarded rather as the backs or sides of the property. Why this should be, when even the frontages of minor lanes were developed, is unclear. One clue is given by the older name of Lower Borough Walls, which was called Rekkestreet or Rack Street in fourteenth- and fifteenth-century deeds. This implies that these open areas, and perhaps the streets themselves, were used for the drying on racks of finished cloth that had been

61 *The High Street today, looking north. The triangular or trapezoidal shape of the market place can still be seen*

fulled (given its last wash or dye). Such racks are shown in Upper Borough Walls in Gilmore's map of 1694 (**52**).

What is clear is the tremendous commercial importance of the High Street/Cheap Street/Stall Street axis (**61**). Compared to other parts of the town, these street frontages are built up, and the number of tenements crowded on to them attests their great value; and this picture is supported by the leases of the thirteenth to sixteenth centuries (which, since most of what has survived has done so because the buildings involved became Corporation property, function as a sort of random sample). In the thirteenth century (and perhaps as early as 1218), references to [market] stalls, which are clearly fairly permanent affairs, are common. They clearly formed long rows all down the street, as references to two shops on either side of a third are common. References to shops rather than stalls becomes the norm in the fourteenth century. Shops were to be found in Southgate Street, inside and outside the gates and especially along the main axis mentioned above. Other streets were perhaps less packed.

A house on the site of the Grapes Inn in Westgate Street probably had its own chapel in the late twelfth century, the future St Michael's Within, granted to the priory by Master Eustace of Bath. Opposite this site was a tavern owned by John Wissy, which we earlier saw him giving to St Mary Magdalen. Along the lanes leading back from Westgate Street were a variety of small shops and workshops, whose purposes, with one exception, have not been recorded. The exception is a dovecote or pigeon house in Bridewell (Plum Tree) Lane which, for a while, gave that lane an alternative name: Culverhouse Lane. This reminds us that much of the open space behind the shops and houses would have been used for keeping animals. Pigs and fowl are the typical urban food animals, kept on a small scale by most families. Pigeons were an extra delicacy. In addition, horses and donkeys or mules would need to be stabled in the town, and most richer houses would have had stables, or at least access to them; so a lease of 1430 records a set located in Paynestwichene (Union Passage), in the hands of the euphoniously named Felicia Yewyll (**62**). Another large plot of land by the Cross Bath was leased to Nicolas Lavender in 1292, and contained a house and what must have been a substantial yard. Stables are mentioned nearby in 1446. St Michael's churchwardens' accounts detail maintenance work on stables in the 1460s and 70s.

The shops were the lifeblood of property investment, but they would occupy only part of a building, and sometimes there would be several on one tenement. In 1313, John Cole refers to his tenement with a hall, solar and cellar in the High Street, as having his *stalls* on it. A large plot in the south-east angle of the later White Hart Lane had a house fronting Stall Street, which would have had a shop. There was an oven, and a yard at the rear which also contained two further 'semi-detached' houses in the mid-thirteenth century. The mention of an oven, as on a number of other properties, reminds us that baking and roasting was done in a small number of communal ovens. The average medieval house had none. A 'common oven' is specifically mentioned in Sutor Street in 1363.

Shops and little shops are commonly described in thirteenth-century leases, and by the beginning of the next century are clearly permanent structures with living quarters, or usable rooms, above, and increasingly cellars below. Indeed, by 1341, a shop in Southgate Street is noted as *not* having a cellar. These shops were never large though: two typical measurements are 14ft x 11ft (4.27m x 3.5m) and 11ft x 16ft (3.35m x 4.88m), and properties could be as small as 12ft x 8ft (3.66m x 2.44m). The usage of property became more complex, with multiple occupancy more common. In 1351 John Champflour sold or leased off a tenement, but reserved for life his right to occupy 'the inner chamber next to the hall door of the tenement he has given up.' Even more complicated was the grant in 1348 by Joan de Salsomarisco which included, among other descriptions and stipulations, 'one inside cellar and the cellar adjacent' to Joan's tenement, 'saving to Joan the corner of the entrance to the under cellar of the outhouse.' The solars could also be revenue raising: in 1323 John Dunster the Tailor rented a solar over a shop in Corn Street (as the junction of Stall Street and Westgate Street was called then), probably as a well-lit workshop. That lighting was of importance is indicated by a lease dated four years later, with a clause forbidding the blocking-up of windows. To some extent this highlights what must have been a growing problem as the tenements became increasingly built up.

Open spaces persisted, however, even on the main streets. In 1377, Thomas Saundres granted a shop with a garden and another garden adjacent in Southgate Street, and in 1454 a plot in that street is described as empty, but previously having had a house on it. However it is more common, and in keeping with the later map evidence, to find references to open ground away from the main streets and along the

62 *Union Passage today, late medieval* Cox's Lane *or earlier* Paynestwichene. *Not many realise this popular shopping street goes back over 1100 years*

city walls. In 1430, a listing of a clutch of valuable properties in High Street and Paynestwichene (also called Cox or Cockes Lane in the later fifteenth century, now Union Passage) concludes with 'a garden against the borough walls, between the barn and another garden.' Along Westgate Street in the thirteenth century there were houses with gardens, a smithy, and, near the west gate, a garden in the hands of the almoner of the priory (still a garden in 1600). One of these gardens must have been the site of the plum tree or orchard that by the thirteenth century had given its name to Plumtreostwichene, or Plum Tree Lane, now Bridewell Lane. The land of St John's will also have lent a more open aspect to this side of town.

It seems clear from one or two descriptions that living quarters were at the rear of and over the property, and were reached by entrance ways along the side or between the stalls and, later, shops. In 1388, an inner cellar and solar were to be incorporated to enlarge a shop in the High Street. The property is described as being between the shops on the frontage, the rest of the hall behind, and north of the entrance passage that ran along the side of the holding. In other words, the property had already been intensively developed and the only way to make the shop bigger was to extend backwards into the living quarters. Another fourteenth-century deed refers to land in High Street as having four shops with solars above, on either side of the door leading to the hall. Again, the house was at the rear of the shops (and the occupant of the house was not necessarily either the owner or the shop keeper). Open space was probably more common in the less important streets: excavations have showed gardens north of the tenements lining Westgate Street and behind Bridewell Lane which lasted throughout the Middle Ages. The gardens were func-tional spaces however, as opposed to solely pleasure grounds. They would be used for growing herbs and vegetables (as much for medicine as food), as well as other useful plants such as teazel, for keeping smaller domestic animals and as outdoor working spaces. An example of this is the *herbarium* granted to St John's by Vincent son of Hugh Galopin in 1260. This was 'next the Bath', probably meaning the Hot Bath. Archaeologically-recovered remains confirm this picture of severe practicality. Seeds recovered from excavations suggest that weeds and grasses of disturbed ground contended for space with wild garlic, *brassicas*, mustard, cole and fennel. Herbs and flavourings such as summer savoury and water parsnip were also grown, along with marjoram, dill and doubtless others.

The gardens and backyards also served another purpose, especially during the period around 1100-1300. The most common medieval 'finds' encountered in archaeological excavations are roughly cylindrical pits, dug in their dozens behind the buildings. They seem to have been used as sunken rubbish bins, and to some extent cesspits for the disposal of night soil. The latter are relatively rare, but their contents indicate that fruit, in season, was eaten by contemporary Bathonians. This is not surprising, but does tell us that their diet included blackberry, strawberry and sloe, pears and apples. The latter, of course, might also have been the remains of perry and cider making.

Both suburbs presented a similar picture to that inside the walls, although the lower end of Broad Street and Walcot Street were more heavily occupied in the Poll

Tax lists of 1379 and 1381, and more impressively built up by 1600, than Southgate Street. The poll tax records confirm the picture of wealth along these streets, and of relative poverty behind, but these divisions were not clear cut. Along Southgate Street, not noted overall for its wealth, were two high tax payers; and earlier the rich dyer Alexander had lived here. Excavations into medieval layers have been very limited in Bath, but as far as they go, they confirm this picture of built-up frontages coupled with more open land in the rear of the properties.

Most houses would have been of timber. In the fourteenth and fifteenth centuries clauses in deeds require the rebuilding of cottages in timber, and references to houses in stone are clearly put in because they are exceptional: in 1395 there is a 'tiled house called stonehous' in Broad Street, and in 1300 Sir Richard Junior inherited a 'house of stone'. Timber would have been used even in the priory. In 1984 the basement of Sally Lunn's Tea Shop was investigated, and remains of a dwarf wall for a timber superstructure and an associated stone floor were uncovered. This was a priory building, perhaps part of the refectory, or more likely one of the service buildings along the north side of the great court. In any event it had been built in the twelfth century, and remained in use until the end of the thirteenth. A few more stone buildings were being erected in the town, and are known from archaeology. The basement of Abbey Church House contains a cellar which is an undercroft of a building that, although undated, was extended in about 1400. This is probably part of a substantial house (whose upper parts could nonetheless have been of timber). In later times it was owned by St John's Hospital, but it may not have been from the first. Fragments of another stone cellar, this time dating to the mid–fifteenth century, were found by chance during limited excavations in 1996 on the corner of Westgate Street and Union Street, in the very heart of the medieval town. A 'depe celeer' is mentioned in a deed of 1303 on or adjacent to this site, and the fragments excavated may have been an addition or extension to this if it is the same holding. It must have been deep to survive the massive cellarage of the Victorian building that now stands on the site. Only the very base of the rear of the cellar walls and the north east corner survived, but packed into the foundations were two sherds of pottery: one was an import from western France, the other a local copy. Both sherds were rare evidence of trade through Bristol, and the house may well have been the shop or workshop of a wealthy merchant in that trade. Since we know where the street frontage was in around 1450, we can say that the house extended 25ft (7.5m) back from the road. It would have been about 21ft (6.3m) wide.

Only one other medieval house is known in Bath, but it has added enormously to our knowledge of such structures in the town. It was only discovered in 2000, during building refurbishment at 21 High Street. The timber-framed side wall of the whole first floor and roof gable of this building survived in the party wall of number 21, a superficially Georgian building (**63**). The gable of the other side of the building was also discovered, incorporated in the other side wall. Such survivals quite frequently turn up in what appear to be much later buildings, but they have been rarer in Bath and this is the first such structure in the city which is almost certainly medieval. The building has a stout oak panel frame with plastered wattle and daub

63 *The timber frame of 21 High Street as it first appeared behind later panelling.* Based on the original drawing by ASI Heritage

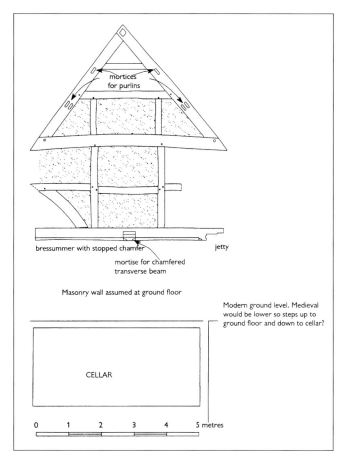

mortices for purlins

bressummer with stopped chamfer

jetty

mortise for chamfered transverse beam

Masonry wall assumed at ground floor

Modern ground level. Medieval would be lower so steps up to ground floor and down to cellar?

CELLAR

0   1   2   3   4   5 metres

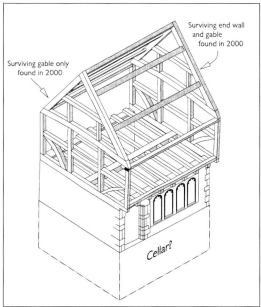

Surviving end wall and gable found in 2000

Surviving gable only found in 2000

Cellar?

64 *A reconstruction of the structure of the house, based on the timbers and the joint holes. The building is just over 5m² in plan, but would have continued to the rear*

65 *The east side of Stall Street just before street widening in 1806. The fourth house up from the Abbeygate Street corner is late medieval or sixteenth- century.* Bath and North East Somerset Council Archives

infill. Curved braces kept it rigid. The first floor was jettied over the street and three beams connected the two sides of the house, and supported each floor. The first floor bressummer or wall beam was decorated with a stopped chamfer, showing that it was meant to be seen from the inside. The roof had a slightly raised tie beam, and was of queen post and collar design. The principal rafters of both gables have been recycled from an older building, shown by extra and unnecessary mortise holes. This timber structure rested on a (now vanished) masonry ground floor. We know this from the complete absence of joint mortises on the underside of the lowest beam, showing there was no timber structure below.

It is possible to reconstruct the front block of this building, and the first thing that is striking is how small it is (**26 & 64**). The rear range has been removed completely, but even so, the building is only two storeys high. In plan it is 16ft 6in wide by 16ft 9in deep (5.03m x 5.11m), probably intended to be square. We might remember that it is on a prime site on the High Street, the commercial heart of the town. Property values might be expected to have indicated a building making more use of the expensive space, i.e. going up higher; certainly in the early seventeenth century, all houses on the main streets in town are shown, perhaps conventionally, as having three full storeys. Such a house was recorded in Stall Street just before its demolition in 1806 (**65**). It is probably late medieval or Elizabethan, and is three storeys plus a loft. Number 21 might have had a front gable, providing a cock loft or garret, but many houses in the less well-developed streets are shown, on the Savile map, for example, with their roofs parallel to the street. This less 'urban' style may have been much more the norm in earlier times.

The house was described above as 'almost certainly medieval' and the style of construction certainly suggests a date of around 1400–1600, while the size certainly suggests a bias towards the early part of this range. There is some documentary evidence which may fit in with this view. The property was a large freehold held in 1354 by Sir William Hussey. In 1446 it was in the hands of a big landowner in the region, William Blount; and in that year it was leased to John Fayrechild for four shillings a year for the first five years, then rising to eight shillings. Such a relief was commonly given in recognition of expenditure on the property by the lessee, such as rebuilding a house. It is almost impossible to resist the temptation to connect this evidence with the house.

The house may have been part of a set of three or four rebuilt together. It certainly occupies only a part of the frontage of the medieval tenement here. In the seventeenth century, as today, it was part of a building continuing out to the south by two more bays. Timberwork extending over the covered alleyway leading to Northumberland Passage suggests it bridged this to continue southwards.

To recap, what does this house tell us about late medieval houses in Bath? If it is typical, then some were built of stout oak timber framing over a ground floor of stone. Upper floor and internal walls were wattle and daub, and the floors were elm or oak boarded. Doors of oak would be fitted with iron hinges and locks, oak window frames with strong hinged shutters; possibly at this date, some contained glass. The basic design is small, very reminiscent of some of the sizes mentioned in ancient deeds. The plan, as far as we can reconstruct it, fits well with the pattern that we have seen in the leases and deeds: a shop with a solar above and some building behind. The present cellar is eighteenth-century, but could be medieval in origin. The roof was just a plain double pitch, of either tile or thatch (more probably the former), but could have contained a garret. The now vanished rear could have been the hall, or main living quarters, but could alternatively have been workshops, for instance for weavers or spinners, or other journeyman craftsmen; or a warehouse, or indeed all these things.

The process of transformation that this building underwent is informative. In this instance the building first had an extra timber storey added, probably in the seventeenth century. Then a new façade was added in the eighteenth, this time in stone. In the nineteenth century the floor levels were changed and party walls were knocked away to open up the ground and first floors for commerce. Thus the original roof, the floors and the ground floor walls on the north and the ground and first floors on the south of the building were removed. Further alterations to the roof and the insertion of chimney stacks and staircases brought more destruction, but the timber frame remained hidden and forgotten behind plaster and panelling until refurbishment in recent times. It is to be hoped and expected that more such fragments will emerge as observation during refurbishment becomes the norm.

Documentary evidence also makes it clear that timber building was the norm in medieval Bath, and remained common into the seventeenth century. St Michael's accounts from the late fifteenth century predominantly mention wood, laths, wattle, daub, planks and beams, wood and lead gutters 'for that work in studding and boarding and plastering:16^d'; 'and the said Godfrey [the carpenter] to repair the stair and party wall in Thomas Bryddes tenement and the floor in William Woodhall's'. There is also reference to Godfrey the Carpenter and his associate 'squaring, sawing, framing and setting up the work'. Much iron work was used. Hinges (hooks and twists), latches, locks (gemmolls) and straps, all figure in these accounts, as do endless nails. It is also clear that the buildings, even cottages, had proper board and lead guttering, louvres if not chimneys (both are mentioned), and windows and shutters (although glass was not yet common).

Streetscape

Between the tenements, linking the shops, workshops, houses, gardens and almshouses, churches and baths, ran the streets of the town. These were carefully planned and to some extent maintained. Mud and dust would have been the predominant impression of the road surfaces, but substantial effort was put into maintenance. There was no system, but both the prior and the corporation would sporadically have taken on the responsibility, and in later times the parish was responsible. St Michael's churchwardens recorded the spending of money on repaving Walcot Street on several occasions in the 1460s and 70s. Otherwise it was still very much up to individual public-spiritedness. Money was left to repair roads and causeways, but gradually a system evolved whereby the property owners were responsible to the parish for the street outside their property. In the absence of strong enforcement, this was a recipe for bad roads and filthy footways.

Physical remains are scarce, but excavation has given us some idea of the quality of at least some of the streets. Alfred's streets were laid out on a foundation of medium-sized stones, as seen in the fragment north of Bath Street. The surface of this one had gone, but was almost certainly of smaller stones packed down on the foundation. This section of it was not long-lived, but the street laid out by John of Tours between the King's Bath and the Cross Bath lasted from around 1100-1790, and the surfaces for the first one or two hundred years survived to be studied in the excavation of the area in 1986, with later layers seen in section but not excavated. The first layer consisted of well-compacted cobbles of limestone, neatly laid (**25**). The sharp edges to the metalling adjoining only dark silts suggest timber buildings alongside the street. However, the variation in width of the later surfacings, some of them consisting of very well-laid cobbles, perhaps better implies a wider street with only a central band given a hard surface. These later resurfacings included a large proportion of iron slags, a waste material which was produced in large quantities by the town's ironworkers, and used increasingly as the twelfth and thirteenth centuries wore on. Some phases of repair were almost exclusively of this material. At its thickest the combined resurfacings amounted to over three feet (1m) thick. They probably represent maintenance from around 1100 until the end of the thirteenth century or later. The earlier levels contained thin spreads of greenish fine silt. This was almost certainly nightsoil and other organic material thrown out on to the streets: a lot of it could have been pig dung. The later levels had much greater thicknesses of this material interleaved with new layers of stone and slag. This suggests either a breakdown in communal urban discipline, or an increase in population and a lack of adequate facilities for disposal of waste (the Corporation did not get around to appointing a refuse collector until 1614!). This picture, however interpreted, is supported by the discovery of rubbish pits dug into the road in the thirteenth century and later. These were filled in quickly, but do not bespeak a strong community feeling – in fact, the pits may have been dug in the first place to steal stone.

The only other road surfaces that have been seen from our period were noted at the southern end of Southgate in the 1950s. Cobbles were seen under a thick layer of black soil with medieval pottery in it, at a considerable depth: over three metres. These are likely to have been buried by the silting mentioned above in relation to the building of the bridge, and probably represent the road leading down to the ford that predated the bridge (and probably continued in use for some time after its construction – Mule Street on the south bank is described as leading to the Avon in the fourteenth century).

Water on tap

Early evidence for the bridge included the mention of the water conduit that passed over it. Several springs rise in the steep hill south of the river, Beechen Cliff, including one on the site of St Mary Magdalen. These were collected and piped across the river and up Southgate Street to a public fountain by the south gate. These fountains came to be called 'conduits' in Bath, and the fountain was eventually named for the church of St James. The water was carried into the priory, and must have fed numerous parts of the complex. We know little about the system, but it seems to have consisted largely of lead pipes and ducts, at least within the town itself. It struck John Leland visiting in around 1534:

> The Cite of Bath . . . is environid on every side with greate Hilles out of whiche cum many Springes of pure Water that be conveyid by dyverse ways to serve the Cite. Insomuch that Leade beyng made ther at hand [on the Mendips] many Houses in the Toune have Pipes of Leade to convey Water from Place to Place.

The system survived into the early nineteenth century as 'The Duke of Kingstons waterworks' (after a later landowner). Maps of the system show lead pipes serving most of the area of the old priory, and a large reservoir just inside the abbey Gate. In detail, this is all post-medieval, but probably indicates the extent and basic layout of the medieval system, which was extensive enough to catch the attention of Leland. Water was also drawn in conduits and lead pipes from the hills north of the town. As well as repairing the St James Conduit, Prior Walter de Anno arranged with the corporation to set up St Peter's Conduit in the High Street just north of the abbey, and this again was used to further feed the monks' needs. The citizens also got their water from these public supplies, but only the richer houses would have a supply. Even in the seventeenth century the domestic supply was available for only a few hours a day through a very small bore pipe, such as a goose quill, to those lucky enough to have such a service. By the end of the Middle Ages there were also 'conduits' outside the north gate and by St Mary de Stalls church. Such systems are known to have existed in several towns, usually those with a monastic presence. The best known is Canterbury, where a thirteenth-century plan of the monastic waterworks survives.

Water supply also requires water disposal, and substantial drains had always been necessary to take off the hot water from the springs (**26**). The King's Bath drained under the bishop's palace, through St James' churchyard and thence through the wall in at least two places: under the Ham Gate and further east, where a late thirteenth- or fourteenth-century conduit was excavated in 1951. Some tenements in Southgate seem to have had hot water from this outfall, and it probably turned the wheel of Isabel Mill by the Ham Gate, as noted by Leland: 'The water that goith from the Kinges Bath turnith a mylle, and after goith into Avon above Bath-bridge.' The mill probably dates from 1135, and is referred to in the later thirteenth century. From the mill, the bulk of it ran into 'Bomdyche', a foul open sewer that led along the back of the tenements along the east side of Southgate Street. Gilmore's map of 1694 shows it lined with privies: it had earned its name of Bum Ditch. We have already noticed the similar ditch which took the overflow from the Hot and Cross Baths and formed the boundary both of the monks' land and the parish of St James.

Citizens made their own arrangements to drain off excess water as needed. In 1433, the mayor gave permission for a drain to be made running from a property inside the walls by the south gate to the Bum Ditch, which seems to have involved punching holes in the city wall. But water usage was very low by our standards, and in fact, not enough was generally used to create an adequate flow for a drainage system in our sense to work at all: with one big exception. The monks and the bishop needed flowing water for the *rere dorter* (monks' lavatories) and the *lavatorium* (the washing place in the cloister), as well as for the generally cleaning of clothes and people, cooking, and watering the animals. It would on the whole not be drunk, but instead be made into beer: we know the priory had a brewhouse, and ale tended to be safer than medieval water. The disposal of all this water seems to have been concentrated into a large covered drain running under present day York Street. The outflow through the walls can be seen in the Savile map (**51**), emptying into an open leat outside the walls and then running off to the river by Monks' Mill. This route, rebuilt and re-engineered, was used by the Victorian excavators of the Roman baths to take off the hot water. It still performs this function today.

Our walled city, then, would be a compact and busy place, by the early fourteenth century intensively developed along its main streets and the northern suburbs. Southgate Street and perhaps Holloway across the river also appear to have been busy, but with more open spaces. Away from the main streets, the buildings are smaller and slightly more dispersed. Three-storey structures were probably rare, most were of timber but probably over stone ground floors and cellars in many cases. Between the houses would be muddy or dusty streets, mostly paved, but not kept in the best of condition. They were seen as much as a handy overflow space for private and commercial activities as for transport, a confusion compounded by the regular markets and fairs held on them. There was a flow of piped water, and public water fountains and the baths were there for the use of the citizens. The parish churches (none of which were very big) and the city gates would tower over the secular buildings that pressed up to them, but all were dominated by the buildings of the cathedral priory and its close. By the end of the fifteenth century the monks, the prior and the bishop had been the most powerful presence in the city for 300 years. The monks had been there for at least another 300 before that. Nobody saw any reason to think it would not always be so.

Further reading

There is little that addresses this subject in detail outside of the primary sources, and archaeological reports referenced at the end of the previous chapter. See Manco 1998 for studies on the hospitals.

66 *Priory Seal showing the cathedral with a spire. SS Peter and Paul are shown carrying their church, which could be merely a conventional rendering, but may represent the actual building. This seal is from the abbot's act of acknowledgement of Henry VIII's supremacy, 1534.* Public Record Office

8 The Later Middle Ages in Bath

The cathedral and its priory, that had been founded by John of Tours and brought to completion by Robert of Lewes, reached their physical and institutional apogee at the end of the twelfth century. After the Glastonbury interlude under Savaric Wells made its claims to the see increasingly felt, and as we have seen, the Pope finally decreed that Wells and Bath were to share the honours of the see, as it were, in 1245. The canons at Wells did not just want parity, however: they keenly felt that Wells, having been the seat of the diocese since 909, should have the precedence and status due to the senior member of the pair. Although never officially granted, this was achieved by degrees, and by 1174 the new church at Wells, clearly intended as a cathedral, was under way. In its startling modernity and originality, it put the old-fashioned church at Bath in the shade. Around 1220, Bishop Joscelin Trotman was building a hall at Wells, the beginning of the bishop's palace there, and the astonishing west front of the church started to take shape under him. His death at Wells in 1242, and burial there against the agreed procedure, led to the final accommodation between the two houses. But clearly he intended to spend much time there, and apparently did so, rather than at Bath; like King Charles II, he had perhaps, after a lengthy exile, no desire to go on his travels again. The Palace at Bath, in the middle of a busy and noisy town, hard up against the church of St James with its parishioners passing under the bishop's window every Sunday at least, must have seemed both a far less attractive option and, by the early thirteenth century, also a very old-fashioned and uncomfortable building. Yet Bath was far from abandoned at this stage, and some work was carried out on the church. Bishop Button I built a Lady Chapel in 1260. This was almost certainly an enlargement of the central eastern apse of the Romanesque cathedral, and a common development in most churches of this plan;,but it might just have been the reordering of another, smaller chapel inside the church. Slight evidence for the former option is the recovery of fragments of stained glass of this date from excavations at the east end in 1979. There is also a suggestion that a spire may have been added to the Norman tower. A seal of about 1300 shows the church held aloft by St Peter and St Paul, with its central tower crowned with such a spire (**66**). There is no other evidence for this, but if it was built, it might well have been of wood and lead as much as masonry.

There is also archaeological and historic evidence for improvements and alterations to the bishop's palace at Bath, albeit in parallel with campaigns at its counterpart in Wells. Bishop John's hall (**32**) was largely demolished, with one end and a later twelfth-century extension retained as the core of a new building. The lower parts of this survived to be excavated in 1984-5. Thin walls with deep buttresses and windows framed with slim purbeck marble shafts show that one of the mid- to late thirteenth-century bishops was rebuilding the palace in up-to-date style. The most likely candidate would be Bishop Robert Burnell (1274-92) who, in 1279, provided a new site for the church of St James and took over its nave as a private chapel, demolishing the chancel. The church, henceforth episcopal chapel, was described as adjacent to the bishop's chamber; and it seems reasonable that the rebuilding of the palace was linked to this re-organisation of the bishop's close. This does not neces-sarily mean that the bishop was intending to spend much time in Bath. Burnell was a builder. He also erected a magnificent three-storey hall on his estates in Shropshire, at Acton Burnell, as well as a new hall at Wells, second only to the princely hall of the Bishops of Durham in size. As Chancellor of England and friend and courtier to Edward I, he spent very little time in his diocese, let alone Bath.

The relative withdrawal of the bishops has been noted above as providing an opportunity for the townsmen to start to acquire a little more control over their affairs. The same applied to the priors. In 1261 William Button I gave the monks permission to elect the prior themselves. The first to be so elected was Walter de Anno, an active administrator who, we have seen, secured the water supply to the town in association with the Guild.

This independence may have gone to their heads. During the Civil War of 1264-6, the monks and prior had supported Simon de Montfort and the barons against Henry III. Finding themselves on the losing side, they were excommunicated for their pains and had to seek absolution from the bishop as a result. However, de Montfort's rebellion did result in the regular calling of parliament, and in 1295 Prior Robert actually sat as the priory's representative in the Model Parliament. Subsequent parliaments were attended sporadically at first, but after 1321, Bath, both city and priory, always sent a representative. Other aspects of Bath's rôle in national affairs were more onerous. Three times between 1311-24 the town had to supply soldiers, equipment and money as part of its feudal dues (and sometimes beyond them) to the Crown, a duty that continued throughout the rest of the century.

The prior's post had always carried with it the responsibility of running the monastery. This was really more like managing a business, and it is not surprising that the incumbent often seems more akin to a capitalist than a cleric. With the bishop away much, if not most of the time, the prior became an increasingly important – and sometimes self-important – figure. This culminated in Richard de Clopcote's self-regarding request to the Pope, John XXII, for the right to bear pontifical insignia, i.e. to put a mitre on his arms and have it carried before him in ceremonies. This was politely refused (though actually finally granted to the priors in 1456). Clopcote's vanity was not matched by his ability, however. Attempts to make the Irish possessions profitable included a visit to Ireland in 1306, but were ultimately unsuccessful. The dependencies were effectively given up on financially in the year of Clopcote's death. Hugh de Dover had been sent in an attempt to make them economically viable, but was recalled for unspecified incompetence.

In 1311, Bishop John of Drokensford set up a commission of enquiry to stop reckless extravagance. The monks were fierce in defending their right not to be inspected (even though the bishop was their titular abbot), and were once again, as a body, excommunicated for their defiance. The fuss blew over, but ten years later the bishop wrote again saying that 'he had heard of the scandalous waste of the revenues and the stinting of the monks' diet'. It seems the monks were denied physical as well as spiritual nourishment by their support for the prior. The bishop rather tamely urged more care on the prior, but later in 1321 another enquiry was set up, and this time some compromise seems to have been made. At least, in 1323, the sub-prior wrote to the bishop to report that the new arrangements for the kitchen were working well. Clopcote upset more than the bishop and his monks' digestions. He ran foul of the king's justice and was fined, before dying in 1332. In his will he left his goods, perhaps with some trepidation, for the good of his soul. He had at any rate outlasted his bishop, who was in fact little better than he ought to have been over finances himself. His relatives had good reason to be pleased at his career success.

Clopcote was succeeded by Robert Sutton. His election was deemed irregular, however, and after papal intervention, he was forced to resign in favour of Thomas Crist. Resignation was not so bad; Sutton received what these days would be called a 'golden parachute'. He was made prior of the dependent house of Dunster, pleasantly situated on the Somerset coast. He was also given a pension of £20 a year and to have with him 'such friends as he desired', and was to be allowed to retire to the chamber he had built in Bath at such time as he became infirm. This he did in 1337. This was no monk's cell; in 1339, after Sutton's death, it is described as accommodating Sir Walter de Rodeneye, his esquire, chamberlain, three grooms and the horses. It may well have been the detached house in its own garden built against the city wall east of the Great Court, and visible in early seventeenth-century maps (**26 & 51**). Crist was involved in the wool and cloth trade, on behalf of the priory, and was a local man with relatives in the business. He was probably trying to repay debts, but was still incurring new ones. His retirement was also pleasantly provided for. His pension was a life interest in the manor and church of South Stoke, just south of Bath, with 'a chaplain, a squire and a groom, sufficient food for all of them and wood for the fire.'

Crist was succeeded in 1341 by John de Iford, who can charitably be described as a colourful character. Despite presiding over a steady increase in the debts of the monastery, Iford provided for friends and relatives out of priory money. Requests for free corrodies, (accommodation in the monastery which were otherwise used to create income), even Royal ones, were met on several occasions with pleas of absolute poverty: 'Sire, we cannot, the substance of our house is wasted'. Iford wasted his substance in other directions. In 1346 he was found to have installed a mistress, Agnes Cubbel, in the Manor of Hameswell in Gloucestershire, some miles north. He was informed on by the Bishop of Worcester who wrote direct to Bishop Ralph, but little seems to have been done about it. One wonders what the mayor's reaction would have been – Agnes was a relative, possibly a daughter. A few years later, Iford gave sanctuary to a Bristol merchant, Robert Gyene, who had been outlawed. This was no philanthropic gesture. The priory owed Gyene £100, and Iford obviously hoped to get the debt forgiven. However, he only got in deeper: he was arrested and charged with having sworn to support an enterprise against the king. Details are frustratingly missing, but Iford was nothing if not a survivor. He emerged unharmed from the affair, as he had from his entanglement with Agnes Cubbel, and, indeed, the Black Death, whose dire effects on the town and priory we have seen. He died 'in post' in 1359.

The priors were not the only 'interesting' people in the priory. In 1324, two monks, William of Nubelly and William Upperhill, went on crusade. Their fate is unrecorded. Much later, in 1445, another monk, the appropriately named Richard Veyse, was found living in adultery at Stokeney. He was imprisoned in the priory for apostasy. One wonders where Prior William Southbrook, who only had about 15 monks, thought he was.

The priors after Iford were mostly less controversial figures, but all struggled with the continuing financial problems and apparent moral laxity. The monk's numbers had been halved or more by the Black Death, and never recovered. In the 1350s, many of the profitable corrodies were unlet. Adjustments to the demographic and economic changes wrought by the Black Death and the general economic crisis of the early fourteenth century caused problems, but they were not fatal. Incomes from land seem to have quickly reached earlier levels, helped by 'fines' – fees – for the taking up of new tenancies from dead tenants (death as always providing opportunities for the living). Feudal services were still enforced, despite a tendency, finally irreversible, to convert all such renders to cash payments. This was resented. In 1381 (reacting to the Peasants' Revolt of that year) the bishop's bondsmen in Wellington refused a service of carrying hay to the bishops manor, and gathered together 'in great force' with staves and swords to resist. Such rebellion melted away or was crushed, but showed that the feudal system was weakening and would eventually be transformed out of existence.

Weaknesses in the administration of the monastery were matched by problems with the physical fabric. In 1324 Bishop Drokensford arranged for diocesan collections for further repairs of the church. The work was consecrated the following year, so could not have amounted to much, but might well have included the paving of the church with encaustic tiles. Tiles of this date have regularly turned up in excavations since the nineteenth century, and a complete floor was recorded in the crossing by Irvine in 1869 (**67**). More substantial work might, however, have been going on in the late 1320s and 30s, as master mason Richard Davy of Farleigh (near Bath) was working here before going to Salisbury in 1334. Little else happened to the church fabric until the next century.

This was not the case with the rest of the priory. The guest house, somewhere on the west range of the cloisters, was demolished in about 1300 and rebuilt. It seems likely that the prior's lodging, along the same range, was redesigned in much grander style at about the same time. In 1305 there is a reference to the prior's great chamber. This probably formed the core of the building shown on the edge of the Gilmore map of 1694 (it survived until 1754), which has clearly undergone major refurbishment or even rebuilding from the late fifteenth century onwards (**68**). Nonetheless,

67 *The tile floor in the crossing found during cellar digging in 1863. It would have been laid in the early fourteenth century.* Society of Antiquaries of Scotland

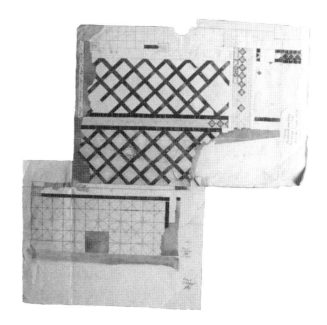

the 1305 building probably contained a hall, chapel and solar over lower rooms, which may have been lodgings or storerooms. The prior was also involved in rebuilding and refurbishing the bishop's palace.

The bishops had finally given up on residence in Bath. In 1328 the prior agreed to rent 'a certain house in the city of Bath called Bishopsboure [which ought to mean something like 'bishop's chamber'] and a place [open area or courtyard] adjoining within the walls of the close of the bishop's palace', at a rent of 20s a year. This reference is expanded in 1336, and we hear more, perhaps exaggerated, about the condition of the Palace:

> . . . that place commonly called Bishopsboure and the place adjacent to it which has been a great burden to us and our predecessors for many years; a heavily expensive building subject to ruin, the repair and restoration of which would be very expensive to make it useful and commodious for us and our successors; considering the location of the place near to the priory of Bath of which only one intermediary wall is adjoining and which said place is near the priory and Chapter; the use of this could provide solace and profit and so the place and the adjacent parts with all the other appurtenances are conceded to the Prior and Chapter for the present with permission to build repair and free to dispose and ordain in perpetuity . . .

The bishop was obviously greatly relieved to get the palace off his hands. What is hard to understand is why the priory wanted it. It can only be that prior Thomas Crist saw what he thought would be a commercial opportunity. The monks themselves had no need of the site, but if it could be refurbished or rebuilt and let out it might solve some of the financial difficulties. In 1347 one Reginald de Buggewell, later Dean of Exeter, was living in and probably renting the 'chamber under the bishop's chamber and the garden and chapel adjoining.' We do not know if the idea worked. There is no clear evidence of its success, but the prior was still paying his rent, at the same rate, at the Dissolution. It may be that the Black Death upset the prior's financial planning, changing everybody's calculations; or on the other hand, he may simply have given in to episcopal pressure.

Excavation on the site of the palace reflected these changes. Burnell's rebuilding provided the framework for the southern end of the site (we are still ignorant about the north), but it seems that floors were ripped up in the fourteenth century and replaced with clay ones, and roofs were falling in (at least in part). Rough subdivisions of the thirteenth-century rooms were being made (**32**); walls were partly dilapidated, and the culverts and drains were filled in. Leland's comments (p.xx) make it clear that nothing very palatial was recognisable in the buildings he saw in around 1534, though many cartloads of stone were taken away from the site in 1563 to construct new houses.

The priory was struggling in the later fourteenth and fifteenth centuries, but the town was doing well. Cloth was still king, and the major players in the town were all primarily cloth merchants. Their civic rôles and responsibilities were confirmed and clarified in the renewal of the charter that the city obtained from Henry VI in 1447. As well as authorising control of trade and general governance the charter enjoins the guildsmen to guard against overpayment of labourers, prevent the clipping and falsifying of coin and to regulate 'workmen, artificers, servants, innkeepers, beggars and vagabonds and other begging men who call themselves travelling-men'. They must also act as the king's Justices of the Peace. The adjuration to look out for 'those that rode in company with armed force against the Kings Peace' both reflects the increasing lawlessness of the times and is a premonition of the Wars of the Roses, the struggle for the crown that led to the ascendancy of the Tudors, and began in the following decade. Bath seems to have avoided the worst of the fighting, but then most places did. This particular dynastic struggle, while it had some very bloody battles, spectacular falls from grace and vicious betrayals, was quite sporadic over many decades. The final battle took place in 1485. The closest Bath came to involvement was the passing by of the army of the Earl of Devon and the Duke of Somerset in 1459, on the way to support Richard of York, far to the north. Bishop Stillingfleet (1466-91) was heavily involved on the losing side, and was briefly imprisoned by Henry VII, but he was an absentee bishop anyway, and his involvement had little effect on the town. The main impact was financial, and the town seems to have been able to cope with that.

We have met mayor and MP Phillips as a type of the successful merchant and conscientious civic leader; and later in the century such men can still be found. A deed of 1492 lists Mayor Robert Batyn and Aldermen: William Haynes, Robert Rogeris, Thomas Chauncellor, William Tyler and John Geffery (aka Cockes or Cox). All had taken their turn as mayor; and all were very wealthy – in fact Chauncellor was the richest man in Bath. In his will he left over £500 in cash, 12^d for each of his outworkers, mostly weavers and tuckers, and 20s for the lady who ran his shop. John Geffryes' will also shows a wealthy man; he left his best scarlet gown to a fellow alderman and another to his wife, and made bequests to the church, including his Cheap Street house to St Mary de Stall. He left £20 for an annual distribution of wheat, barley, beans and malt to poor citizens. Like Chauncellor, he remembered his staff and workers, and in addition left a silver gilt spice plate to the Corporation.

From the next generation of clothiers, three names were mentioned by Leland of leading men in living memory in the cloth trade '[by which] the town hath of a long tyme syns bene continually most mayntainid': Style, Kent and Chapman. Since their death the cloth trade is said to be 'sumwhat decayed'. The decay had been accelerating in the early sixteenth century: the changing attitudes of the fifteenth and sixteenth centuries were not conducive to the corporatist attitudes of the Middle Ages. Ambitious men were anxious to carve their own paths, and in this climate the Guild's control of trades was becoming oppressive. Trade was 'going out of town', and businessmen were setting up in small towns and villages where the Guilds' writ did not run; an early example of investment following cheap labour and lack of regulation. Bradford, Frome and Trowbridge were coming up at this time, but Bath's cloth trade was entering a terminal decline, although it did not die until the later seventeenth century.

An example of the extreme tendency towards independence and self-aggrandisement is given by the career of a particularly unpleasant character, Thomas Crouch. Even by the standards of the fifteenth and early sixteenth century, Crouch was unscrupulous, grasping and totally ruthless. He started his career in Bath as an agent of Prior Holloway. He duped the prior into making a creature of his the master of St John's Hospital, giving him control of its lands and wealth. Crouch then claimed the right to appoint the next master. This was too much, and a lawsuit followed, in which feelings ran high: Crouch was forcibly ejected from the cathedral after trying to serve a *subpoena*, and later found himself in the stocks. A mob of priory servants tried to burn his house down, and he retaliated with flights of arrows. However, it emerged that he had habitually rampaged around town with his gangs of paid thugs and reduced the town to such disorder that two mayors of Bath and important cloth manufacturers (presumably Styles and Kent) had left the town in fear of their lives and 'to its great impoverishment'. Crouch lost the case, but continued to profit from his scheming long after the prior had been forced out by the Dissolution.

In the decades when the town's trade was, despite the excitements of such as Crouch, on a gentle slope of decay, the cathedral and the priory were on a roller-coaster of change. The monks had been sleeping in the dormitory built under Robert of Lewes for 300 years when Bishop Bekyngton (1443-66) took pity on them and paid for a new one out of his own pocket (even this level of assistance was unexpected, as he was building extensively in Wells). The bishop's liberality only points up the priory's inability to maintain the fabric of the monastery. The old claustral buildings were certainly in a pretty bad way. Prior John Dunster found himself faced with the necessity of rebuilding the refectory sometime in the 1470s, and under a far less liberal bishop. He raised over £600 by various stratagems which so financially embarrassed the monastery that his successor, John Cantlow, sued him for the losses (Dunster had been promoted to Abbot of St Augustine's at Canterbury). There seems to have been no substantial work on the cathedral itself after the early fourteenth century until the first quarter of the fifteenth, when Bishop Bubwith gave 328 marks (£218 13s 4ᵈ) for work at the church. Although a not inconsiderable sum, this was only enough to scratch the surface of the cathedral if we compare it with the £300 plus *per annum* for the rebuilding under Bishop King (p159). It was probably used to refit a chapel in the south aisle, but it did not begin to match what later events show was required.

Cantlow's suit against Dunster contains a description of the state of the priory that seems to imply not only lack of funds, but a serious and sudden structural failure as well. The costs of recent rebuilding, says the document, are a burden, but the house 'was in grete povertie for manye causes', with 'the soden ruyn of the most of the church of the seid priorye [and] the charges and costs of repare' being a major issue. This implies that a large part of the church had literally collapsed. Perhaps the tower had fallen or the high vaults in the choir. Perhaps the wooden roofs had rotted and fallen. We do not know how much damage the church had suffered, nor whether Cantlow was exaggerating to support his case. Superficially, his statement suggests that he was attempting to repair or rebuild the church, and the priory was certainly excused taxation between 1485-96 because of its poverty and ruinous condition. However, he was also spending money on projects elsewhere, and it is hard to see that much could have been achieved at the church. For example, the Hospital of St Mary Magdalen, just south of the town, was likewise ruinous, impoverished and in debt. By agreement, Cantlow had taken it over, completely rebuilt it, and assumed its debts (**48**). He also rebuilt the chancel of St Catherine's Church, east of Bath and, it seems, a major portion of the Prior's Lodging, which survived into the eighteenth century as Abbey House (**68**). On balance, Cantlow seems to be telling the truth. The church, or parts of it, had collapsed, but little was done to rebuild it. When Oliver King became bishop and visited the city in 1499, he indeed found the church 'ruined to the foundations'.

King had been translated to the see in 1496, but his workload as Henry VII's secretary meant that he could not visit until 1499. An energetic man, used to achievement and success (he had negotiated the violent and dangerous transitions between three kings and two dynasties in both his worldly and spiritual careers and come out on the winning side), he at once decided that here was a task suited to his drive and his gifts. He blamed the prior and his predecessors for the problems, stating that it was 'through the laxity of many priors that the church had not been repaired or rebuilt'. This was technically correct, but an almost totally absentee bishop followed by a short-lived one had not helped, although King was not about to blame his episcopal forebears. King also berated the poor moral condition of the priory. There was feasting in the refectory, the monks were not fulfilling their duties and women were found to be in the precinct at unseemly hours. Cantlow conveniently died just a month after King's visitation, and William Bird was elected

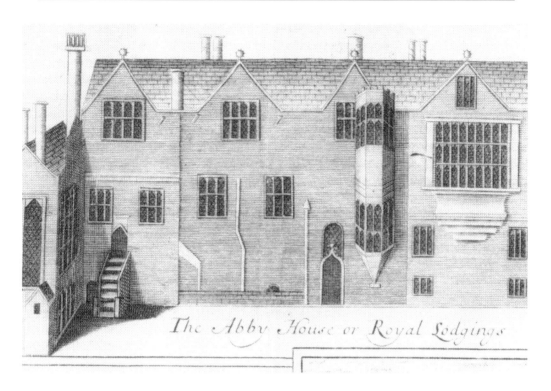

68 *The Prior's Lodging from Gilmore. The western range of the cloister survived until 1754 as a private house. The building here is probably broadly as left by Prior Cantlow in the 1480s.*
Victoria Art Gallery, Bath

prior. Bird was King's willing assistant in the rebuilding project but proved to be much more than this. He outlived King by 22 years, and his passion for the rebuilding ensured that the project did not falter despite its patron's death. King rapidly got things moving. He informed the prior that he was resolved to rebuild the church anew. He had calculated the monks' income at £480 a year. Out of this he would reserve £300 *per annum* for the rebuilding fund, and undertook to raise extra finance himself. Henry VII had visited Bath in 1496 and again in 1497, and his intense interest in church affairs is likely to have led him to inform his servant and bishop that there was a task awaiting him at Bath. Something of this sort is certainly needed to explain the bishop's priorities. But later writers, and the church itself, tell us of another reason that certainly would appeal strongly to the medieval mind: Bishop King had a dream.

Sir John Harington was squire at nearby Kelston, and a catalytic figure in the later sixteenth-century restoration of the Abbey Church, as it was by then known. He wrote that 'while lying at Bathe' King dreamt he saw a vision of the Trinity, with angels descending and ascending a ladder, at the bottom of which was an olive tree with a crown on it. He heard a voice saying 'let an olive establish the crown and a king restore the church'. This call to action is, of course, famously recorded

159

69 *Oliver King's* rebus *or visual pun on the west front of the new cathedral.* "Be to us the olive king". *Compare* **71**, *before the restorations*

in the sculptures of the present west front of the church (**69**), although these are now in such poor condition that the texts cannot be read, as well as having suffered three major restorations between 1890 and 1990. The general scheme however is still apparent: the ladders with ascending and descending angels, the heavenly host high in the gable and the olive trees with their encircling crown. The main text continued the theme of pun and rebus: 'Trees going to chuse their King said 'be to us the Olive King'.

King immediately set about realising his dream. The king's masons Robert and William Vertue were called in as architects, a scheme was prepared and foundations were being dug as early as 1502. The rate of building was astonishing: demolition of the old nave must have started in 1501 or 1502; in early 1503 the walls were rising and King wrote that the building would be roofed by November. It seems likely that the shell was being rushed up. Certainly the east end with its great square-headed window must have been up to the eaves by early or mid-1503 (**70**). It is clearly designed for a flat timber ceiling or roof: the slots for the horizontal timbers are still visible above the present stone vaulting. The vaulting, however, had already been decided on in 1503, when the Vertues promised King a vault in comparison to which there should be 'none so goodely neither in England nor in France' (**70**). King's death in July 1503 is the latest possible date for the change in plan: it was probably decided upon early in the year. The west end of the nave was nearly as far along. The great west window shows signs of a change in design to accommodate a vault just at the springing of its arched head. Like the east end it was also originally designed to fit below the horizontal tie beams of a low timber roof. The faithful

70 *The inside of the east end of King's church, the great east window and the poor fit of the vaulting to it, the result of a change of plan in 1503*

71 *The west front of the Abbey Church in 1798, in a drawing by John Carter commissioned by the Society of Antiquaries. Much detail lost to later aerial pollution and consequent re-carving is visible*

72 *The heraldic bosses in the choir aisle vaults. The escutcheons of Prior Bird (1496-1525), left, and Bishop Adriano de Castello(1504-18), right*

fulfilment of the original west front design, commemorating King's dream, is also an indication that much was completed in his lifetime (**71**). However, up in the high west front, among the heavenly host, one can just see, after the recent cleaning, a cardinal's hat: the insignia of King's successor, Cardinal Adriano de Castello (and conveniently, his successor, Wolsey). Castello never visited England, let alone Bath, but Prior Bird faithfully added the arms and insignia of all officially involved in the project. In fact, Bird's placing of both the cardinal's and his own blazons on the east end vaulting, both in the choir and the side aisles, rather suggests that even the lower vaults were built after King's death (**72**). The early rush was just to get the walls up and the roof on; King wanted to establish 'facts on the ground' to enforce his vision on those who came after. The subsequent history of the building shows him to have been brilliantly right.

What was this vision? The old church, ruinous or not, was intensely unfashion-able. Compared to contemporary buildings it was heavy, dark, low and with crude and poor quality stonework. It was also huge and, we should remember, it was uniquely one of *two* cathedrals in the diocese. King wanted a state-of-the-art, modern, high-technology status symbol, but of a size that fitted his funds, his timescale, and the peculiar circumstances of Bath and Wells. With striking design and the best architects, he could get a lot of presence in a small space (**73**). The unity of the building is also striking, with repetition of a few standard design elements being the key to the relationship of parts to whole, typical of late Gothic. One is reminded of the hi-tech, high-profile, but small-scale Spa building going up in Bath as these words are being written. But that building is hidden away; King wanted his new building to be seen. Today it still manages to dominate many views of Bath, near and far, despite the insults of the nineteenth and twentieth centuries. How overwhelming must its presence have been when none of the buildings around it were more than two or perhaps three low storeys.

Inside, even now, the visitor to the church is struck by the light flooding in through the large windows, a defining feature of late Gothic English architecture.

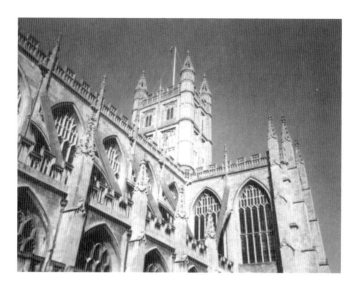

73 *A dramatic, hi-tech, high-profile building. Bishop King's statement, the new cathedral of Bath*

How much colour King would have introduced is not known: all of the pre-Dissolution glass went in 1539. Totally plain clear glass to the extent we see now would not have been part of the plan, we can be sure. The fan vaults are among the finest in England, and gather up all the lower accents as the eye travels up (**70**). In the aisles the vaults are of the logic-defying pendant variant, a trademark of the Vertues. However, the nave vaults had to wait 250 years for their completion. They were finally installed by Sir Gilbert Scott in the 1860s – and wonderful they are.

The new church was built on the nave of the old one. The outer walls served as footings, and much of the old stonework was recycled into the inner and hidden parts of the new walls. It also served as material for those new footings that were required: the transepts and the new arcade piers. The old east end seems to have been left standing. When Leland visited in the 1530s, he described the ruined east end with its abandoned bishops' tombs as 'onroofid, and wedes grew about this John of Tours sepulchre', but 'the walles yet stande.' Clearly, the plan was to keep the east end standing until the new church was ready; and indeed, an ordination took place in the old east end in 1502. By Leland's visit the old choir was obviously not in use, and the archaeological investigation that revealed the plan of the east end of the old church showed that the building was not fully removed until the mid-sixteenth century. Access to it was provided from the new church by keeping open two arches that had originally led from the nave aisles into the transept. These were incorporated into the new east wall of the new cathedral, and survive today, along with the walling around them, simply blocked in when the old east end was finally demolished. The arch at the east end of the south choir aisle can easily be seen today, and

74 *The Norman arch in the present south choir aisle, revealed during restoration work in 1863-71*

was partly exposed during the restorations of the 1860s (**74**). The arch at the east end of the north aisle is more difficult to see, as it is merely a plain row of voussoirs in the wall, but much of both these fragments of wall are essentially of John of Tours' Church, the only parts still fully above ground.

On the basis of a very untrustworthy depiction on Smith's map of 1568, it has been claimed that the east end of the present abbey was originally supplied with a projecting Lady Chapel. This may well have been planned; patched scars on the masonry either side of the great east window suggest that the stonework here was left unfinished, to allow the dogging in of masonry. Such a chapel would have been difficult to build until the old east end was removed. But the scars are not extensive enough to represent the wall that would need to have abutted here if it had been built and removed; and more importantly, no signs of footings were seen when the fourteenth-century crossing pavement was uncovered by Irvine here in 1867 (**67**). If the chapel had existed and still stood in 1568, it is surprising that it was not mentioned in the extensive references to the restoration of the abbey church in the 1590s and 1600s. Finally, Leland's description of the old east end makes no mention of it.

With new claustral buildings having been erected in the previous 50 years, little needed doing to the buildings in the priory, but the cloisters had to be reworked to fit the new building. The major problem was the new south transept, which projected right into the north walk of the cloisters. Rather than rebuild the whole thing, King's masons simply rebuilt the north walk far enough south to pass in front of the transept. The footings for the new work were uncovered in excavations in 1993, and in the same excavations the base of the south-east corner of the transept was seen resting on the twelfth-century paving of Robert of Lewes' north walk, effectively blocking it. This re-jigging resulted in a very odd layout. The east walk of the cloister was now reached from a door east of the transept, in the south choir aisle. This entrance can still be seen, though the cloister vanished in the sixteenth century; it is now the entrance to the early seventeenth-century clergy vestry which was built on to the outside of the door in 1613. The other door, leading from the nave into the west walk, also still exists, forming the entrance to the book shop in the early twentieth-century choir vestry. Incidentally, the door to the prior's lodging still exists in the south-west corner of the nave aisle just west of the cloister door. It now leads nowhere.

The church was largely completed by Bird, and seems to have been completely finished by his successor, the last prior, Holloway (or Gibbs: it seems he used both names). It is now sometimes said that the church was unfinished by the Dissolution of the Abbeys in 1539, but although we have no record of its consecration, it does seem to have been substantially completed. Leland, writing around 1540, says:

> Oliver King Bisshop of Bath began of late dayes a right goodly new chirch at the west part of the old chirch of S. Peter and finished a great peace of it. *The residue was syns made* by the priors of Bath: and especially by Gibbes, the last prior ther, that spent a great summe of mony on that fabrike. [my italics]

Given the huge early progress made, this is perhaps not really surprising. Nothing of the internal fittings survives the vicissitudes of the last 500 years, except the splendid chantry chapel that Prior Bird built on the south side of the chancel (**75**). This small stone room, defined by its delicate tracery and dainty vault, is more like a richly-decorated tent, or even a draped bed. It would have been magnificently gaudy in its original colours, some slight trace of which survives in pockets in the mouldings. Bird would have confidently expected prayers to be said here for his soul until doomsday. In the event politics and reform meant they were said for less than 14 years.

75 *Prior Bird's chantry. The last monument of the Middle Ages in Bath*

The 'passing away of the present order of things' happened in short order once Henry VIII had squared his conscience with political necessity and broken with Rome. The smaller monasteries were suppressed in 1535. Henry's commissioners then embarked upon the investigation of the larger ones. These investigations were hardly impartial. In 1535, Dr Layton reported to Thomas Cromwell, the king's minister:

> Hit may please yor godness to understand that we have visited Bathe, wheras we found the prior a right virtuose man and I suppose no better of his cote, a man simple and not of the greteste wit, his monkes worse than any I have fownde yet both in bugerie and adulterie sum one of them having x women sum viii and the rest so fewer. The house well repared but foure hundrethe powndes in dett.

It is hard to know which was most exaggerated, Gibbs' simplicity, or the monks' degeneracy. We know that individuals throughout the past history of the priory had been caught in carnal sin, but it seems hardly likely that the whole establishment was little more than a bawdy house. At any rate, Gibbs clearly thought he might buy favour, perhaps unable to comprehend the full extent of Cromwell's relentless determination. Layton continued: ' . . . the prior of Bathe hath sent unto yow for a token a leisse of Yrishe laniers (hawks), brede in a cell of hys in Yrelande no hardier can be as he saythe'; and later in the year Gibbs sent Cromwell a book from the cathedral library, while in 1537 he made him an offer of a pension of £5 a year. Nearer the end Gibbs had obviously realised that the king and his minister were not to be diverted. Despite instructions not to do so, he had started dispersing the priory's property, reducing the catch for the king. In the end, as with nearly all monks and friars nationally, the prior and his monks went quietly. On the 27th January 1539, the prior surrendered the priory to Tregonwell and Petre, the king's representatives. The prior signed the surrender, and so did the subprior, the prior of Dunster and the 18 monks who made up the community. The inmates were treated well, as long as they co-operated. The prior was granted a pension of £80 a year and a house in Stall Street, while the subprior got £9. The monks were rewarded according to seniority, and received pensions ranging from £4 13s 4d to £8. Most were still alive in 1553, although Gibbs had died by this time; and one, William Clement, became vicar of St Mary de Stalls. The generosity was easily afforded. When it surrendered, Bath was the second richest monastery in Somerset (after Glastonbury, whose unfortunate last abbot was hanged), worth £617 2s 3d.

Further reading

For a general background to the period, see, *inter alia*, King 1988 and Keen 1998. The *VCH* gives a detailed ecclesiastical history. Britton 1825, on the abbey, is remarkably good for its date and has informative illustrations of the present abbey building before any of the major restorations. Irvine 1890 and Bligh Bond 1918 should be consulted for details of the discoveries of remains of the Norman building, and Rodwell and O'Leary 1991 for the uncovering of the plan of the east end of the Norman cathedral. Shickle 1921, Green 1888 and Bush 1877, 79 and 80 deal with city records from the period. Manco 1993 gives a good account of the layout of the abbey, largely from documentary sources, but this author differs from her interpretations in some areas. Manco 1998 is especially useful for the hospitals and some background. *The Dictionary of National Biography* is increasingly useful for more important individuals.

Epilogue

The priory had always existed. It had been there for longer than the city. How would the city function with this void at its centre? At first the destruction just went on, as the king's commissioners set about matching the institutional void with a real one. The roof was stripped and the lead sold. The glass and iron glazing bars went; the building materials from the refectory, dormitory and cloister were sold, and the entire roof of the nave dismantled. Nor was this all: in 1542 an act of parliament was passed creating the diocese of Bristol, based on the old St Augustine's Abbey and partly carved out of Somerset. As part of this tidying up, Bath's cathedral was stripped of its status: Wells had finally won back all its pre-eminence. The citizens, the 'mayor and commonality of Bath' must have been in many minds about these events, and this uncertainty was reflected when they refused an offer from the king's commissioners to buy the priory and all its lands for £500. Later sources tell us that this was so cheap that the Guild felt they might be accused of defrauding the king. Local individuals did not hesitate nonetheless to buy the building materials that were on offer. It is hard to imagine the city fathers turning away such a bargain, and while there might have been a fear of benefiting from such an act against the church, it was probably, more pragmatically, fear of a future change in policy.

If so, the fear did not last long. Humphrey Colles, from Taunton, bought the close and lands and in 1548 they passed into the hands of Matthew Colthurst, of Wardour Castle in Wiltshire and MP for Bath. He or his son Edmund turned the prior's lodging along the west cloister range into a private dwelling (it would have needed little conversion), and transformed the cloister into a private garden. Its two parterres, perhaps laid out as fashionable knots, can be seen in the Savile and Speed maps (**50 & 51**). The amount of work necessary was seen in the 1993 excavations. The garden wall was formed from the outer wall of the cloister, and the paved paths were built up half a metre (1ft 8in) on the dumped rubble either from the demolition, or that part of it that could not be sold as building material. By the end of the sixteenth century, all the claustral buildings had gone except for the Abbey Gate at the end of Abbey Gate Street, and the house on the walls that is probably the one built by Robert de Sutton in the 1320s. It was not until Colthurst sold up in 1612 that development started. But elsewhere things had not been so slow.

Colthurst had given the shell of the cathedral, now usually referred to as the Abbey Church, to the city in 1572, and almost immediately the city built new houses on the strip of land along the north side of the church, valuable properties facing the market place. These houses were removed in the early nineteenth century, but the scars they left in the church fabric can still be seen. The gift of the church was with a view to it becoming the parish church of the city. Queen Elizabeth I's minister, Burleigh, was petitioned in 1572 for Her Majesty's permission for the scheme, and to allow a nationwide appeal for funds for the restoration. This was granted in 1573 and the Queen visited the town in 1574. In the petition the Corporation gave a clue as to why they were no longer satisfied with the old parish churches. Clearly they had decided that the economic salvation of the town lay in the tourist trade and the exploitation of the springs, certainly at first for their medicinal qualities. For, 'There is in the springtime and at the fall of the leaf yearly great repair to the city of noble men, men of worship and others *for relief at the Baths*' [my italics]. This repair to the city had clearly been going on in pre-Dissolution days, but is largely undocumented. It was certainly deliberately encouraged by the physicians who appeared in large numbers in the later sixteenth century to provide a medico-scientific slant to the pleasures of the bath. Dr William Turner was the most influential of these. He wrote a book published in 1557 on the spas of Europe and 'I have also writen so well as I can of the bath of Baeth in England to allure thither as manye as have need of such helpe as almighty God hath graunted it to gyve'. Turner established a practice in Bath to assist the God-given healing powers of the springs. John Jones' *Bath of Bathes Ayde* followed in 1572, and ex-Abbot Feckenham (of the short-lived Marian re-establishment of Westminster Abbey) established a poor leper's hospital near the Hot Bath, and published works extolling the baths and prescribing the correct rules of behaviour.

The baths themselves saw investment. Leland's descriptions of the three springs are probably of buildings little changed since the earlier Middle Ages. The Cross Bath 'is temperate and pleasant having 11 or 12 arches of stone in the sides for men to stande under yn tyme of reyne'. The bath was extensively remodelled in the 1590s, and this is how it appears on the corner of the seventeenth century maps (**50, 51 & 52**). The same had happened to the Hot Bath, ('lesse in Cumpace withyn the Waulle then the other, having by 7 Arches in the Waulle') and it had the 'lazars'' (lepers') bath added to the west side by Feckenham in around 1576. The King's Bath was extended by the creation of a new bath to the south, later called the Queen's Bath, in around 1590. Not only baths and church had to be provided for the influx of visitors. Lodgings were required, and much new building took place. The West Gate was rebuilt and extended to the north in 1572 to provide high status accommodation: Queen Elizabeth stayed there in 1574.

The Guild took the lead in all this activity. It was a wealthy body, and in 1551 built a market hall in the High Street on the site of the market cross. In 1552 it acquired the prior's rights to the baths and the remnants of monastic property. This was officially to finance the hospitals and the new free school (King Edward's School, still functioning today), but although the hospitals were conscientiously run, the money inevitably became remarkably difficult to disentangle from the city's general finances. In 1590 the city fathers acquired a new charter from the Queen, which confirmed their new status as the only significant corporate body in town. From this date on we can properly refer to the *Corporation* of Bath.

The abbey church needed more time to sort out; it took until 1581 to reroof the choir and north transept, and the nave was not completed until 1613. The parish had been formed by the granting of the petition of 1572, but the first incumbent was not in place until 1583. St Mary's by the Northgate was abandoned by that date, but St Mary de Stalles remained in use for worship until 1593, and the last burial in the churchyard was not until 1606. By then all the parish churches within the walls, except St James, were abandoned. The sites were leased out as commercial properties, or in the case of the St Mary's by the Northgate as a school and prison. St Mary de Stalls finally disappeared in 1659, St Mary's by the Northgate in 1772.

The city was now completely its own master. The church had gone, the cloth trade was still an important industry but in decline; the tourist trade was clearly the future. The late sixteenth and seventeenth centuries were periods of both solid growth in the spa trade and of physical development, interrupted only by the civil war in the 1640s, when the city was besieged. In these years the foundations were laid for the almost magical transformation of Georgian times. The medieval city vanished, gradually at first, and then with increasing speed and completeness, before the dazzling success of the eighteenth-century spa and the concomitant almost total redevelopment of the town by the construction of classical buildings.

Almost all that is left of the medieval achievement to the casual observer is the 'abbey'. Though smaller than its predecessor, it is still one of the largest buildings in the city. Yet somehow it remains invisible, or at least, unrecognised, a hulk left behind by the receding tide of the past; admired yet barely recognised for what it is, the last medieval cathedral built in England, a last survivor of a lost city.

Appendix I
Mayors of Bath in the Middle Ages

I am very grateful to Elizabeth Holland for making available her researches into the mayors of Bath.

c.1230	John de Porta (of the Gate)	1299	William Cook	1338	Roger Crist
1230–62	David Little (?)	1300	William Cook	1339	William Cubbel
	Walter de Falc	1301?	John Pistor (Baker)	1340	Adam Whyteson
	Henry the Tailor	1302	Peter Le Brevitor	1341	Alexander Dyer
1262	Henry the Tailor	1304	William Serrel	1342	Roger Crist
1277	Henry the Tailor	1305	William Serrel	1343	John Cole
	Nicholas Biscop	1307	Peter Le Brevitor	1344	William Cubbel
c.1279–83	Roger of Dichegate	1309	William Cook	1345	Adam Whyteson
	Henry the Tailor	1310	Adam Whyteson	1346	Alexander Dyer
Undated (later thirteenth century)			(Miller)	1347	William Cubbel
	Gilbert Cissor	1311	Walter Falconare	1348	William Cubbel
	(Tailor)	1312	Richard Whyteson	1349	Roger Crist
	John de Combe	1313	Peter Le Brevitor	1350	Thomas Stote
	(a tailor from	1314	Richard Whyteson	1351	Robert le Dyer
	Combe Down)	1315	William Cook	1352	William Cubbel.
	Thomas Sweyn	1316	John the Baker		Only
	Nicholas Clerk	1317	John Cole		documented
	Walter Sewall	1318	Richard Whyteson		survivor of BD
	(Serrell)	1319	John Baker	1353	Thomas Stote
	Richard Everard	1320	John Cole	1354	Walter Carpenter
	Richard Taverner	1321	John Cole	1355	John Wittokesmede
	Peter le Brevitor	1322	Adam Whyteson	1356	William Serrel
1283	William Cocus	1323	John de Wyk	1357	William Cook
	(cook)	1324	Roger Cole	1358	John Sheory
c.1280s	John de Dover and	1325	Richard le Boye	1359	Robert le Dyer
	Walter Ring –	1326	John Cole	1360	John Wittokesmede
	Cofferers	1327	John de Wyk	1361	Walter Carpenter
1290	Stephen Baker/de	1328	Richard le Boye	1362	John Gregory
	Devizes	1329	Adam Wyteson	1363	John Gregory
1291	John le Venar	1330	William Cook	1364	John Wittokesmede
1292	John Le Tayleur	1331	Roger Cole?	1365	John Wittokesmede
1293	William Cook	1332	Alexander Dyer	1366	John Gregory
1294	John de Combe	1333	William Sweyn	1367	John Gregory
	(Tailor)	1334	Alexander Dyer	1368	—
1295	William Serrel	1335	Adam Whyteson	1369	John Wittokesmede
1296	Thomas Sweyn	1336	Roger Cole	1370	William Drayton
		1337	Alexander Dyer	1371	John Grigory

1372	Robert Wattes	1412	John Savage	1452	William Dreyton
1373	John Gregory	1413	—	1453	William Abell
1374	—	1414	Ralph Hunt	1454	Thomas Abell
1375	John Compe	1415	—	1455	John Austell
1376	John Gregory	1416	Walter Rytche	1456	—
1377	John Compe	1417	Ralph Hunt	1457	—
1378	John Natton	1418	Richard Widcombe	1458	—
1379	Robert Wattes	1419	—	1459	—
1380	John Natton	1420	Richard Widcombe	1460	—
1381	John Gregory	1421	—	1461	John Thomas
1382	Richard Bedul	1422	Ralph Hunt	1462	—
1383	—	1423	William Philipps	1463	—
1384	—	1424	John Savage	1465	—
1385	John Natton	1425	John Savage	1466	—
1386	—	1426	William Hodgkyns	1467	John Steere
1387	—	1427	Richard Widcombe	1468	William Stanburgh
1388	Robert Waspray	1428	W Phillips	1469	—
1389	—	1429	Ralph Hunt	1470	—
1390	Robert Draper	1430	—	1471	William Hayne
1391	William Rous	1431	—	1472	—
1392	Robert Waspray	1432	— Phillips?	1473	William Stanburgh
1393	William Rous	1433	William Phillips	1474	Robert Rogers
1394	Robert Waspray	1434	William Phillips	1475	Robert Batyn
1395	John Waspray	1435	William Hodgekyns	1476	William Stanburgh
1396	Thomas Swayne	1436	—	1477	Robert Rogers
1397	—	1437	William Phillips	1478	Thomas Chauncellor
1398	Thomas Plomes	1438	Walter Rich	1488	William Tyler
1399	Robert Waspray	1439	—	1492	Robert Batyn
1400	Roger Testwode	1440	—	1497	Robert Rogers
1401	Roger Testwood	1441	William Hodgekyns	1498	William Stanburgh
1402	Roger Waspray	1442	William Phillips	1503	Richard Chapman
1403	Roger Testwood	1443	Walter Ryche	1533	Richard Covell
1404	Richard Widcombe	1444	William Phillips	1534	William Horsington
1405	—	1445	—	1540	Robert Style
1406	—	1445-	—	1543	John Chapman
1407	Roger Testwood	1447	William Hodgekyns	1544	Anthony Scrope
1408	Ralph Hunt	1448	—	1551	Edward Ludwell
1409	John Savage	1449	William Cubbell	1553	John Davis
1410	Ralph Hunt	1450	—	1555	Thomas Ash
1411	Robert Waspray	1451	—	1567	John Pearman

Appendix II
Abbots, Bishops and Priors of Bath

Abbots/Abbesses

Berta	675–c.681
Bernguida	fl.681
Wulfgar	fl.950s
Æscwig	fl.965-70
Ælfeah	c. 980
Wulfwold	before 1061–c.1084
Ælfwig	before 1061
Sæwold	c.1060-6
Ælfsige	1066-87

Bishops

John of Tours (or de Villula)	1090-1122
Godfrey	1122-35
Robert of Lewes	1136-66
Reginald FitzJoscelin	1174-91
Savaric (Bishop of Bath and Glastonbury)	
	1192-1205
Joscelin Trotman	1206-42
Roger of Salisbury	1244-7
William Button I	1247-64)
Walter Giffard	1264-7
	Promoted to York
William Button II	1267-1274
Robert Burnell	1274-92
William de la March	1293-1302
Walter Haselshaw	1302-09
John of Drokensford (Droxford)	
	1310-29
Ralph of Shrewsbury	1329-63
John Barnet	1363-7
John Harewell	1367-86
Walter Skirlaugh	1386-8
Ralph Ergum	1388-1400
Richard Clifford	1400-01
Henry Bowett	1401-07
Nicholas Bubwith	1407-25
John Stafford	1425-43
Thomas Beckington (Bekynton)	
	1443-66
Robert Stillington	1466-91

Richard Fox	1492-6
Oliver King	1496-1503
Adriano de Castello	1503-18
Thomas Wolsey	1518-23
John Clerk	1523-41
William Knight	1541-8
William Barlow	1548-54
Gilbert Bounre	1554-60
Gilbert Berkeley	1560-84
Thomas Godwin	1584-93
John Still	1593-1608
James Montague	1608-13

Priors

John fl.	1122
Benedict	fl. 1151
Peter	fl. 1157
Hugh	1174-80
Gilbert	1180- before 1191
Walter	Before 1191-8
Robert	1198
Thomas	1223-61
Walter de Anno	1261-after 1263
Walter de Dune	fl. 1266, 1283
Thomas de Winton	fl. 1290
Robert de Clopcote	1301-32
Robert Sutton	Irregular election, resigned 1332
Thomas Crist	1332–40
John de Iford	1340–59
John de Berewyk	1359-77
John Dunster	Died 1412
John Tellesford	1412-24
William Southbrook	1425–47
Thomas Lacock	1447
John	fl. 1468
John Dunster II	fl. 1481–2
	May be same John
John Cantlow	1482-99
William Bird	1499-1525
William Gibbs, alias Holloway	1525–39

Biographical notes of the more significant or interesting bishops

John of Tours

John of Tours, or de Villula, was a native of Tours in the Loire Valley. His date of birth is unknown, as is how he came to England, although presumably he took advantage of the opportunity presented by the Norman court after the conquest of 1066. He was a friend and confidant of William Rufus (1087–1100), and seems to have been his physician. He was certainly known as a skilled doctor. He became the first Bishop of Bath in 1088, buying the city and probably the honour from William. His love of learning was marred by his contempt for the English monks, whom he probably judged on their lack of French rather than their command of Latin. He was high-handed in his dealings related to the reorganisation of the priory, but relented in later years. He was described as a man of 'cheerful and courteous disposition'.

John le Tours was busy in church matters generally, being present at several important events such as the consecration of the new cathedral at Old Sarum (a resited church like his own), and the dedication of Battle Abbey, a monastery founded on the very site of the Battle of Hastings. Presence here showed public and prudent commitment to the Norman cause. He was also, perhaps surprisingly, at the side of the Bishop of Durham in his last illness in 1095/6, presumably in the capacities of both priest and physician. We know he was present on at least one occasion at the king's Council in his position as bishop, and was there asked for his support by the Archbishop of Canterbury (1097), but we know little more of his detailed involvement with temporal affairs. He was at the Synod of Westminster in 1102, and in Canterbury as a senior bishop at the consecration of five others in 1107.

Le Tours died in Bath on 29 December 1122, after being taken ill, perhaps with a heart attack, after Christmas dinner. He was described as being elderly when he died, and this would support a date of birth in the 1050s or early 1060s.

Robert of Lewes

Very little is known about this important bishop. His surname derives from his being previously a monk at Lewes, but Britton claims he was of Norman origin. He attracted the patronage of the Bishop of Winchester, the powerful Henry of Blois, King Stephen's brother who, after securing preferment for him in Winchester, was instrumental in his translation to Bath. Patronage from the royal family is enough to explain Robert's adherence to the king in the civil wars. His rôle is not clear, except that he was the temporal lord of a city fortified for the king. He was captured during fighting in the 1140s and exchanged for a high-ranking rebel prisoner. When Stephen heard this he was so angry he was minded to strip Robert of his temporalities. This is not so physically painful as it might sound, but the loss of all income not directly from church fees would be painful in other ways. What it tells us about the bishop's favour with the king is also unclear.

Robert's greatest achievements were both in relation to the priory at Bath. He completed the ambitious building programme of John of Tours and confirmed the legal status of Bath as the only cathedral in the diocese and the head of the see. The canons at Wells had no say in the new arrangements. He died in 1166 and was buried in the cathedral at Bath.

Reginald Fitzjoscelin

Reginald was the son of the Bishop of Salisbury, and this irregular position probably accounted for his upbringing in Lombardy (North Italy). He was sometimes referred to as Reginald the Lombard or the Italian because of this. Born in 1139 or 1140, he was well connected, his father being a Bohun, one of the great Norman families. His father acknowledged him and it was later accepted that Reginald was not illegitimate but was born before his father took the cloth. This was the cause of much delay in his later elevation to the episcopacy.

He mixed early with those in power and was a friend of Thomas à Becket during his ascendancy. However, Becket excommunicated Reginald's father during the quarrel with Henry II and this turned him to the king's side. He went as the king's ambassador to the Pope in 1167 and 1169, which roused Becket's anger to great heights. When Becket was murdered, Reginald was sent to Rome to plead the kings' innocence. As a reward for these services, he was elevated to the see of Bath in 1173. He had to travel to Rome to get papal confirmation and this came only after long argument, his taking oaths on his lack of complicity in Becket's death and his legitimacy, and, of course, much bribery. Reginald was finally confirmed in May 1174. Returning home he met the king in France, and was finally enthroned by the archbishop in November.

Reginald was a very active diocesan bishop, regularising and confirming procedures and safeguarding incomes, and he oversaw some of the rebuilding of Wells Cathedral. He gave Wells town two charters, and at Bath founded The Hospital of St John. He also set in train the close links with Glastonbury that led to Savaric's short-lived see of Bath and Glastonbury by inviting the Abbot of Glastonbury to sit on the cathedral chapter.

He remained throughout deeply involved in national politics. Reginald was a regular attender of the king's councils in the 1170s; and he also, less attractively to our eyes, sat on a commission to suppress the cathar heretics in the south-west of France. He seems to have had a natural affability and was friends with Henry's illegitimate son Geoffrey, and also apparently with Hugh of Avalon, whom he had brought back from France and helped obtain the see of Lincoln. He had a conspicuous rôle in the coronation ceremonies of Richard I, but failed to buy the Chancellorship in that year despite the huge sum of £4000 he offered for it. However affable he may have been, he had a harder edge. In 1191 he was involved in conspiring to replace Longchamp, who had secured the chancellorship. He also plotted with the monks of Christ Church, Canterbury in their argument with the archbishop. His kinsman, and successor, Savaric, was also heavily involved. When the archbishop died the monks elected Reginald to the archiepiscopal see. He returned to Somerset to secure Savaric's election as bishop there, but died on the way back to Canterbury. He was buried in Bath Cathedral on the 29 December 1191.

Savaric

Reginald's successor in the see was a hard-nosed, ambitious and clever prelate, whose pursuit of power and wealth and lack of moral scruple seem very unpleasant to us now but were exceptional even then. He was Reginald's father's cousin, and connected to powerful Norman families, as well as being the cousin of the Holy Roman Emperor, Henry VI. Savaric first comes to notice in 1172, when as a young cleric he was fined £26 3s 4^d for stealing a bow from the king's foresters in Surrey.

A wealthy young man's high jinks: if he had been of a lower status he would have been maimed or executed. He was first an archdeacon at Canterbury, then Treasurer at Sarum and finally Archdeacon of Northampton in 1180. He managed to upset Henry II, who sent complaints to the Pope about him in 1186. The dispute may have been about money.

Savaric went off on crusade in 1189 with Richard I, a move which seems to reflect his restless, ambitious nature. He got Richard to write a letter from Sicily to the Justiciars in England as part of the wrangle with the Archbishop of Canterbury. At this juncture he left the Crusade and went off to Rome to intrigue some more in the schemes to make Reginald primate and himself bishop of Bath. His high connections helped. Savaric was supported at Rome by Philip of France and the Emperor. As we know, he was successful and was elected by the monks at Bath and consecrated bishop by the Pope in August 1192.

He did not return to England until late in 1193, as he was involved in the negotiations over the release of Richard I from his captivity by the Emperor (Savaric's connections were immensely useful to him here). Nevertheless he revealed his colours by pressing Richard to write to England from his captivity to support his promotion to Canterbury, in return for his good offices in the release. Richard repudiated this letter as soon as he could. The Emperor was also pressing for a clause in the release treaty confirming Savaric as Bishop of Bath *and* Glastonbury. During these negotiations, Savaric showed divided loyalties by acting as a hostage for Richard during the last stages of the negotiation at the same time as he was employed as the chancellor of the county of Burgundy for his cousin the Emperor.

On his return to England Savaric confirmed his possession of Glastonbury and informed the unhappy monks that he was their abbot. The monks appealed repeatedly to the Pope against this, encouraged at least once by a clearly angered Richard. Savaric won all his cases, but reinforced his position by particularly savage beatings of the monks who opposed him: one allegedly died. The legal arguments continued, the monks supported by the king, Savaric by the Pope. King John's accession in 1199 swung the balance, and in 1202 the monks surrendered. At this point, Savaric became a gracious lord, confirming the charter to Wells and protecting the cathedral plate in Bath from the collection for Richard's ransom. Both Wells and Glastonbury were given money grants and other privileges. In 1205 he was again in Rome, campaigning for Peter de Roche's claim as the Bishop of Winchester. He died there in August, but was brought back to Bath for burial in the cathedral.

Most medieval churchmen had to be tough and calculating characters to survive what was unashamedly a political career. Savaric seems to outdo them all in sheer brazen ambition and self-promotion, with not even a nod towards the more Christian aspects of his position. It is perhaps a little satisfying that all his schemes were undone after his death.

Joscelin of Wells (Trotman)

Joscelin was born at Wells into a remarkable family: his brother was Hugh of Lincoln, a great prelate of the thirteenth century. By 1203 he was senior enough in the church hierarchy to be one of the custodians of the see of Lincoln during a vacancy. From 1203–05 he was a senior judge at Westminster, and by this time held a canonry at Wells. In February 1206 he was elected Bishop of Bath and Glastonbury, in succession to Savaric. For a change there was no conflict between Bath and Wells in this election.

King John was in dispute with the Pope, and the quarrel became serious enough in 1208 for five bishops, including Joscelin to go into exile. He was one of those who attempted to negotiate a deal in 1209, but unsuccessfully. The dispute was resolved in 1213 and henceforward he served as one of the kings advisors. Joscelin is named in Magna Carta, and in 1216 he was present at the crowning of Henry III. He was one of the circuit judges for Somerset, Dorset, Devon and Cornwall in 1216, also the year the Glastonbury question was solved; Glastonbury's status was restored and the see reverted to Bath and Wells (as in theory it had been between 1176 and 1193, but not in practice).

In the 1220s the bishop held the royal castles in the diocese for the young king. He was involved in successive tribunals to settle ecclesiastical disputes in the west, and in 1234 had to deprive the abbot of Glastonbury for misconduct. He was increasingly focussed on the diocese in these later years, pushing forward the building of the cathedral, the bishop's palace, a manor at Wookey and a new hospital at Wells. He also much reformed and improved the institutional arrangements at Wells. Joscelin died at Wells in November 1242 ('full of days', he was probably born well before 1180), and was buried in the cathedral there.

The Buttons

Confusingly there were two Bishop William Buttons at Bath in the thirteenth century, uncle and nephew separated only by the short reign of William Giffard (to whom they were also related).

William I's family came from Bitton a few miles west of Bath. He was elected bishop early in 1247; later in the same year an earthquake severely damaged the new cathedral at Wells. Button was present at the parliament of 1253 which vainly sought to achieve free elections for bishops, and successfully confirmed the rights in Magna Carta. He went on an embassy for Henry to Castile but does not otherwise seem to have been much involved in affairs of state. He seems to have been quarrelsome in diocesan affairs, always attempting (but frequently failing) to extract some pecuniary advantage. He was more successful in promoting his family, and five of his close family obtained lucrative posts in the church, including his namesake and successor-but-one, William II, whom he started on his ecclesiastical career. William I died at Wells and was buried there in 1264.

William II was elected bishop in 1267. Despite his nepotistic ascent in the church he seems to have been a pious man, as different from his uncle as possible. When Robert Kilwardby, an ascetic friar, was about to be consecrated Archbishop of Canterbury he declared he would have no other than the Bishop of Bath at the ceremony on account of his 'eminent piety'. After his death he was seen as a saint by the local laity, and offerings were made at his tomb at Wells. The money was put to completing work on the cathedral. As late as the seventeenth century 'Saint' William was invoked for toothache in Somerset.

Robert Burnell

Burnell came from a knightly family who had made good in the dangerous but profitable marches of England and Wales in the late twelfth and early thirteenth century. The family seat was at Acton Burnell in Shropshire, which Robert inherited as the eldest survivor of four brothers, and to which he remained attached all his life, probably for dynastic and economic reasons as much as for any sentimental considerations. He entered the service of Prince Edward, later Edward I, and seems to have become a friend and companion as well as servant to him. Robert's church career saw him starting to collect offices, and his royal service was also lucrative. He accompanied Edward to France in 1260 and on the Welsh campaigns in 1263; in the same year he was adding to his lands in Shropshire; and in 1265 he was on diplomatic service into Wales.

In 1270 Edward and Robert both signed up for the Crusade of that year. Before he left, Edward made strenuous efforts to get his protégé elected as Archbishop of Canterbury. This was both astonishing and unrealistic: Burnell had only reached the heights of the archdeaconry at this point, and the Pope settled the dispute accordingly. Edward went to Palestine, but it is not clear if Burnell went with him: if he did he was back in England by later that year, as he was one of those acting as Edward's agent in England in his absence. When Henry III died in 1272 these agents became regents. Actually ruling the realm was rather tough but effective training for the post of Chancellor that Burnell received from the king on his return in 1274, a post he held for the rest of his life.

In 1275 he finally received his bishopric, becoming Bishop of Bath and Wells in January. Edward attempted once more to get Burnell promoted to Canterbury, and then when that failed to Winchester. In both cases, the Pope simply refused for unknown but obviously strong reasons to countenance any such promotion.

Burnell's civil career was more fruitful. His appointment to the Chancellorship coincided with a series of major legislative reforms which he is likely to have been instrumental in planning. He also fixed the Chancery in London rather than following the king, and greatly improved its efficient operation, although Burnell himself was constantly on attendance on the king or his business: we find him in Wales, France, then Scotland. His influence is difficult to detect clearly, but it has been claimed that Edward's policies in most respects became harder and less 'politic' after Burnell's death. His standing is seen in his involvement in all the king's Welsh and Scottish affairs, and especially in Prince Llewellyn's request that Burnell stand hostage for him when he visited Edward in London. His importance to the legal system is shown by its apparent collapse during his three year absence in France, 1286-9, and the reorganisation he undertook on his return. His personal significance to Edward is seen in his performance of the baptism of Edward's grandson Gilbert in 1291. Burnell died at Berwick-on-Tweed during negotiations with the Scots in October 1292. His body was brought back to Wells for burial.

Considering his constant employment on the king's business, and the rarity of his visits to Bath, Burnell was an active bishop. Building at Wells was underway, particularly the great hall at the palace, and much was done in increasing the wealth of the see. It is likely he rebuilt the palace at Bath as well.

Burnell's public persona seems reasonably attractive – but in private he was no better than other prelates. He was ever-eager to acquire wealth for himself and his family, and at his death he held estates in 19 counties and 82 manors. His plural holdings of church benefices added both to his wealth and to the problems he had with Archbishop Peckham, who was a from a poor order of friars and objected greatly to wealthy churchmen. Burnell's surviving brothers were killed fighting the Welsh but he passed on much of his wealth to his daughters, whom he married off to noblemen tempted by the inheritance. His legal heir was his nephew, who seems to have squandered his uncle's accumulations in one generation.

Burnell left little lasting in the material or spiritual fields, but he was the most outstanding national politician of all the bishops of Bath, making a major impact on the politics and legislative system of his day.

Ralph of Shrewbury

Ralph's date of birth is unknown, but he died old and infirm in 1363 so must have been born at the latter end of the thirteenth century, which makes it unlikely that he had been a prebendary at Salisbury in 1297 as has been reported. By 1328 he was Chancellor of Oxford University, and from there was elevated to Bath and Wells in 1329. However, the king had other ideas and although he was soon mollified, this led to a dispute where the Pope was not disposed to accept Ralph's election. It took much diplomacy and even more money (which is said to have impoverished the see) before the Pope relented.

Ralph was an active diocesan bishop, 'visiting' his see extensively in 1333. He insisted on reforms at several abbeys, and had a similar dispute with Wells as Drokensford previously had with Bath over irregularities he discovered in a visitation there in 1337. He was jealous of the see's rights, and a dispute with the town of Wells led to the revocation of their charter in 1343. He was active in general in the see's behalf and was largely responsible for the present form of the bishop's palace at Wells, and for ridding himself and his successors of the Bath palace. Ralph instituted the vicars college buildings at Wells, and largely completed the work on the east end of the cathedral there after 1338. He also instituted a lecture series to be given by the Chancellor, to increase knowledge of theology and church law. On a more practical level he secured the *disafforestation* of two of his Mendip manors, freeing his tenants from the terrors of forest law.

The central event of his reign was the Black Death. On hearing of its approach he ordered processions and services to avert the wrath of the Lord. In the absence of priests in many parishes through death or desertion, he authorised measures allowing clerks in minor orders, lay people, and even women to hear confession, and communion to be made by deacons. He presented 228 priests at this time, the greatest majority of whom would be replacements for plague victims. During this time Ralph stayed at his manor of Wiveliscombe, where he died in 1363. He was buried under an alabaster tomb in Wells Cathedral.

Thomas Bekynton

Bekynton (modern Beckington) was born around 1390, in the village 15 miles south of Bath whose name he bears. He was educated at Winchester from 1404 and went to New College, Oxford in 1406. His parentage is unknown but was obviously well-connected and wealthy. In 1420 he entered the service of the king's brother Duke Humphrey, and from here his career took off. He spent the next 20 years gathering church offices and benefices, and seems to have built up a reputation in church legal matters. He was much involved in several high-profile heresy cases, which had important political overtones at this time with the rise of Lollardy, and was the author of several important church documents.

Bekynton was also much involved in temporal matters. In the 1330s and '40s he went three times to France with embassies to negotiate over the French Wars, and was one of the hosts of an embassy from Armagnac. During this time he became the king's secretary and Lord Privy Seal. This success with the king led to his preferment to the see of Salisbury in 1443, but the incumbent refused to leave and Beckington was made Bishop of Bath and Wells instead (his predecessor there, John Stafford, being more easily persuaded to move by the carrot of the Archbishopric of Canterbury). Our cynical age is amused at the resulting confusion over bribes paid at Rome for the elevation to Salisbury being charged, after much confusion, to the see of Bath and Wells.

Bekynton's temporal career stalled after his elevation, although he was still present at Parliament in less important capacities from 1444-53. He obtained an exemption from attendance due to old age in 1452, which was confirmed in 1461 by Edward IV; and his main energies from here on seem to have been directed at building in Wells and (to a lesser degree) in Bath. His character is difficult to describe. He was unpleasant to those he was in conflict with, but kind and generous to his protégés. His skill in diplomacy is likely to have obscured his personality. Bekynton died in 1465 and was buried in a tomb he had built himself at Wells Cathedral.

Robert Stillingfleet

Stillingfleet was born near York some time before 1420. He was educated at Oxford, and was principal of Deep Hall (one of the precursors of colleges at Oxford) in 1442. In 1445 he became a canon at Wells, and was made chancellor by 1447. His ecclesiastical progression ran in parallel with a secular career, and by 1448 he was already involved in negotiations with Burgundy. Like many of his contemporaries he went office and benefice hunting, collecting an impressive collection of profitable holdings. He became Archdeacon of Wells in 1465. Politically aligned with the Yorkists in the Wars of the Roses, Stillingfleet was made Lord Privy Seal in 1460 and was well-positioned to prosper after the accession of Edward IV in 1461. In 1465 he was elected Bishop of Bath and Wells, and two years later he became Lord Chancellor. He fell from office on the short-lived restoration of Henry VI in 1471, but bounced back with Edward IV's successful counter coup in the same year. In 1475 he resigned the Chancellorship but later in the year was employed in negotiations to obtain the surrender of the Earl of Richmond, then living in exile in Brittany. This was a move with long-term consequences, as the earl was the future Henry VII who had a tenacious and unforgiving memory. Despite his service, Stillingfleet was imprisoned in the tower in 1478 for 'uttering words prejudicial to the king' and may have been involved in injudicious plotting with Richard of Gloucester, the future Richard III. Since his claim that he had married Edward to a woman before his marriage to the queen would have supported Richard's later claim that Edward's children were bastards, he was lucky to have escaped at all. The story is perhaps substantiated by his support for Richard after Edward's death, and his involvement in the declaration of the princes' illegitimacy.

His career ended with the accession of Henry in 1485. His diplomatic skills saved his skin; he was arrested but pardoned three months later. That he was an inveterate plotter is shown by his support for the rebellion of Lambert Simnel in 1487. He was arrested after its failure and imprisoned at Windsor, where he died in 1491.

Stillingfleet was a typical example of the late medieval great prelate more interested in political influence and power than religious works. Of his personal life we know less. We may not be surprised that he is said to have had a son, who was captured by the French and died in captivity. His reaction to this event is unknown.

Oliver King

Like so many of the bishops who rose to prominence from relatively humble origins, King's birth date is unknown. He was born in London and became a scholar of Eton in 1449 (implying that he must have been born around 1435), and was later a fellow of King's College, Cambridge. It is curious, or perhaps no coincidence, that his life was bound up with three of the great perpendicular gothic churches of England. He seems to have started his temporal career as secretary to Edward, Prince of Wales, who was killed in battle in 1471. In 1476 he had successfully negotiated the change in dynasty and became Edward IV's chief secretary in French for life. His church preferments were few at this stage and in 1480 he exchanged a prebend at Hereford for a canonry at Windsor, where he was registrar of the Order of the Garter. In 1482 he was made Archdeacon of Oxford, but on the accession of Richard III was sent to the Tower, and only released on the death of Richard, when he was reinstated as secretary by Henry VII. He was sent on an Embassy to the commissioners of Charles VIII of France, and again at a later date to enquire of the king's rights in his posses-sions in France.

King's connections with Windsor were obviously strong; in 1488 he was granted the reversion of a canonry there and was involved in setting up a Guild of the Holy Trinity in that town, a religious society that suggests he had at least a strong conventional piety. His connection with Bath and Wells began in 1489 when he became Archdeacon of Taunton. In 1492 he was made Bishop of Exeter, but seems never to have visited his see. His relationship with Henry was strong, and the king's favour is shown by the prominent rôle assigned to King in the cere-monies surrounding the creation of Prince Henry as Duke of York. In 1495 King was made Bishop of Bath and Wells.

It is uncertain whether he would have visited this see either unless political events had propelled him. Perkin Warbeck's rebellious army had landed in 1497 in Cornwall, and King accompanied Henry on his march against the rebels into Somerset, entering Wells in April of that year. He did not visit Bath until 1499. King's lack of either concern for the see or interest in Bath up to this point suggests that the story of a dream compelling him to rebuild the church may have some truth in it. He certainly rushed into things with a will once the decision to rebuild had been made.

King did not live to see the church finished, and Harington relates the story that he was much depressed by the death in 1502 of Henry's eldest son, Prince Arthur. Whether this is true or not, King died in August 1503, possibly at Bath. There is uncertainty about this and, curiously, about where he was buried. His will directs him to be interred in the north choir aisle at Bath, but a tomb appears to exist in the King chantry at St George's Chapel, Windsor, to where, as we have seen, he had close ties.

Appendix III
Pounds, shillings and pence

Sums of money have occasionally been quoted in pounds shillings and pence (£ s d). No attempt is made to give equivalent purchasing value, but some clarification is probably necessary for younger and perhaps foreign readers. Up until 1971 the pound sterling was divided up into 20 shillings (20/ or 20s). The shilling was divided into 12 pennies or pence. (12 d – the modern 'p' was invented to distinguish the new unit). Amounts of money were therefore expressed as £x ys zd. To complicate matters, the mark was often used, though not since the Middle Ages. This was two thirds of a pound or 13s 4d. Half of this was 6s 8d, and this, too, often figures as a sum in documents.

For conversion into modern currency (but not value), a shilling is equivalent to 5p and a penny to just over 0.4p. Pounds are the same. Thus Alexander the Dyer's tax assessment in 1340 of 13s 4d, or a mark, is 66.67p. Needless to say, such a sum would buy a very considerable amount more in his time than it would today. In the late fourteenth century $\frac{1}{4}$d would buy $1\frac{3}{4}$lb of apples: Alexander's tax assessment therefore would buy over half a ton (and apples were probably relatively more expensive then). Another comparison is that a free farmworker at that time would have to work for over four years to earn that much. Allowing for a small amount of inflation, we can begin to get a sense of the magnitude of Thomas Chancellor's cash worth of over £500 in the late 1400s, or the £300 *per annum* King reserved for rebuilding the abbey.

Bibliography

Arnold, C.J. 1984 *Roman Britain to Saxon England*. Indiana.

Aston, M. 1986 'The Bath Region from Late Prehistory to the Middle Ages', *Bath History* I, 61-89.

Bassett, S. 1989a 'Churches in Worcester Before and After the Anglo-Saxons.' *Antiquaries Journ.* 69, 225-56.

Bassett, S. (ed.) 1989b *The Origins of the Anglo-Saxon Kingdoms*. Leicester.

Bassett, S. 1992 'Church and Diocese in the West Midlands: The Transition from British to Anglo-Saxon Control' in J. Blair & R. Sharpe (eds) *Pastoral Care Before the Parish*, Leicester.

Bede (trans.) 1968 *A History of the English Church and People*. Trans. by Leo Sherley-Price, Penguin Classics.

Bell. R. 1996 'Bath Abbey: Some New Perspectives.' *Bath History* VI, 7-24.

Biddle, M. & Hill, D. 1971 'Late Saxon Planned Towns.' *Antiquaries Journal* LI, 70-85.

Blair, J. and Sharpe, R. (eds) 1992 *Pastoral Care Before the Parish*, Leicester.

Britton, J. 1825 *The history and antiquities of Bath Abbey Church*, London.

Bush, T.S. 1877, 79 & 80 'Churchwardens' accounts St Michael's Bath.' *PSANHS* vol xxiii, xxv & xxvi.

Campbell, J. 1991 *The Anglo Saxons*, London.

Chapman, M. 2000 'The development of the Saw Close from the Middle Ages' *Bath History* VIII, 56-79.

Chapman, M. *et al.* 1995 'The Precinct of the bishop's palace at Bath' *Archaeological Journal* 152, 95-108.

Chapman, M. *et al.* 1998 *The J. Charlton map of Lyncombe and Widcombe*, Bath.

Chapman, M. and Holland, E. 2000 *'Bimbery' and the Southwestern Baths of Bath*, Bath.

Coates, R. 1988 *Toponymic Topics*, Brighton.

Cochrane, L. 1991 *Adelard of Bath First English Scientist*, London.

Cunliffe, B. 1983 'Earth's Grip Holds Them' in Hartley & Wacher 1983.

Cunliffe. B. 1984 'Saxon Bath' in Haslam 1984.

Cunliffe. B. 1986 *The City of Bath*, Gloucester.

Cunliffe, B. 2000 *Roman Bath Discovered* 3rd edition, Stroud.

Cunliffe, B. & Davenport, P. 1985 *The Temple of Sulis Minerva at Bath,* Oxford.

Dark, K. R. 1994a *Discovery by Design: The Identification of Secular Elite Settlements in Western Britain AD 400-700*. Brit. Archaeol. Rep. Brit. Ser. 237, Oxford.

Dark, K. R. 1994b *From Civitas To Kingdom: British Political Continuity 300-800*, Leicester.

Dark, K.R. 2000 *Britain and the End of the Roman Empire,* Stroud.

Davenport, P. 1988 'Bath Abbey.' *Bath History* II, 1-26.

Davenport, P. (ed.) 1991 *Archaeology in Bath 1976-85*, Oxford.

Davenport P. 1996 'The Cathedral Priory Church at Bath' in Tatton-Brown & Munby, 19-30.

Davenport, P. 1999 *Archaeology in Bath: excavations 1984-89*. Brit. Archaeol. Rep. Brit. Ser. 284. Oxford.

Davenport, P. 2000 'Aquae Sulis: The Origins and Development of a Roman Town.' *Bath History* VIII, 1-26.

Eaton, T. 2000 *Plundering the Past. Roman stonework in medieval Britain*, Stroud.

Esmonde Cleary, A.S. 1989 *The Ending of Roman Britain*, London.

Faulkner, N. 2000 *The Decline and Fall of Roman Britain*, Stroud.

Galliou, P. & Jones, M. 1991 *The Bretons*, Oxford.

Gildas see Winterbottom 1978.

Green, E. 1889 'A Bath Poll Tax , 2, Richard II.' *Proc. of The Bath Nat. Hist. and Antiq. Field Club*, vol VI (3), 294-315.

Greening, P. 1971 'The Origins of the Historic Street Plan of Bath.' *A Second North Somerset Miscellany*, 7-16. Bath.

Grinsell, L.V. 1973 *The Bath Mint: An Historical Outline*, London.

Hamer, R. 1970 *A Choice of Anglo-Saxon verse,* London.

Hartley, B. & Wacher, J. 1983 *Rome and her Northern Provinces,* Gloucester.

Haslam, J. 1984 *Anglo Saxon Towns in Southern England,* Chichester.

Hill, D. 1969 'The Burghal Hidage: the establishment of a text' *Medieval Archaeology* 13, 92–4.

Hodges, R. 1982 *Dark Age Economics: The Origins of Towns and Trade A.D. 600-1000.* London.

Holland, E. 1988 'The Earliest Bath Guildhall' *Bath History* II, 163–180.

Holland, E. 1994 'The 1524 tax roll' *The Survey of Bath and District* vol. 1.

Holland, E. and Chapman, M. 2000 *Bath Guildhall and its neighbourhood: 800 years of local government,* Bath.

Holland, E. 2001 'This Famous City: The Story of the Chapmans of Bath' (for comments on the 1379 Poll Tax) *The Survey of Bath and District* vol 16, 33–34.

Hunt, W. 1893 *Two Cartularies of Bath priory,* Somerset Record Soc. 7.

Irvine, J.T. 1890 'Description of the Remains of the Norman Cathedral at Bath' *Journ. of the Brit. Archaeol. Assoc.* 1st Series, 46, 85–94.

Keen, M. 1983 *English Society in the Late Middle Ages 1348-1500,* London.

Keevil, A.J. 1996 The Barton of Bath. *Bath History* VI, 25–53.

Keevil, A.J. 2000 'Barrack(s) Farm, Wellsway, Bath: the estate and its holders' *Bath History* VIII, 27–55.

Keynes, S. (trans.) 1983 *Asser's Life of King Alfred.*

King, E. 1988 *Medieval England 1066-1485,* London.

Leach, P. 1991 *Shepton Mallet: Romano-Britons and Early Christians in Somerset,* Birmingham.

Manco, J. 1993 'The Buildings of Bath Priory'. *Proc. Somer. Archaeol. & Natur. Histor. Soc* 137, 75–109.

Manco, J. 1998 'Saxon Bath' in *Bath History* vol VIII, 27–54.

Manco, J. 1998a *The Spirit of Care,* Bath

O'Leary, T. 1981 'Excavations at Upper Borough Walls, Bath in 1980' *Medieval Archaeology* XXV, 1–30.

Pearce, S. (ed.) 1982 *The Early Church in Western Britain and Ireland.* Brit. Archaeol. Rep. Brit. Ser. 102. Oxford.

Platt, C. 1978 *Medieval England. A social history and archaeology from the Conquest to 1600AD,* London.

Rahtz, P. 1991 'Pagan and Christian by the Severn Sea.' in L. Abrams & J. Carley (eds) *The Archaeology and History of Glastonbury Abbey,* 3–38, London.

Rahtz, P. *et al.* 1992 *Cadbury Congresbury 1968-73: A Late/Post-Roman Hilltop Settlement in Somerset.* Brit. Archaeol. Rep. Brit. Ser. 223, Oxford.

Rahtz, P. 1993 *English Heritage Book of Glastonbury,* London.

Rahtz, P., Wright, S. & Hirst, S. 2000 *Cannington,* London.

Shickle, C.W. 1921 *Ancient Deeds of Bath,* Bath Records Society.

Sims-Williams, P. 1974 'Continental influence at Bath monastery in the seventh century.' *Anglo-Saxon England* 4, 1–10.

Steane, J. 1984 *The Archaeology of Medieval England and Wales,* Athens, Georgia.

Stenton, F. 1971 *Anglo-Saxon England,* London.

Tatton-Brown, T & Munby, J. 1996 *The Archaeology of Cathedrals,* Oxford.

Victoria County History of Somerset, esp vol II.

Watts, L. & Leach, P.J. 1996 *Henley Wood, Temples and Cemetery Excavations 1962-1969 by the late Ernest Greenfield and others,* York

Welch, M. 1992 *Anglo-Saxon England,* London.

Whitelock, D. 1959 *The Beginnings of English Society,* Pelican History of England vol 1, London.

Whitelock, D. *et al.* (trans.) 1961 *The Anglo-Saxon Chronicle.*

Wilson, D. 1971 *The Anglo-Saxons,* London.

Winterbottom, M. 1978 *De excidio Britonum,* 22, in Gildas, *The Ruin of Britain and Other Works,* London.

Woodward, A. & Leach, P.J. 1993 *The Uley Shrines: Excavation of a Ritual Complex on West Hill, Uley, Gloucestershire 1977-79,* London.

Ziegler, P. 1998 *The Black Death,* London.

Index

Entries in **bold** refer to figures

21 High Street 137, 142, **63, 64**
abbey(s) 165, 31, 34, 36, 37, 40, 43, 44, 47, 49, 51-3, 57, 60, 64-9, 71, 72, 74, 88, 89, 91, 94, 108, 132, 166, **16, 27**
abbey church 34, 69, 54, 75, 79, 95, 159, 166, 169, 171
Abbey Church House 100, 142
abbey churchyard 89, **26**
abbey gate 147, 169, 77, 89
Abbey Green 79, 89
Abbey House 158, **68**
Abbey Orchard 115, 128
Abbey Street 66, 90
Abbeygate Street 21, 22, 66, 77, 79, 89, 131, 169
abbot(s) 40, 56, 94, 67, 69, 71, 109, 153, 158, 168
Abbot's Bath 109
Abbot Feckenham 170
accountant 104, 114
accounts 110, 112, 145
Acemannesceastre 24
Achamanni 24
Acton Burnell 152
Adam le Muleward 104
Adam the Barber 105
Adam the Blacksmith 112
Adam the Tanner 110
Adam Whiteson 104, 102
Adelard(us) 85, 90, 91, 91
Adriano de Castello 163, **72**
Ægelmær (II), monk 67
Ægelmær, monk 67
Ægelric, monk 67
Ægelwine, monk 67
Ælfheah 61
Ælfmær, monk 67
Ælfric, monk 67, **24**
Ælfsige 67, 69, 71
Ælfwig 67
Æscwig 61
Æthelferth, moneyer 51
Æthelmær 62
Æthelræd Unræd (Unready) 51, 64, 66, 60, 61, 62, 63
Æthelric, moneyer 51
Æthelwald 57
Æthelwold 57, 58
Aethelwulf 39
Æthesyge, moneyer 51
Agnes Cold 120

Agnes Cubbel 153, 154
Agnes 104
Akeman Street 24
Aldermen 156, 157
Alexander the Dyer 102, 104, 107, 112, 142
Alfred (reeve) 48, 97
Alfred, king of Wessex 50, 39, 40, 41, 48, 57, 62, 126, 130, 146
Alfred's successors 41
Alfredian 42, 49, **12**
Alice 104, 117
All Saints 49, 65
almoner 141
almshouses 116, 119, 120, 125, 146
Alron's Bath 104, 109
Alsi's bath 69
altar 16, 86
Alured 70
Ambrosius Aurelianus 20
Ambry 128
ambulatory 83
Amicia 104
amphorae, mediterranean 17
Anarchy 91
angels 159, 160
Angles 67
Anglo-Saxon Chronicle 26, 19, 62
Anglo-Saxon England 37, 38
annual fairs 109
apostles **38**
apprentice 104
Aquae Sulis 19, 13,15, 20, 24, 37
Aquaemann 24
Aquaemannia **8**
Aquamania 24
Arabic 90
arcade piers 164
archaeology 63, 75, 123, 126
Archbishop 38, 58, 93
Archdeacon 94
architects 160, 163
architectural fragments 19, 88
archives 100
aristocracy 80
Armorica 20
arms 163
army workshops 16
Arnold, physician 115
artefacts 109, 110
artificer(s) 110, 105, 112, 114, 133, 156
artists 90
ashlar 58, **17, 21**
Asia Minor 31
astrolabe 90
astrologer 90
astronomy 90
Athelney 40
Augustinian 28, 117
Avon 28, 29, 35,107, 115, 147-8
Aylmer the Weaver 108

BAÐ mint mark 50
Baðan (Baðon, Baðum) 24, 50
bailiff 97, 99
bakehouse (baker, baking) 89, 102, 105, 139
baptistery 33
barbarians 19
Barbury 26
barley 115
barn 141
Barnsley Park 25
baron(s) 131, 152
barracks 22
Barton Farmhouse 97
Barton Lane 26, 37, 49, 60, 63, 67, 69, 97, 99, 115, 129, 130, 132
Bath and Glastonbury 94
Bath Hundred **42**
Bath mill 107
Bath of Bathes Ayde 170
Bath Street 19, 22, 44, 69, 109, 146
bath suites 23
Bathampton 38, 25, 57, 70, 99, 112
Bath-bridge 148
Batheaston 107, 120, 70
Bathford 57, 70, 99
bathing 36,109, 117
baths 13, 16, 22, 24, 32, 34, 36, 149, 170
Bathwick 70, 130, 132
Beacon Hill 115
Bear Flat 19, 49, 65, 102
Beckington/Bekyngton 109, 157
Bede 19, 28, 32, 36, 108
bedesman 119
Beechen Cliff 133, 147
Beehive Yard 74
beer 148
beggars 156
Bell Tree Lane 49
bells 92, 110, 120, 137
Benedict Hercy 110
Benedictine 58, 70, 88, 109
benefactors 118
Beornwyth 31
bequest(s) 107, 118, 119, 137
Berewick 110, 102
Bernard Lens 133, **58**
Bernguida 31
Berta 31-2, 34
Betriche Marleward 104
Bilbury/Bimbury Lane 44, 49, **13**
Bimbery/Binbury 44, 49, **10**
binnanburh 49
Biorhtulf, moneyer 51
Bird 166
bishop(s) 71, 80, 92-5, 97, 99, 109, 115-7, 128, 137, 148-9, 152-6, 158-9
Bishop John's hall 151, **32**
Bishop of Bath and Wells 94

Bishop of Bath 70-1
Bishop of Durham 70, 152
Bishop of Wells 71
Bishop of Worcester 35, 153
Bishop's Bower/hall 64, 79, 90
bishop's close 152
bishop's court 89
bishop's palace 74, 77, 79, 89, 109, 132, 148, 151, 155, **33, 30**
bishopric 93
Bishops of Sherbourne 71
bishops' tombs 164
Black Alms 119
Black Death 105, 116, 119, 120, 154, 156
blacksmith 13
Bligh Bond 75, **27**
boarding 146
Bomdyche 148
bondsmen 154
bone 22, 88, 109
bookbinders 114
borough walls 132, 141
boundary(ies) 97, 129
Brade Street 133
Bradford-on-Avon 30, 58, 157
brassicas 141
Brentford, Synod of 35
bressumer 144
brethren 35, 109, 117
Bretwalda, 38
brewers 105
brewhouse(s) 89, 148
Bridewell Lane 138, 141
bridge 133, 147
Bridgewater 25
Brihtwold 67
Bristol 91, 102, 107-8, 110, 129, 133, 142, 153, 169
Bristolians 92
Britain 17, 83
Britannia 15, 19
British zone 26
British/Britons 19, 26, 28, 30
Brittany 25, 30
Broad Street 47, 108, 112, 132, 141-2
broadcloth 132
bronze buckle 16
Brunel 134
Bubwith 158
building(s) 86, 123, 137, 141, 144, 146, 148, 151, 163
Bull Garden **31**
Bum Ditch 148
burgage plot 116
burgess(es) 51, 69, 89, 92, 97, 104, 120, 132
Burghal Hidage 40-2, 51, **11**
Burhs 40, **11**
burial ground(s) 77, 88-9, 128
burial(s) 54, 65, 86, 89, 86, 90, 116, 151, 171

Burleigh 170
Burnell see Robert Burnell
buttress(es) 84, 151

Cadbury Castle 25
Cadbury Hill, Congresbury 25, 29
Cadbury 30
candlemakers 114
Cannington 25
canon(s) 71, 93, 95, 117, 151
Canterbury 50, 62, 85, 94, 148, 158
capital messuage 100
capitalist 152
cardinal's hat 163, **71**
Carfax, Oxford 43
Carpenters 110
cathedra 93
Cathedral Close 42, 44, 74, 77, 129, 149, 155, 169
cathedral library 115, 167
cathedral precinct 44
cathedral priory 35, 71-2, 74, 89, 92, 120, 132, 149
cathedral school 91
cathedral(s) 31, 72, 74, 80, 85-6, 88-90, 102-3, 108, 112, 120, 134, 137, 151, 157-8, 163-4, 169, 171, **34-6, 38, 73**
cathedral, Exeter 13
cattle 115
causeway 133, 146
Ceawlin 26, 28
celeberrimus monasterium 35
cellar(s) 100, 128, 139, 142, 145, 148
cellarage 142
cemetery(ies) 25, 28, 77, 86, 88-9, 116
Cenwalh 30
Ceolwulf 40
cesspits 141
chamberlain 153
chancel 80, 152, 158, 166
Chancellor 99, 120, 152
chantry chapel 166, **75**
chapel(s) 47, 89-90, 99, 100, 116-9, 137-8, 151-2, 155-6, 158, 165-6
chaplain 117, 153
Chapman 157
chapter house 74
Chapter 155
charcoal burials 53
charity 119, 120
Charlemagne 38
Charmy Down 24
charter 31, 35-6, 92, 98, 109, 165, 170, **41**
Chaucer 103, 108
Cheap Street 44-5, 54, 65, 72, 77, 109, 114, 138, 142, 157, **26, 14**
Cheddar 38, 57, 60
Chelles 31

children 88
Chippenham 40
choir 83, 86, 88, 158, 163-4, 171
Christianity 15, 25
Christians 15, 120
church porch 103
church(es) 47, 74, 80, 83-4, 86, 88-90, 92, 95, 97, 99, 109, 115-6, 119-120, 137, 146-7, 151-4, 157-160, 163-4, 166, 169-171
churchwardens 110, 112, 114, 139, 146
churchyard 90, 148, 171
cider 141
circular bath 36-7
Cirencester 13, 20, 26, 28
cistern 133
cithara 91
Citizen House 21-2
citizens 92, 99, 104, 108, 114, 116, 120, 131, 134, 148-9, 169
city 97, 99, 116, 120, 126, 128, 132, 152, 169-171
city ditch 132-3
city fathers 169-170
city gates 32, 72, 120, 129, 149
city wall(s) 15, 32, 44, 83, 99, 108, 112, 126, 128, 137, 141, 148, **54, 55**
civic centre 13
civil war 91-2, 126, 134, 152, 171
civitas dobunnorum 22, 26, 28
civitates 19-20
claustral buildings 166
Claverton Down 80
clergy 89, 105, 107
cleric 117, 152
cloister(s) 74-5, 77, 85-6, 88-9, 148, 154, 166, 169, **29**
Clopcote 153
cloth trade etc 55, 99, 102, 105, 107-9, 112, 114, 132, 137, 156-7, 171
clothes 148
clothiers 157
Cnut 63-4, 66
cock loft 144
Cockes, Cox 156
cofferers 98
coffin cover, stone 65
coinage/coins 17, 37
Cold Ashton 57
coliberti 68, 69
Combe Down 70
commerce 99, 145
commercial activity 55-6
commissioners 167, 169
commonality 92, 137
commons 115
community 13, 58, 89, 117, 168

conduit(s) 24, 147-8
Congresbury 25
consecration 88, 166
Constantine I 15
Constantine III 16, 19
continuity 32
convent 13, 31-2, 34-5
cooking pots 57
cooking 148
cordwainers 99
Corn Street 109, 139
Cornish 39
Cornmarket 109
Cornwall 17, 20, 25
coronation of Edgar 58, 60, 63
Corporation 89, 92, 120, 137-8, 146-7, 170
Corrody(ies) 115, 153-4
Corston 57
Cotswolds 99, 107
cottages 119, 125, 142, 146
Council of London 71
Counter's Tower 131
country estates 25
country houses 13
court(s) 91, 97-8, 120
covered markets 128
Cox (Cockes) Lane 141
Craft guilds 99
craftsmen 105, 112, 114
Cross Bath 46, 69, 104, 108-9, 112, 116, 129, 139, 146, 148, 170
cross heads 64, **23**
crossing (of cathedral) 80, 83, 154, 166, **67, 68**
Crown 152
crown 159, **69**
Crusade(s) 92, 103, 154
crypt 77, 85
Crystal Palace public house 66, 90
Culverhouse Lane 139
culvert(s) 80, 109, 131
Cuna 70
curfew 120
curia 85

Danegeld 62-4
Danes 40, 57
Dark Ages 16-7
dark earth 22-1, 32
daughters 105
David de Berewyk 99
David, son of Goldriana 97
de Berewyks 102, 107
De Eodem et Diversa 90-1
de Westons 102
Dean 156
Death and taxes 104
death rate 105
debts 153
dedications 47
deed(s) 103, 125, 132, 137, 141-2, 145, 156
Deerhurst 61

defences 26, 51, 83, 126, 131, **54, 55, 56, 57**
demesne 115, 117
demolition 34, 132, 160, 169
Deorham 20, 26
destruction 169
Devon 25
diet, high status 80
dill 141
diocese 95, 99, 107, 120, 151-2, 163, 169
Diocletian 15
Dissolution 31, 35, 66, 123, 156-7, 164, 166
ditch 13, 42, 131
Dobunni 26, 28, 31
Domesday (Book) 32, 48, 68-70, 107, 116, 132
doomsday 166
Dorchester 39
dormitory 86, 89, 157, 169
dovecote 138
Dover 97
dower 103
Dr Layton 167
drain(s)/drainage 24, 148, **26**
draper 105
drapery 108
dream 159-160
dues 120, 129
Duke of Kingston 79, 147, **31**
Duke of Somerset 156
Duke 105, 114
Dumnonia 25
Dundry Hill 29
Dunstan 57-8, 60-1
Dunster 107, 118, 153, 168
dye 138
dyers 104-5
dyestuff(s) 107-8
dynasties 158
Dyrham 20, 26

Eabae 28
Eadgyvu 53, **17**
Eadric, monk 67
Eadwig, monk 67
Eafe, see Eabae
ealdormen 35, 66
Eanulf, ealdorman 67
Earl of Devon 156
Earldoms 66
early church 32
earthen bank 13-4
earthquake 90
East Anglia, Great Army in 39
east end 160, 164-6
east gate 37, 44, 72, 100, 130, **26, 57**
east window 160, 165, **70**
Easter 114, 120
Ecgbryht 39
economic basis 16

economic crisis 154
economy 109
Edelina 103
Edith 67, 69
Edmund Colthurst 169
Edmund Ironside 64
Edmund, ealdorman 67
Edstan, moneyer 51
Edward I 99, 152
Edward III 130-1
Edward the Confessor 66, 85
Edward the Elder 50, 57
Edward, weaver 108
elder 55
election 94, 153
Elias the Grocer 105, 109
Ellen de Bathon 104
elm 114, 145
Empire Hotel 42, 72, 128
empire, under attack 15
emporia 37
endowment 118, 120
England 30, 39, 90, 105,
    152, 160, 164
English architecture 163
English settlement of Severn
    Valley 28
entrepreneurs 99
epidemic 105
episcopal palaces 95
episcopate 91
estates 25
Eston 70
Ethelnoth 67
Ethelweard, ealdorman 67
Euclid 90
eweflocks 115
excavation(s) 13, 34, 75, **77**,
    79, 85, 88-90, 110, 112,
    115, 128, 130-1, 133,
    141-2, 146, 151, 154,
    156, 166, 169, **28, 29**
excommunicated 152
Exe, river 42
Exeter 13, 41-2, 156

Façade of the Four Seasons,
    used as paving 14
Fair(s) 74, 97, 109, 116, 149
falconry 90-1
fallow deer 80
fan vaults 164
Farleigh 154
farms 24
farrier(y) 112, 131
Fastrad 91
feasting 158
fee farm 99
fees 115
Felicia Yewell 139
fennel 141
feudal 103, 152, 154
fields 24
fine 91
fire 88
fire-reddening 88
fish 115

fishponds 115, 131
Flanders 58
Fleury 58
Folcburg 32
Fons Sulis, 32
fontem 133
food 22, 109
footings 164, 166
ford(s) 110, 133
Forda 70
Foreign Hundred 97, **43**
forest laws 103
forinsecum 97, **43**
fortifications 92
forts 40
Fosse Dyke 42
foundation(s) 86, 89, 112,
    146, 158, 160, 171
fountain(s) 147, 149
fowl houses 89
fowl 115, 139
France 142, 160
Frankia 31
freehold 145
French pottery 110
Freshford 64, 70
friars 168
Frocester Court 25
Frogge Lane 132
Froggmere 132
Frome 117, 157
frontage(s) 133, 137-8,
    141-2, 145
fruit 115, 141
frumenty 114
fuller 104, 105
fullers' earth 112
fulling 107-8

Galen 115
game birds 80
gaol 131
garden(s) 114, 116, 119, 128,
    139, 141, 146, 156, 169
garlic 141
garret 144
Gascoine's tower 131
gate(s) 92, 126, 130-1, 134,
    138
Gaul 24
Gaunt 108
Geoffrey of Bath 103
Geoffrey Talbot 91-2
geometry 85, 90
Georgian 123, 130, 133-4,
    142, 171
Geraint, king of Dumnonia
    29
Gesta Stephani 86, 108
giant's work 28
Gibbs 166-8
Gilbert Scott 164
Gildas 19-20, 25
Gilmore 123, 133-4, 138,
    148, 154, **52**
Giso, death of 71
glass 13, 145-6, 164

Glastonbury 25, 29-30, 54,
    58, 75, 94, 99, 151, 168
Gloucester 20, 26, 35
Gloucestershire 153
glovemaker 110
Godfrey, carpenter 146
Godwin, Earl of Wessex 66-7
Godwine, monk 67
Goldriana 97
gospel books 67
Gothic 163
governance 92, 156
governors 92
Grapes Inn 138
grave markers 52, **17**
graveyard 86, 137
Great Bath 23, 36
great chamber 154
great court 89, 131,
    142, 153
Greek 90
grid 43
grist 107
guest house 154
Guild(s) 92, 97-9, 102-3,
    107, 120, 152, 157,
    169, 170
Guildhall 100, 137, **44**
guildsmen 98, 100, 156
Gunkel 63
Gunnar 63
Gunnilda 104
Gyldehall 100

Hærlewine, monk 67
half-timbered 89
hall(s) 79, 95, 100, 139,
    141, 145, 152, 155
Ham Gate 108, 128,
    131, 148
Ham Green 110
Ham 115, 128-9, **51**
Hameswell 153
Hampshire Wiltshire border
    20
Hamtona 70
Hamwic, see Southampton
Harold Godwinsson, Earl of
    Wessex, 67
Hartley Farm 24
Hastings, battle of 67
Hat Bathu 31, **10**
hats 110
hawks 167
healing 86, 170
hearths 64
Heathored 35
Helgi 63
Henley Wood 25
Henry Gervase 103
Henry Hurel 104
Henry I 91
Henry III 152
Henry Marshall 112
Henry Peytevin 103
Henry the Smith 105
Henry the Tailor 98, 102

Henry VII 156, 158-9
Henry VIII 166-7
Henry Wells 120
Henry, goldsmith 108
heraldic bosses **72**
herbarium 141
herbs 141
heresy 120
Herewis, moneyer 51
Hexham, 33-4
hides 110
Hiedewulf, monk 67
high altar 88
High Street 43, 45-6, 97,
    102, 109, 138-9, 141,
    144, 147, 170, **14**
Hildebert, at Wells 71
Holloway 117, 133,
    148, 166
Honorius 16, 19
horn 109
horses 139
horseshoes 80
horticulture 74
Hospital of St John 108
Hospital of St Mary
    Magdalen 102, 118, 158
hospital of the baths
    109, 116
hospital(s) 117-9, 170, **49**
Hot Bath 46, 69, 116, 129,
    141, 148, 170
hot baths 33, 109
hot spring(s) 16, 36, 74, 86,
    108, 116
hot water 13, 117, 148
house(s) 11, 13, 39, 142,
    144-6
households 116
Hugh de Dover 152
Hugh Galopin 141
Hugh of Lincoln 118
hulk 171
Humphrey Colles 169
Hun, ealdorman 67
hundred 48, 97-8, 104
hundred court(s) 48, 103
Hundred, Foreign 26, 32,
    48-9, **43**
hundred of Bath 132
Hundred of la Buri 97
hunting dog 80
Hwicce 28, 31

Iford 154
imports 110
Improvements 123, 137
incumbent 152, 171
independence 152
industrial town 16
industry 107, 171
infirm 117
infirmary 74, 86, 116-7
inheritance 97
inhumation 89
inner precinct of temple 14
innkeepers 156

gnia 163
sulae 43
terlaced style 64
vestment 110, 139
pswich 37
reland 94, 152, 167
rish possessions 152
ron knife 22
iron slag 146
Iron working 55
ironworkers 146
Irvine, James 75, 83, 85, 112, 154, 166, **37**
Isabel Mill 108, 148
Isabella 88, 92, 103
Italy 107

Jacobean 97
jettied 144
Joan de Salsomarisco 139
John Champflour 139
John Cole 139
John de Bathon 115
John de Berewyk 103
John de Combe 102
John de Dover 98
John de Drokensford 152, 154
John de Iford 153
John Dunster 139
John Fayrechild 145
John Fowler 114
John Geffery 156-7
John Harington 159
John Jones 170
John Le Veniur 102
John Natton 105
John of the Gate 98
John of Tours 67, 70-2, 74, 79-80, 83, 85-6, 88, 91, 93-4, 108-9, 118, 126, 130, 132, 137, 146, 151, 164-5, **28, 34, 35, 36, 38**
John Pistor 102
John the Innkeeper 102
John the Plumber 114
John Wi(y)ssy 102, 119, 138
John Wood 128, 129
John, Prior 71, 102
Johnson 125, **53**
joiners 114
Joscelin Trotman 94-5, 151
journeyman 104, 145
Juliana Jay 103
jury 99
Justice of the Peace 156
Justiciar 70

Kelston 26, 159
Kent 39, 157
Keynsham 67, 133
keys 112
king 71, 92, 97, 99, 103, 120, 128, 154, 167, 169
King 158-9, 163, 166, **73**
King Æthelbald 35
King Æthelwulf 39

King Alfred (see Alfred)
King Athelstan 50-1, 57, 60
King Beornulf 38
King Burhred 38-40
King Cenwulf 38
King Ceolwulf 38
King Charles II 151
King Cynegils 28
King Eadred 58
King Eadwig 58, 60
King Ecgbryht 38
King Edgar 24, 58, 60, 62-3
King Edmund 60
King Edward (the Confessor) 68
King Edward (the Elder) 57, 60
King Edward's School 170
King Henry I 74, 79, 97
King Henry II 93
King Henry VI 156
King Henry VIII 74
King John 95, 131
King Offa 35
King Osric 26, 28, 31
King Richard I 80, 94, 97
King Richard II 108
King Stephen 86, 91-2, 126, 129
King's Bath 32-3, 36-7, 44, 65, 69, 72, 74, 77, 79, 86, 90, 108-9, 137, 146, 148, 170 **25, 26, 39, 40**
King's Bath spring 47
king's lodging 90, 99
Kingsmead 99
Kingston Estates map 123
kitchen 89, 100, 153

laborar(i) 105, 112
labourers 156
ladders 92
Lady Chapel 151, 165
Lady Gundreda 104
landowner 145
Lanfranc 85
Lansdown 109, 115, 117
Late Antiquity 15
Latin 90
latitude 90
lavatories 148
lavatorium 148
lawsuit 157
lazars 170
lead pipes 147
lead 114, 169
lease(s) 112, 125, 137-9, 145
leat 148
leather 109, 110
legislation 107
Leland 74, 79, 109, 128, 134, 147-8, 156-7, 164, 166, 170
Leofwig, monk 67
Leper(s)/leprosy 109, 118-9, 170
Leuthere 31

Lincoln 85
Lindinis 25
Lindisfarne 39
linen smoother 55, **19**
linen 105
Little Orchard Street 128
living quarters 139, 141, 145
loans 108
Locking 117
locks 112, 145-6
locksmiths 114
lodgings 155, 170
Lollardy 120
London 13, 37-8, 50, 62-3, 92, 129
loom weight 55, **19**
looms 132
lord of the manor 97
Lot Gate 72, 100, 130
Lot Lane 72, 128-9
Lower Borough Walls 49, 137
Lower Common 13
Lower Pitts 110
ludgeat 130
Lundenwic, see London
Lyncombe 109, 115

Magna Carta 120
main streets 144
maintenance 114
Malmesbury 41
Manor(s) 47, 99, 153-4
manual workers 112
manufacture/ing 105, 109
manumission of slaves 68
manuscripts 67
map(s) 123, 125, 137, 147-8, 154
Margaret Little 103
marjoram 141
market(s) 37, 72, 97, 107, 109, 116, 138, 149, 169-170
marriage(s) 103
mason(s) 110, 154, 160, 166
masonry 144, 165
masses 117
Master Edward 119
Master Eustace 138
master plan, of city 48, **26**
Master Roger, *medicus* 115
Master 117, 157
Mathilda of Champfleur 103
Matilda 91-2
Matthew Colthurst 169
Mayor and Commonality 99-100, 120, 169
Mayor (of Bath) 92, 100, 102, 104-5, 107, 112, 114, 119, 148, 153, 156-7
Mayor of Bristol 102
mayoral lists 107
Mayor-making 100
mead halls 22
medicine 70, 115, 141
medieval villages 24

medieval, sites in northern Europe 22
Mediterranean 25
mendicants 105
Mendips 69
merchant(s) 92, 97, 99, 100, 102, 107, 142, 156
merchant-moneyers 56
Mercia 28, 38-41, 57, 60
Mercians 28, 36
messuage 112
middle men 107
migration of Britons 20
Miles Dennison 79
mill 69
millkeeper 104
Milsom Street 63
minister 167, 170
ministri 91
minor orders 91
minster(s) 34-5
Mint 50, 57, 69, 92
mira fabrica 58
mistress 153
mitre 152
moat 42, 131
Model Parliament 152
monarchs 131
monastery(ies) 25, 34-5, 40, 57-8, 85, 88-9, 91, 94, 99, 103, 117-8, 152, 153-4, 158, 167-8
monastic cemetery 86
monastic community 69
monastic houses 32
monastic precinct(s) 72, 99, **26**
monastic property 170
monastic reform 58
monastic town 49
money 99, 152
moneyers 50-1, 92
monk(s) 31, 37, 40, 53, 67, 74, 86, 88-9, 91, 95, 107-8, 115-7, 131, 148-9, 152-4, 157-8, 167-8
Monks' Mill 72, 107-8, 130, 148, **26**
Monmouth 134
Monnow 133
Mons Badonicus 20
Moorish civilization 90
moral condition 158
mosaic(s) 13-4
MP 119, 156, 169
Mule Street 147
mules 139
mummers 114
murder 102
musician 90
mustard 141
mysteries 85

nave 80, 83, 85, 89, 134, 152, 160, 164, 166, 169, 171
Nennius 32, 36

nettles 55
New Bond Street 51
Newtonian 90
niches 88
Nicholas de Dyer 104
Nicholas Lavender 139
Nigel Pontarius 133
night soil 141, 146
Norman arch **74**
Norman(s) 72, 75, 80, 84, 112, 151, **27, 30**
Normandy 62, 66
Norsemen 37, 39, 62
north gate 37, 44, 72-3, 104, 108-9, 112, 129, 131-2, 137, 148
North Parade Passage 89
North Sea 19
north transept 84
north Wales 20
north wall 130
Northampton 94
Northumberland Passage 145
Norton St Philip 120
Nottingham 39
Nowhere Lane 116
nuns 34

occupation(s) 104-5, 132-3
Odierna 103
Odo 71
Offa 35-8, 57-8
Olaf Tryggvason 61-2
Old Bridge 133-4
Old Orchard 115
Old Palace Yard 79
Old Pallace 79
Old Sarum 26
olive tree 159, **69**
Oliver King 158, 166
open field system 115
Orange Grove 80, 88-9
oratory 133
Ordgar, ealdorman 67
Osric 35
Oswald 57, 58, 67
outlawry 102
outwork 131
oven 139
Oxford 41, 51, 72
Oxfordshire 20

paddocks 132
pagan worship 14
palace 22, 72, 77, 89-90, 95, 99, 137, 151-2, 156
palatium 38
paragon 90-1
parchment 110
Paris 31
parish boundary 129
parish church(es) 47, 65, 114, 120, 134, 149, 170-1
parish(es) 35, 47, 97, 105, 134, 137, 146, 148, 171
parishioners 89, 99, 151
parks 117

Parliament 102, 152, 169
Parret, river 30, 67
pasture 99, 117
patients 119
patron saint 33
patron(ess) 88
paving 166, **3, 4, 7**
Paynestwichene 139, 141, **62**
pears 141
Peasants' Revolt 154
Penda, king of Mercia 28-9
pennant sandstone 23
Penselwood 30
pension 115, 153, 167-8
Petre 168
pewter 13
physician(s) 115, 170
pig(s) 22, 139, 146
pigeon 138-9
pigsties 89
Pillory Lane 112
piped water 149
pitchers, beer or wine 57
Place of Water 24
plague 28, 107
planks 145
planning 43, 137
plasterers (ing) 110, 114, 146
play 114
players 114
Plum Tree Lane 138, 141
plumber 114
Plumtreostwichene 141
podium 33
politics 94, 166
Poll Tax 105, 108, 110, 112, 116, 133, 141-2
pontiff 93
pontifical insignia 152
Pope 68, 88, 93-5, 151-2
population 69, 105, 107, 116, 132, 147
Porchester 41-2
porter 89
Portishead 110
Portland Bay 39
post Roman sites 22
postern 130
post-medieval 147
post-Roman 22, 86
Pottery 17, 22, 57, 74, 110, 132, 142, 147
poverty 116, 142
precinct 13, 22
pre-Dissolution 170
prelate 74
priest(s) 105, 120
prior(s) 67, 80, 99, 107, 109, 115, 117, 126, 132-3, 146-7, 149, 151-9, 166-8, 170
Prior Bird 163, 166, **72**
Prior Cantlow 119, 158
Prior Holloway 157
Prior John Dunster 157-8
Prior Park 80

Prior Robert 152
Prior Thomas Crist 155
Prior Walter 94
Prior William Southbrook 154
Prior's Bath 109
Prior's Kitchen 115
prior's lodging 85, 109, 154, 158, 166, 169, **29, 68**
priory 72, 74, 77, 85, 88-9, 99, 107-9, 112, 115-6, 118, 120, 123, 128-9, 131, 134, 137, 141-2, 147, 151-8, 166, 168-9
Priston 57
private chapels 47
privies 148
professional classes 114
professions 104
property(ies) 103, 105, 110, 116, 118-9, 123, 125, 132, 137, 141, 146, 167, 169
property boundaries 125-6, 131, 137
property deeds 103
Provost 71
Pucklechurch, royal palace 60
Pulteney Bridge 107
Pump Room 53
purbeck marble 152
Purgatory 120

Quaestiones Naturales 90
Quarr Ground 110
quarries 74, 110, 112, **46**
Queen Elizabeth I 170
queen 91, 170
Queen's Bath 170

Rack Street 137
racks 137
radiocarbon dating 51
Ralph 116, 153
Ralph le Hoper 104-5
Ralph the Taylor 104
Ralph 92, 108
Rampires 137
ransom 94, 103
Ranulf Flambard 70
rebellion(s) 71, 74, 152, 154
rebuilding 74, 119, 157-160
rebus 160, **69**
reconquista 91
reconstruction 77, 83, 100
Rector of Stalls 137
rectores 20
reeves 39, 48, 51, 57
refectory 74, 89, 142, 157-8, 169
reform 166
Reformation 65
refuge 131
refuse 147
Reginald de Buggewell 155
Reginald Fitzjoscelin 80, 93-4, 115-8

Regularis Concordia 58
regulation 157
Reiner the Goldsmith 98, 108
Rekkestreet 137
relics 85
religious centre 13
religious observance 16
religious rites 16
Remigius 84
renaissance 90
rent(s) 104, 115
rental 137
repaving 146
rere dorter 148
reredos **38**
reservoir 147
resistance 25
restoration(s) 159-160, 164, 166, 170
Rev. Lockey 129
Richard Davy 154
Richard de Berewyk 115
Richard de Clopcote 152
Richard de Forde 99, 103
Richard Glover 110
Richard II 105, 131
Richard le Vingour 104
Richard of Combe 117
Richard of Cornwall 103
Richard of York 156
Richard Tanner 114
Richard the Lionheart 92
Richard Veyse 154
Richard Whyteson 102
ridge tiles 110, 114
river 117, 131, 133
road 146-7
Robert Batyn 156
Robert Burnell 99, 115, 152, 156
Robert Curthose 71
Robert (de) Sutton 153, 169, **31**
Robert Draper 102
Robert Gyene 153
Robert Little 102
Robert of Gloucester 91
Robert of Lewes 74, 86, 88, 93, 91-2, 129, 151, 157, 166
Robert Rogeris 156
Robert the Dyer 107
Rode 63
Roger Crist 107
Roger Mowbray 71
Roger of Salisbury 95
Roger the Tanner 104, 110
Roger, son of Algar 116
Roman(s) 13, 26, 42-3, 83, 86, 88, 112, 126, 130-2, **54**
Roman Bath 13, **5**
Roman Baths 36, 115, 148
Roman Britain 15
Roman buildings 21-2, 34, 43, 112

Roman ditch(es) 42, 126
Roman fortified sites 41
Roman gates 42
Roman masonry building 38
Roman outflow 36
Roman ruins 74, 112
Roman spring reservoir 37
Roman street pattern 42
Roman towns 15, 21
Roman wall 42, 88
Roman, stone coffin,
    recycled 63
Romanesque 80, 151
romanitas 31
Rome 166, 93
Romsey 54
ropemaker 114
royal estate 63, 97
royal palaces 60
Royal Warrant 80
royalty 91
rubbish bins 141
rubbish dump 55
rubbish pits 64,
    109-110, 147
rubbish 131
Ruin, The 13
ruins 99
runes 63
rushes 55

Sæwold 67-9
Sæwulf, monk 67
saints, Welsh and West
    Country 25
Salisbury 26, 93, 154
Sally Lunn's Tea Shop
    89, 142
sanctuary 102, 116
Savaric 94, 151
Savile 123, 129, 133-4,
    144, 148, 169, **51**
Saw Close 112, 133, **26, 51**
saw dust 112, 133
saw pits 112, 133, **47**
Saxon 13, 20, 22, 24, 34,
    37, 63, 72, 89, 97, 108,
    126, 130-2
Saxon advance 20, 25
Saxon church 54
Saxon control 26
Saxon England 64, 67
Saxon mercenaries 19
Saxon poet 14, 22
Saxon Street 44, 54, **25, 18**
Saxon town plan 42, 43, **14**
Saxon wall 34, 47, 85
Scandinavia 51
scars 165, 170
sceat 38, **15A**
scholar 91
scholars 85, 90
scriptorium 67
scrivener 98
sculptures 160, **71**
seal 58, 98, 100, 151, **45**
secretary 158

see 48, 71, 88, 92, 94, 117,
    132, 151
seeds 141
sepulchre 164
Serlo the Skinner 110
Serlo the Tailor 108
Serlo's Lane 108
servant(s) 88-9, 95, 105,
    156-7, 159
servi 68-9
Seven Dials 112, 126, 128
Severn 26
sheep 22, 115, 131
Shepton Mallet 25
Sheriff of Wiltshire 117
Shockerwick 99
shoemaker(s) 105, 114
shop keeper 141
shop(s) 112, 133, 138-9,
    141-2, 145-6, 157
Shropshire 152
Shury stables 131
shutters 145
Sicily 90
sickness 116
siege 134
silting 133
silver gilt 157
Simon de Montfort 152
Sir Richard Junior 104, 142
Sir Walter de Rodenaye 153
Sir William Hussey 145
sisters 117
skinners 110
slag 112, 147
slaves 68
Slippery Lane 104, 132
slips 88
sloe 141
slype 86
small town 15
smith 112, 132
Smith's map 165
smithy 112, 132, 141
solar 139, 141, 145, 155
soldiers 152
Somerset 25-6, 28-9, 48,
    63-4, 69, 71, 80, 99, 107,
    110, 123, 153, 168, 169
Somerset/Wiltshire border 29
sons 105
Souter Street 114
south gate 72, 117, 126, 128,
    130-1, 148
South Stoke 26, 153
South Street 133
south transept 85, 166
Southampton 37
Southgate Street 102-4,
    107, 110, 133-4, 138-9,
    142, 147-8
Southgate 147-8
spa(s) 115, 163, 170-1
Spain 90-1
spearhead, seventh-century 38
Speed 123, 129, 133-4, 169,
    50

spinners 105, 145
spinning 107
spire 151, **66**
spring(s) 24, 34, 43, 86, 90,
    115, 133, 147-8, 170
SS Peter and Paul 35, 95
St Alban's 24
St Alphege 61
St Augustine's 158, 169
St Bartholomew **38**
St Benedict 35
St Bertin 60
St Catherine 26, 100, 112,
    119-120, 125, 158
St Helen's, Malmesbury 65
St James 44, 47, 66, 89-90,
    99, 129, 132, 134, 147-8,
    151-2, 171, **33, 59**
St John's Hospital 100,
    116-7, 141-2, 157
St Lawrence 58, 65, 133
St Mary de Stall 47-8, 65-6,
    77 , 89, 100, 134, 137,
    148, 157, 168, 171
St Mary in the Churchyard
    89
St Mary Magdalen 47, 110,
    117, 138, 147, **48**
St Mary 47
St Mary's by the north gate
    65, 137, 171
St Mary's 86
St Michael's Within 46, 48-
    9, 65, 137-8
St Michael Without 47,
    110, 112, 114, 132, 137,
    139, 145-6
St Michael 47
St Michael's Passage 108
St Michael's, Oxford 65
St Patrick 25
St Paul 151
St Peter 35, 47, 58, 74, 97,
    129, 151, 166
St Peter's Conduit 147
St Peter's gate 77
St Peter's, Bradwell 33
St Vincent **38**
stables 89, 131, 139
stained glass 151
Stall Street 37, 44, 46, 49,
    65, 72, 77, 79, 109-10,
    112, 137-9, 144, 168, **26,
    53, 65,**
Stalls Church 119
Stalls churchyard 103
stalls 139, 141
Star Chamber 90
status 163, 169-170
Stephen de Devizes 102
Stillingfleet 156
stocks 157
Stokeney 154
stone buildings 24, 104, 142
stone recycling 34
stone 14, 112, 142, 147-8
stonework 75, 164-5

stonhouse 142
stop line 20
storerooms 155
strawberry 141
street(s) 37, 123, 137-8,
    146-7, 149
Streetscape 146
strong rooms 100
strongholds 25
Style 157
sub-prior 153, 168
sub-Roman archaeology 25
subsidy of the ninth 104
suburb(s) 72, 110, 115-6,
    118, 126, 130, 132, 137,
    141, 148
Sulis Minerva 13, 16, 44
Sultan of Egypt 103
summer savoury 141
surgery 105
surnames 105
surrender 168
Sutor Street 139
Swallow Street 22, **32**
Sweden 63
Swein Godwinsson, Earl of
    Wessex 67
Sweyn 62-3
Swindon 26
sword, Scandinavian 63, **22**
synod, of Brentford 35
Syria 90

tabernarius 102
tailor 105, 112
tanner 110
tannery 110
Taunton 169
tavern 138
taverner 102
tax collectors 99, 102
tax dues 104
tax of the ninth 105
tax payers 104, 142
tax rate 105
tax return(s) 102, 116
tax(es) 15-6, 97, 107
taxation 158
teazel(s) 55, 114, 141
temple courtyard 86
temple forecourt 32
Temple of Sulis Minerva 13,
    16, 22-3, 32, 34, 37, 65, **1**
temples 15
tenants/tenancies 48, 115,
    120, 154
tenement(s) 104, 112, 132,
    138-9, 141, 145-6, 148
Terrace Walk 128
Thames 39
thatch 145
thatchers 114
The Bear 102
the Crown 102
thegn 70
Theodore 28, 31, 35
Theodosius 15

Theodwold, monk 67
therapy 117
thermal water 109
Thomas à Becket 93
Thomas Brydde 145
Thomas Chauncellor 156
Thomas Crist 107, 153
Thomas Cromwell 167
Thomas Crouch 157
Thomas Leche 115
Thomas Roberd 103
Thomas Saundres 102, 139
Thomas the Mason 104
Thomas the Tyler 114
thread picker 55, **19**
thugs 157
Thured, monk 67
Tidenham 57
tile(s) 13, 114, 145
timber (in buildings) 19,
    21, 24, 88, 100, 142,
    145, 148, 160, **63**
timber coffin 88
timber palisade, ditch
    revetment 51, **12**
timber 34, 112, 134
tithe 115
tofts 132
Toledo 90-1
tolls 129
tombstones 15
topography(ies) 123, 125-6
Touraine 80
tourism 13, 16, 170-1
Tours 83, 91
tower(s) 80, 83, 92, 130,
    133, 151, 158
town 41, 69, 71, 92, 123,
    125, 129, 151, 154,
    156, 170
townscape 123
townsmen 120, 152
townspeople 108
trade(s) 37, 57, 89, 92, 104-
    5, 107, 110, 142, 156-7
trader(s) 99,104
tradesman/men 92, 104
tradespeople 114
trading 109
traffic 129
transept(s) 77, 80, 83, 85-6,
    89, 164, 171
transformation 15
transport 110, 149
Treatise on the Astrolabe 90
Tregonwell 168
trigonometry 90
Trinity 120, 159
Trotman 94

Trowbridge 157
tuckers 156
tucking 107-8
Tudors 156
Turkey 31
turrets 133
twichens 44-5

Uley 25
undercroft(s) 85, 100, 142
underfloor heating 13-4
unfree 120
Union Passage 139
university 91
Upper Borough Walls 42,
    51, 63, 128, 138, **22, 55**
Upper Pitts 110
urban 132

vagabonds 156
vault(s) 28, 63, 74, 84, 160,
    163-4, 166
vegetables 115, 141
Vegetius 43
Vertues 160, 164
vestry 85, 166
vicar 168
Vicaridge Lane 102
Victorian 142, 148
victuals 89
Vikings 38-9, 62, 68
villas 13, 25
vines 115
vintner 104
Vinyards 115
vision 163
visitors 108, 131, 170
Vortigern 19-20, 24

Walcot church 99
Walcot Street 13, 47, 109,
    115, 132-3, 141, 146
Walcot 13, 16, 112, 115
wall(s) 14, 63, 92, 128,
    148 169
walled area 33, 132
walled city 134, 148
Wallingford 41, 62, 72
Walter Brian 104, 107
Walter de Anno 147, 152
Walter de Falc 98
Walter Hussey 117-8, 131
Walter le Carpenter 112
Walter Ring 98
Walter 119
Wansdyke 29, **9**
war 92
Wardour Castle 169
Wareham 43, 41

warehouse 145
Warfare 38
Warleigh 26
Wars of the Roses 156
waste 147
water parsnip 141
water supply 133, 148, 152
water 147-8
waterlogged 133
Waters of Sulis 24
waterworks 148
Watling Street 40
wattle and daub 142, 145
wattle 133
wealth 69, 105, 108-9, 142
weaver(s) 105, 108, 120,
    133, 145, 156
weaving 107
Wedmore, Treaty of 40
weeds 141
weights 108
weirs 110
Wellington 154
Wells cathedral 94
Wells Road 133
Wells 48, 54, 71, 91-5, 99,
    107, 117, 133, 151, 157,
    163, 169
Wellsway 110
Welsh marches 20
Welsh 39
Wessex 1, 28-9, 35, 38-40 ,
    49-50, 57, 60, 62, 67
west end 160
west front 160, 163, **71**
west gate 37, 44, 112, 129-
    131, 133, 141, 170
West Saxon kingdom 28
West Saxon, knife and
    brooch 28
west window 160, **71**
Westgate Street 43-5, 49,
    108, 112, 138, 141-2, **14**
Westminster Abbey 85, 170
Weston 57, 61, 102
Weston-super-Mare 25
wheat 115
White Hart Lane 69,
    139, **25**
whitewash 88
Wica 70
Widcombe 115
widow 103
widowhood 103
Wife of Bath 103, 108
Wilfrid, church at Hexham,
    33-4
will 133
William Abingdon 114

William Bird 158-9
William Blount 145
William Button I 151-2
William Clement 168
William de Berewyk 99
William Galwyne 114
William Gascoigne 131
William Haynes 156
William of Malmesbury
    36, 74
William of Nubelly 154
William Phelippes (Phillips)
    119-20
William Rufus 70-1,
    74, 94
William the Clothmonger
    108
William the Conqueror 68
William the Cooper 105
William the Goldsmith 88,
    92, 108
William Turner 170
William Tyler 156
William Upperhill 154
William Woodhall 146
William, Vicar 117
wills 107, 114, 125
Wiltshire 91, 107, 110, 169
Winchester 20, 40, 50, 54,
    57-8, 65, 72, 92, 125
windows 139, 145, 163
wine merchant 104
wine 25, 110
Witan 57, 62
woad 107
Wolsey 163
women 103-4
wood 145
Woodwick 70
woodworking 112
Wool 99, 107-8, 153
Worcester 28, 31, 58
workers 112
working man 114
workmen 55, 138, 142,
    145-6, 156
Wroxeter 24
Wulfan, wealthy Saxon 64
Wulfbald, moneyer 51
Wulfgar 60
Wulfrich 114
Wulfwold 67
Wynstan, moneyer 51

Ymma 104
York Street 148
Ypres 108